Rhetoric, Persuasion, and Modern Legal Writing

Rhetoric, Persuasion, and Modern Legal Writing

The Pen Is Mightier

Brian L. Porto

LEXINGTON BOOKS
Lanham • Boulder • New York • London

Published by Lexington Books
An imprint of The Rowman & Littlefield Publishing Group, Inc.
4501 Forbes Boulevard, Suite 200, Lanham, Maryland 20706
www.rowman.com

6 Tinworth Street, London SE11 5AL, United Kingdom

British Library Cataloguing in Publication Information Available

Library of Congress Cataloging-in-Publication Data
Library of Congress Control Number: 2020930448

ISBN 978-1-4985-6891-3 (cloth)
ISBN 978-1-4985-6892-0 (electronic)

To two thoughtful Hoosiers who eased my transition
from law student to lawyer:

Leonard Fromm—the law student's advocate;

Patrick Baude—teacher, scholar, inspiration.

Contents

Acknowledgments

Nobody writes an academic monograph alone, even when only one author's name appears on the front cover. The advice and counsel of colleagues almost always shape and guide the author's thinking, improving the product that finally emerges from the writing process. This book conforms to that rule. Discussions with many colleagues clarified its focus and enhanced its prospects for publication. I am indebted to Steve Dycus, Ross Guberman, Greg Johnson, Reed Loder, Phil Meyer, Sean Nolon, Dave Schultz, Kristen Tiscione, and Rebecca Zietlow for the insights they offered at various stages of the project. I am also indebted to the wonderful partnership between the Legal Writing Institute (LWI) and LexisNexis that has supported my work with an LWI Scholarship Grant.

Others deserve honorable mention too. My students at Vermont Law School, in our regular class sessions, provide a warm and supportive, yet intellectually rigorous, forum for presenting and testing both substantive ideas about legal writing and methods for teaching it. Our discussions, framed by the verdant beauty of the Green Mountains, have helped to inform this book. Also at Vermont Law School, librarian Michele LaRose located numerous research materials for me expeditiously, and my research assistant, Hannah Clarisse, ensured that my quotations and citations were accurate and complete, which they would not have been without her diligence and skill. The anonymous reviewer who read the manuscript for Rowman & Littlefield also deserves my thanks because the resulting critique prompted me to shorten the book while also rebalancing it to include more rhetorical analysis and less biography.

I am grateful for several opportunities that became available during the writing process to discuss material pertinent to the book, in venues that ranged from informal faculty gatherings at Vermont Law School to the annual meeting of the New England Consortium of Legal Writing Teachers (NECLWT) to the pages of the Vermont Bar Association's quarterly journal. And I am grateful to the two editors at Rowman & Littlefield with whom I worked: Emily Roderick, who acquired the book and Becca Beurer, who guided it to completion. Each editor was a pleasure to work with.

Finally, I extend a deeply appreciative thank you to my wife, Sherrie Greeley, for her steadfast love and support and her sharp proofreader's eye. This book is more pleasant to read and easier to understand because of her efforts. Any lingering errors or omissions, substantive or mechanical, are my responsibility alone.

Chapter One

The Power of Rhetoric in Supreme Court Opinions

A. Rhetoric and Persuasion

Aristotle observed long ago that it is not enough to know *what* to say; one must know *how* to say it.[1] Great orators and writers seem to know that instinctively. Instead of producing oratory or writing that is merely a utilitarian means to an end, they create compelling arguments, featuring evocative prose, and arrange those arguments to maximize the persuasive effect. The Roman statesman and orator Cicero, one of the foremost classical rhetoricians, acknowledged that stylistic distinction is impossible to achieve without worthy ideas, but quickly added that ideas are lifeless without stylistic distinction.[2] To borrow an old metaphor, itself a classical rhetorical tool, great orators and writers show us the difference between a "master" and a "journeyman" in the venerable craft of persuasion.

Some American presidents have been masters of persuasion.[3] They understood Aristotle's message perfectly. They knew "how to say it," meaning how to devise arguments and to order them in a speech in a logical way that ensured comprehension by the reader or listener and how to use words and expressions likely to inspire and to endure in the public consciousness. For example, the words of President John F. Kennedy's Inaugural Address, delivered on a cold January day in 1961, still warm the heart and stir the spirit more than a half-century later.

> Let the word go forth from this time and place, to friend and foe alike, that the torch has been passed to a new generation of Americans, born in this century, tempered by war, disciplined by a hard and bitter peace, proud of our ancient heritage, and unwilling to witness or permit the slow undoing of those human

> rights to which this nation has always been committed, and to which we are committed today at home and around the world.[4]

Why are President Kennedy's words still so powerful today? One likely reason is their subject: the timeless quest for human freedom and the call to action in pursuit of it. But an equally important reason is Kennedy's use of rhetorical techniques to highlight that subject and enliven his description of it. Employing the rhetorical canon known as *invention*, which concerns the creation of arguments, he developed an argument from *circumstance*, which encourages an audience to act by showing its members what is possible if they work together.[5] That argument exhorted "a new generation of Americans," of which Kennedy was part, to seize the torch of leadership and carry it forward to expand human freedom around the world. The Peace Corps, founded during the Kennedy administration, embodied the promise in the president's words.

The other rhetorical technique evident in President Kennedy's speech is *style*, which refers to the speaker's or writer's word choices in a particular discourse.[6] A prominent feature of style is the *figure of speech*, which the rhetorician uses to enhance language, either by presenting words in an unconventional order or by placing them in an unfamiliar context. In other words, writes Professor Michael Smith, figures of speech "achieve eloquence by intentionally deviating from the normal or literal use of language."[7] President Kennedy used *alliteration* ("friend and foe alike") and *asyndeton* (". . . a new generation of Americans, born in this century, tempered by war, disciplined by a hard and bitter peace . . .") to aid comprehension and convey a sense of urgency to the listener. Alliteration is the repetition of initial (as in this case) or medial consonant sounds in two or more adjacent words.[8] Asyndeton is the deliberate omission of conjunctions (and, or, but, etc.) between a series of related clauses. Its principal effect is to hurry the rhythm of a sentence.[9] Kennedy hurried the rhythm of his words to convey an urgent message to Americans—especially young Americans—to join him in working for peace, freedom, and international understanding, thereby countering the influence of the Soviet Union among developing countries.

Thus, the application of rhetorical devices to a grave and preeminent subject has ensured the continued vitality of President Kennedy's Inaugural Speech. To grasp the importance of rhetoric in that speech, consider the likely effect if Kennedy had expressed the same ideas by saying, "A new generation of Americans must now assume the responsibilities of leadership and promote around the world the human rights we hold dear." Would those words be remembered as well and quoted as often as the words he actually spoke? It seems unlikely.

In exhorting Americans, through rhetoric, to join forces and pursue a brighter future together, President Kennedy honored a tradition established by his predecessors in the White House. One of those predecessors, Abraham Lincoln, was among our most talented rhetorician-presidents. He also used an argument from circumstance to persuade Americans to work together to make peace possible, in Lincoln's case, peace between the North and the South after the Civil War. At the close of his Second Inaugural Address, delivered on March 4, 1865, as war raged on, President Lincoln spoke the following words, which still stir the emotions more than 150 years after he spoke them.

> With malice toward none, with charity for all, with firmness in the right as God gives us to see the right, let us strive on to finish the work we are in, to bind up the nation's wounds, to care for him who shall have borne the battle and for his widow and his orphan, to do all which may achieve and cherish a just and lasting peace among ourselves and with all nations.[10]

In President Lincoln's Address, as in President Kennedy's, figures of speech help to ensure the endurance of the message. The opening of the first sentence: "With malice toward none, with charity for all, with firmness in the right . . . ," illustrates *parallelism*—a similarity of structure in a pair or series of related words, phrases, or clauses.[11] Even novice legal writers use parallelism regularly, as when writing that "Judge Smith explained the law to the jury clearly, completely, and concisely"; the parallelism in that sentence lies in its use of three adverbs to characterize the judge's instructions to the jury. Lincoln's use of parallelism not only serves his purpose to link together charity, conviction, and the absence of malice, but also injects into the sentence a rhythm that makes it inspiring to read and easy to remember.

The call to "bind up the nation's wounds" is a *metaphor*, an implied comparison between two things that are dissimilar, yet have something in common.[12] Like parallelism, metaphor is familiar to most legal writers, who might use it to describe a particularly assertive litigator as being "a pit bull in court." In the example from Lincoln's speech, the implied comparison is between physical wounds sustained in battle and the psychic wounds of a nation divided by an armed—and prolonged—rebellion. The companion call to "care for him who shall have born the battle and for his widow and orphan" illustrates *synecdoche*, a figure of speech in which a part stands for the whole, as in the ship captain's classic call for "all hands on deck."[13] Each hand, of course, refers to a sailor. Similarly, the soldier, widow, and orphan to whom Lincoln refers stand for all the soldiers on both sides who were killed in the Civil War and the widows and orphans they left behind.

The figures of speech that President Lincoln used summoned the audience to assist him in rebuilding the United States and strengthening its international ties after the war. The promises of "malice toward none," "charity for all," and aid to the families of the fallen set a tone of magnanimity at a time when the urge for vengeance was powerful.

Taken together, the quoted passages from the Kennedy and Lincoln Inaugural Addresses show the power of rhetorical devices to enhance the persuasive capacity of language. For legal writers, whose work must persuade, familiarity with these devices is paramount. Some devices, such as alliteration, metaphor, and parallelism, are likely familiar already and will require little additional study. Other devices, such as invention and the more obscure figures of speech, will be less familiar. They deserve the close attention of legal writers because of their power to enhance persuasion.

B. Rhetoric in Legal and Nonlegal Settings

1. A Happy Convergence

This book aims to introduce professionals, scholars, and students who are interested in the Supreme Court, legal writing, or rhetoric to the important role that rhetorical techniques, in particular *invention* (discovery of potential arguments), *arrangement* (organization), and *style* (word choice, including figures of speech), have played and continue to play in producing iconic Supreme Court opinions. That goal derives from a convergence of lessons I have learned in three separate professional roles: law professor, practicing lawyer, and political scientist. During thirteen years of teaching legal writing to law students, I have become increasingly aware of the wisdom of the quotation from Aristotle that began this chapter. In a world of pedestrian legal prose, an argument that features a solid intellectual core and that is clear, concise, and garnished with a sprig of rhetorical elegance can stand out and perhaps win a case that a less vibrant discussion of the subject at hand would have lost. The comments of Judge Murry Cohen of the Texas Court of Appeals support this view:

> Is good writing rewarded? I used to think it doesn't matter much, in comparison with legal authority, justice, and the like. Now I know better. Good writing is rewarded so automatically that you don't even think about it.[14]

My continuing legal practice as a writer of appellate briefs causes me to take to

heart both Aristotle's observation about good writing and Judge Cohen's acknowledgement of its power. The outcome of a close case may well turn on the superior persuasiveness of one advocate's writing because, as legal scholar and former federal judge Richard Posner has noted, "Many legal questions cannot be resolved by logical or empirical demonstration."[15] Posner equates judges' arguments to those of literary critics, writing that both often "fall short of being conclusive."[16] Under these circumstances, the use of rhetoric in a judicial opinion "may have great persuasive force."[17] Indeed, Posner has observed, "It is no accident that the most influential judges and literary critics have been effective stylists."[18]

Finally, the years I spent reading and analyzing Supreme Court opinions as a political scientist showed me the power of language in the hands of rhetorical masters such as Justices Oliver Wendell Holmes and Robert Jackson long before I ever drafted a legal document or taught students to do so. The happy convergence of these three factors is the conclusion that anyone who studies the Supreme Court, whether lawyer, political scientist, or scholar of rhetoric, can benefit from a compact, engaging discussion that shows how some of the Court's best writers have used rhetorical techniques to conceive, construct, and enliven their opinions. My method for making that discussion engaging is to (1) identify five of the Supreme Court's best writers; (2) explain what characteristics make their writing outstanding; and (3) extract from that writing the rhetorical devices the featured justices used to convey their ideas persuasively.

The first task was the most difficult, perhaps because selecting the justices one thinks are the Supreme Court's "best" writers is an inherently subjective enterprise. We all have our favorites, and they do not necessarily correspond to our colleagues' or students' favorites. Recognizing that some subjectivity was inevitable, I established two parameters designed to make selection manageable. One parameter was the exclusion of justices currently serving on the Court, in part because their body of work is incomplete, hence not available in its entirety, and in part to avoid appearing to have chosen justices whose ideological orientation I share. If the selection of particular justices appeared to be an ideological choice, literary craft would be subordinated to judicial politics, which is contrary to this book's intent. The book accounts for judicial politics, but its focus is literary craft. The other parameter was a limitation of the number of featured justices to five—the number needed to win a case—thereby underscoring the power of their writing and making the book short enough that busy professionals and students would have time to read it.

Two essential criteria informed the selection process for the featured justices: the views of established scholars and Supreme Court watchers as to who have been the Court's best writers, and my own estimation of which justices wrote in a way that would speak most clearly to modern readers. As it happens, compiling lists of the Supreme Court's best writers seems to be a favorite indoor sport of Court watchers, most of whom are law professors, journalists, or both.[19] Based on my first criterion, then, I read selected opinions written by John Marshall, Joseph Story, Benjamin Cardozo, Louis Brandeis, Oliver Wendell Holmes, Jr., Robert Jackson, Hugo Black, William Brennan, and Antonin Scalia. Justice Scalia died while this project was in its early days, so he was the last justice whose writings I considered.

Based on the second criterion, I chose to feature Holmes, Jackson, Black Brennan, and Scalia. Their writings reflect a shift over time, to be described in detail in chapter 2, from the *Asiatic* rhetorical style (complex sentence structure, ornate language, many figures of speech) to the *Attic* style (shorter sentences, plain language, fewer figures of speech) and from an authoritative to a conversational tone.

2. The Personal "Voice" in Judicial Writing

Professor William Popkin uses the term *tone* to refer to the relationship conveyed in a judicial opinion between the author and the audience, which can be authoritative or conversational.[20] The judge who speaks in a conversational tone relies less on logic and more on insight into contemporary community values as a source of law. In these circumstances, the judge's own voice speaks with fellow members of the community through the medium of judicial opinions.[21] No jurist was more adept at speaking conversationally than Holmes. Indeed, his opinions epitomize a conversational tone, frequently expressed through aphorisms. An *aphorism* (or maxim) is a short, pithy phrase or sentence that makes a true general statement about human actions, such as "A fool and his money are soon parted."[22] It is not included among the figures of speech generally recognized by rhetoricians, but it serves the same end: to highlight key points in a concise, vivid way.

One famous Holmesian aphorism stated: "The most stringent protection of free speech would not protect a man in falsely shouting fire in a theater and causing a panic."[23] Another example, perhaps equally memorable, but now much maligned, upheld a forced sterilization program for cognitively impaired individuals by declaring: "Three generations of imbeciles are enough."[24] Although the first example continues to command adherence today, while the second provokes disdain, both reflect Holmes's use of a conversational tone to communicate with his fellow Americans, through his Court opinions, based on widely shared values. In using this tone, Holmes wrote in a style that came naturally to him, so that his personality shone through the text of his opinion, allowing the reader to see "the real person behind the document."[25]

The conversational tone has become increasingly evident in judicial opinions during the late twentieth and early twenty-first centuries. Writing in 1995, Judge Patricia Wald, then of the United States Court of Appeals for the District of Columbia Circuit, noted:

> The "impersonal" style ("the court this" and "the court that," or the imperial "we") was designed to advance the notion that the court is a corporate body involved in declaring what the law is rather than three or nine or twelve individuals. Of late, however, it is not so unusual to see judges speaking in the first person, setting forth bits of their own experience or views—more fre-

> quently in the trial courts than above, and more in dissents than in majority opinions.[26]

Judge Wald added,

> [S]ome judges have already broken the [storytelling] mold and write in a folksy way, interspersing the facts and legal analysis with homespun observations. By bringing the author down nearer to the human level of the litigants, such techniques force her to think about the human facets of the case, the "beyond the law" aspects, and perhaps to factor them into an ultimate conclusion that must then make sense in ordinary human terms, not just "the law says so."[27]

Despite differences in their respective writing styles, Justices Holmes, Jackson, Black, Brennan, and Scalia all adopted a modern, conversational tone in their writing. Holmes, Jackson, and Scalia wrote in a more playful and metaphorical manner—amply sprinkling their prose with figures of speech—than Black and Brennan. Still, Professor Yury Kapgan's assessment of the tone used in Justice Scalia's writing also applies to the writing of the other justices featured here.

> His tone is personal and conversational rather than detached and formalistic, certain rather than tentative, rhythmic rather than stilted. He speaks with his own tongue, employing metaphors that help connect him to [an] audience [beyond the Court].[28]

The writing styles of the featured justices will highlight for readers the role of classical rhetoric in Supreme Court opinions. Their disparate biographies will simultaneously identify the forces that shaped those writings (such as Holmes's early exposure to poetry and literature at home and Jackson's literary instruction from his high school teacher, Mary Willard) and describe the role that each justice played on the Court during his tenure. Before discussing the book's plan to marry biography and rhetoric, though, I must introduce the less familiar partner in this union: rhetoric.

3. Rhetoric and Writing: An Introduction

Rhetoric is the ancient art of persuasion. Rhetoric as the ancient Greeks invented it and the Romans refined it is referred to as "classical rhetoric," which is distinct from modern variants that offer many alternative means of evaluating the effectiveness of a speech or an essay.[29] When this book uses the term "rhetoric," it refers to the classical form. Sadly, because rhetoric ceased to be a prominent subject in American schools and colleges long ago, Americans now most often use the word to denote empty promises, usually made by politicians, or the proliferation of mere words, again usually by politicians, when action is needed.

Originally, rhetoric took the form of persuasive speech, but with the invention of the printing press in the fifteenth century, persuasive writing also became a part of rhetoric. Whether oral or written, though, rhetoric has always been aimed at persuading an audience to think or act in a certain way. The ancients divided it into five "canons": the previously introduced invention, arrangement, and style, along with *memory* (techniques for memorizing oral arguments) and *delivery* (techniques for delivering oral arguments).[30]

Memory and delivery pertain to oral, not written, persuasion; hence, they are not addressed here. Accordingly, because this book aims to highlight the connection between rhetoric and persuasion in written works—specifically, Supreme Court opinions—it will focus on invention, arrangement, and style. To paraphrase Aristotle, this book will stress not what is written, but rather, how it is written.

Classical rhetoricians' attention to invention, arrangement, and style reflected their wish to devise arguments that were clear, engaging, and memorable. In other words, argumentative strategy—the means of "winning over" audience members—was as important to them as the logic of their position. Likewise, clear and engaging judicial opinions are most likely to persuade and be remembered.

Justice Cardozo recognized the importance of rhetorical devices in achieving such opinions when he wrote:

> [A]n opinion [needs] persuasive force, or the impressive virtue of sincerity and fire, or the mnemonic power of alliteration and antithesis, or the terseness and tang of the proverb and the maxim. Neglect the help of these allies, and it may never win its way.[31]

More recently (and simply), Judge Ruggero Aldisert underscored rhetoric's, especially style's, contribution to writing when he observed, "Effective writing has a beat, or rhythm."[32] That is because, as lawyer and legal writing professor Brett Rappaport notes, "We hear what we read."[33] Readers do not just extract words from the page; rather, they hear in their minds what they are reading.[34] Therefore, a written text is best understood when its words are arranged to convey a pleasing rhythm to the reader.[35] As a result, a rhetorically effective judicial opinion can shape the development of the law, not only because of the substance of its arguments, but also because the power of its rhetoric may influence the frequency with which that opinion is cited in other cases, hence the opinion's ultimate influence on the law.[36]

4. Rhetoric in Prose and Politics

Nonlegal examples, however, may be best able to illustrate the importance of rhythm to writing. Again, a presidential speech is instructive. In March 2015, President Barack Obama delivered a speech in Selma, Alabama, to commemorate a fifty-four-mile march from Selma to Montgomery, Alabama, in March 1965 that led to Congress's passage later that year of the Voting Rights Act, ensuring voting rights for African Americans. The president delivered his speech near the Edmund Pettus Bridge, where the march, led by Rev. Dr. Martin Luther King, Jr., was aborted on its first two attempts because of armed resistance by local authorities. President Obama used a rhythmic cadence to underscore the historic significance of the Selma march, which followed by just two years the bombing of a black church in Birmingham on a Sunday morning that killed four young girls. Referring to Congressman John Lewis (D-GA), a hero of the Civil Rights Movement whose speech preceded his, Obama said:

> As John noted, there are places and moments in America where this nation's destiny has been decided. Many are sites of war—Concord and Lexington, Appomattox, Gettysburg. Others are sites that symbolize the daring of America's character—Independence Hall and Seneca Falls, Kitty Hawk and Cape Canaveral. Selma is such a place. In one afternoon fifty years ago, so much of our turbulent history—the stain of slavery and anguish of civil war; the yoke of segregation and tyranny of Jim Crow; the death of four little girls in Birmingham; and the dream of a Baptist preacher—all that history met on this bridge.[37]

Several rhetorical devices account for the rhythm in this passage. Besides using parallelism, it uses parallelism's cousin—*isocolon*—to powerful effect. Isocolon occurs when the parallel elements in a sentence are similar not only in structure, but also in length, meaning they have the same number of words or even the same number of syllables.[38] Note, for example, the rhythm achieved by the references to "Concord and Lexington, Appomattox, Gettysburg" and to "Independence Hall and Seneca Falls" and to "Kitty Hawk and Cape Canaveral." The same rhythmic effect results from references to "the stain of slavery and anguish of civil war," "the yoke of segregation and tyranny of Jim Crow, and "the death of four little girls in Birmingham and the dream of a Baptist preacher" (Dr. King). Rhythm also results from the varying of sentence lengths by using two longer sentences as bookends for the short sentence: "Selma is such a place." Together, these rhetorical devices convey with a captivating rhythm the message that Selma is not just a place, but rather, a formative—indeed transformative—event in American history.

Rhythm is important in fiction writing too. Ernest Hemingway's fiction writing has endured in part because it employed rhetoric to achieve rhythm in prose. In the following example, Hemingway achieved rhythm by repeating words, hence sounds, within a sentence and by varying sentence lengths within a paragraph. The repetition of a certain word or group of words at the beginning of successive clauses is a figure of speech known as *anaphora*.[39] The repetition of a word or group of words at the end of successive clauses is *epistrophe*,[40] and the repetition of the last word of one clause at the start of the following clause is *anadiplosis*.[41] In the first chapter of *For Whom the Bell Tolls*, protagonist Robert Jordan has just received an assignment to blow up the enemy's supply bridge during the Spanish Civil War. Hemingway wrote:

> *That was* not his *business*. *That was* Golz's *business*. He had only one thing to do and that was what he should *think* about and he must *think* it out clearly and take everything in as it came along, and not to *worry*. To *worry* was as bad as to be afraid.[42]

The repetition of "that was" in the first two sentences illustrates anaphora, and the repetition of "business" illustrates epistrophe. The repetition of "worry" at the end of the second sentence and the beginning of the third is anadiplosis. Hemingway knew that repeating words and phrases enhances retention by the reader because the repetition of sounds cues mental recall.[43] He also knew that short sentences are different from longer sentences, not only in length, but also in character. Short sentences are dramatic. Longer sentences are calmer, emphasizing description and explanation rather than drama. Too many short sentences in succession can annoy readers with a staccato rhythm, diminishing the dramatic force of each sentence, whereas too many long sentences in succession can be soporific, causing the reader to lose focus.[44] Therefore, Hemingway mixed long and short sentences together, as in the example above. The result was a pleasing rhythm that conveyed drama when necessary, while still holding the reader's attention and facilitating comprehension.

Another twentieth century novelist who knew the importance of rhythm in prose was Willa Cather, who wrote several classics rooted in her girlhood on the Nebraska prairie. One of those novels, *My Antonia*, includes the following passage:

> The first snowfall came early in December. I remember how the world looked from our sitting-room window as I dressed behind the stove that morning: the low sky was like a sheet of metal; the blond cornfields had faded out into ghostliness at last; the little pond was frozen under its stiff willow bushes. Big white flakes were whirling over everything and disappearing in the red grass.[45]

Cather's rhythmic technique is different from Hemingway's. She does not vary sentence lengths as much as he does. Instead, she omits conjunctions, writing, "the low sky was like a sheet of metal; the blond cornfields had faded out into ghostliness; the little pond was frozen under its stiff willow bushes" to hasten the pace of the sentence. In so doing, she accentuates the speed with which the snowstorm has altered the landscape overnight. Recall that the omission of conjunctions indicates the use of asyndeton. Cather's word choices also convey the speed with which the snowstorm has changed the landscape; note her reference to snowflakes *whirling* over everything and *disappearing* into the red grass.

Rhythm is important in nonfiction writing, too, even the writing of lawyers and other professionals. Indeed, rhythm can aid the comprehension of complex, technical, nonfiction writing by maintaining the reader's attention to the text. Nobody knows that better than William Zinsser, whose memorable writing guide, *On Writing Well*, reflects his appreciation for rhythm in its conversational style and variation of sentence lengths. He writes:

> Writing is hard work. A clear sentence is no accident. Very few sentences come out right the first time, or even the third time. Remember this in moments of despair. If you find that writing is hard, it's because it *is* hard.[46]

Thus, rhetoric is all around us in our everyday lives, whether we recognize it or not. To be sure, it is embedded in our politics, such as when President George W. Bush spoke of his "compassionate conservatism" (alliteration) or when libertarians sport a bumper sticker that says, "There's no government like no government." The latter is an example of *antanaclasis*, the repetition of a word in two different senses.[47] Outside of politics, leaders in disparate fields use rhetorical devices to educate and motivate, as legendary UCLA basketball coach John Wooden did in admonishing his athletes, through the use of *antimetabole* ("the repetition of words in successive clauses in reverse grammatical order,") that "[f]ailing to prepare is preparing to fail."[48] And rhetoric is ubiquitous in advertisements, such as the alliteration that describes the soft drink Sprite as "tart, tingling, and even ticklish."[49] Despite its image of academic obscurity, rhetoric is everywhere.

5. Rhetoric in Legal Persuasion

Legal writers have less freedom than novelists to create protagonists and antagonists and to mold language, because the aims of legal writing are to resolve disputes and to justify the resolutions, not to entertain. But this book will show that the most persuasive Supreme Court writers are those who master the art of storytelling and the rhythm of legal prose. Consider, for example, the following excerpt from Justice Jackson's concurring opinion in *Brown v. Allen*, in which the Court held that a confession obtained by state authorities during a period of detention preceding a preliminary hearing and appointment of counsel was admissible at trial.[50]

> Whenever decisions of one court are reviewed by another, a percentage of them are reversed. That reflects a difference in outlook normally found between personnel comprising different courts. However, reversal by a higher court is not proof that justice is thereby better done. There is no doubt that if there were a super-Supreme Court, a substantial proportion of our reversals of state courts would also be reversed. We are not final because we are infallible, but we are infallible because we are final.[51]

The concluding sentence makes the passage persuasive and memorable because of the rhythm provided by Jackson's use of *antithesis* to distinguish one idea from another and of antimetabole to highlight the relationship between finality and infallibility. Antithesis is the juxtaposition of contrasting ideas, often in parallel structure, as in astronaut Neil Armstrong's description of his historic walk on the moon in 1969: "That's one small step for a man, one giant leap for mankind."[52] In both the Jackson and Armstrong examples, two similarly structured clauses house a dramatic contrast. In Jackson's case, had he instead written, "We are not perfect, but we have the last word, so we appear to be perfect," his words would probably not be recalled today. Antithesis, antimetabole, and other figures of speech will appear in the judicial writing to be discussed in detail later in this book.

The judicial writing of Robert Jackson, like the fiction writing of Ernest Hemingway and Willa Cather, shows a remarkable ear for the rhythm of language. Rhythm is a tool of rhetoric because rhetoric is, in Aristotle's words, "the faculty of discovering in the particular case what are the available means of persuasion."[53] Lawyers need rhetoric because most of the claims they make in their arguments are neither self-evident nor empirically verifiable. Therefore, lawyers must persuade the judges and juries before whom they argue during the course of a career that their arguments are reasonable or their clients will lose. That is, what a lawyer argues, in combination with what the judge or jury knows and believes, must seem reasonable.[54] And what seems reasonable today may not seem so tomorrow, as evolving attitudes toward same-sex marriage and the legalization of marijuana, among other social phenomena, illustrate. Lawyers make claims orally and in written pleadings to the court that they cannot prove are completely and unalterably true. One must assume, then, that the adherence won today from judge or jury will be partial and revocable.[55] Thus, for lawyers, the need to persuade is constant, and the value of rhetorical skill is inestimable.

To be sure, rhetorical skill, like athletic ability or musical talent, comes naturally to some people, as the examples from Ernest Hemingway, Willa Cather, and Robert Jackson illustrate. Whether these writers could define "anaphora" or "antanaclasis" is unclear, but they did not need to do so. All three had an innate sense of linguistic rhythm, no doubt refined by their diligent practice of their respective crafts, which made rhetorical devices accessible, whether or not they could name each device they used. This book will examine the writing of five members of the Supreme Court for whom rhetorical tools were accessible and useful. It will identify and explain those tools along the way, and it will show the reader the persuasive power of rhetorical mastery.

C. The Plan of the Book

Chapter 2 will discuss the origins, historical development, and principal teachers and teachings of classical rhetoric—specifically, invention, arrangement, and style—from its roots in Syracuse (modern Sicily) in the fifth century, BCE, through ancient Greece and Rome, with a nod to its modern descendants.[56] Later chapters will show invention, arrangement, and style at work in the opinions of Justices Oliver Wendell Holmes, Jr., Robert Jackson, Hugo Black, William Brennan, and Antonin Scalia, respectively. The book will devote a chapter to each man's life, times, and judicial writings.

Accordingly, chapters 3 through 7 will begin by describing first the life experiences that shaped the featured justice and next his particular role on the Court. In this way, the book will introduce readers to the human beings behind the illustrative opinions and to the societal conditions that spawned those opinions. This discussion will occupy approximately one-third of each chapter. The balance of the chapter will then examine its featured justice's creation and arrangement of arguments, and use of figures of speech, to produce opinions that remain noteworthy long after they were written.

Chapter 8 will complete the book by recounting the value of rhetoric to legal persuasion, by comparing the contributions the featured justices made to legal writing, and by showing how their opinions can serve as models for legal writers and instructional materials for teachers of legal writing. The book will predict that rhetorical skill will likely flourish at the Supreme Court for years to come, judging by the sprightly opinions of Chief Justice John Roberts and Associate Justice Elena Kagan. It will conclude by noting that neither doctrinal analyses by legal scholars nor empirical studies by political scientists can explain why certain Supreme Court opinions become iconic in the American mind. Significantly, neither mode of analysis concentrates on the words in Supreme Court opinions or, more precisely, on the rhetorical devices those words represent. The words still matter. Reflecting that reality, this book shows the need to study justices' rhetorical choices as well as their votes and their doctrinal justifications for those votes.

John Wooden not only taught his athletes that success demands preparation, but also that creativity demands competence; that is, a thorough grasp of the fundamentals of one's task.[57] The same principle applies to persuasive writing. To fully appreciate the rhetorical creativity of Justice Holmes in chapter 3, readers should become familiar with the history and fundamentals of rhetoric, which is the business of chapter 2.

NOTES

1. Aristotle, *On Rhetoric*, Trans. H. Rhys Roberts (New York: Barnes & Noble Books, 2005), Bk. 3, Ch. 1, p. 397. The precise translation is, "It is not enough to know *what* we ought to say; we must also say it *as* we ought."
2. 3 Marcus Tullius Cicero, *De Oratore*, Trans. H. Rackham (Cambridge, MA: Harvard University Press, 1942), Bk. 3, vi. 24, p. 21.
3. This elite fraternity includes Thomas Jefferson, James Madison, Abraham Lincoln, Ulysses S. Grant, and Theodore Roosevelt, whose writings and speeches are analyzed in Julie Oseid, *Communicators in Chief: Lessons in Persuasion from Five Eloquent American Presidents* (Durham, NC: Carolina Academic Press, 2017).
4. Inaugural Address of President John F. Kennedy, January 20, 1961, accessed May 29, 2019, https://millercenter.org/the-presidency/presidential-speeches/january-20-196.
5. Edward P. J. Corbett and Robert J. Connors, *Classical Rhetoric for the Modern Student*, 4th ed. (New York: Oxford University Press, 1999), 108.
6. Ibid., 21.
7. Michael R. Smith, "Rhetoric Theory and Legal Writing: an Annotated Bibliography," *Journal of the Association of Legal Writing Directors* 3 (2006): 134.
8. Corbett and Connors, *Classical Rhetoric for the Modern Student*, 4th ed., 388–389.
9. Ibid., 387.
10. Second Inaugural Address of President Abraham Lincoln, March 4, 1865, accessed May 29, 2019, https://millercenter.org/the-presidency/presidential-speeches/march-4-1865-.
11. Corbett and Connors, *Classical Rhetoric for the Modern Student*, 4th ed., 381.
12. Ibid., 396.
13. Ibid., 397.
14. Bryan A. Garner, *Garner on Language and Writing* (Chicago: American Bar Association, 2009), 62.
15. Richard A. Posner, *Law and Literature: A Misunderstood Relation* (Cambridge, MA: Harvard University Press, 1988), 286.
16. Ibid., 288.
17. Ibid.
18. Ibid.
19. See Jeffrey Rosen, "Strong Opinions," http://www.newrepublic.com/article/politics/magazine/92773/elena-kagan-writings; Jonathan Turley, "The 9 Greatest Supreme Court Justices," *American History*, http://www.historynet.com/the-9-greatest-supreme-court-justices.htm; Ruggero Aldisert, *Opinion Writing*, 3rd ed. (Durham, NC: Carolina Academic Press, 2012); Posner, *Law and Literature*; and Bernard Schwartz, "The Judicial Ten: America's Greatest Judges," *Southern Illinois Univ. Law Journal* 4 (1979): 405.
20. William D. Popkin, *Evolution of the Judicial Opinion: Institutional and Individual Styles* (New York: NYU Press, 2007), 3. I am indebted to Professor Popkin (my law school professor) for the concept of "tone," but I have modified his formulation somewhat. He distinguishes between "voice" (the relationship between the judge and the source of law from which the judge draws) and "tone" (relationship between judge and audience). He also distinguishes between two varieties of tone, the "authoritative" and the "exploratory." To simplify matters, I discuss only tone, not voice, and distinguish between "authoritative" and "conversational" tones.
21. Ibid.
22. Aristotle, *On Rhetoric*, Bk. II, Ch. 21, pp. 339–340. See also *Corbett and Connors, Classical Rhetoric for the Modern Student*, 4th ed., 116–117.
23. *Schenck v. United States*, 249 U.S. 47, 52 (1919).

24. *Buck v. Bell,* 274 U.S. 200, 207 (1927).
25. Linda H. Edwards, *Readings in Persuasion: Briefs That Changed the World* (New York: Wolters Kluwer, 2012), 26.
26. Patricia M. Wald, "The Rhetoric of Results and the Results of Rhetoric: Judicial Writings," *University of Chicago Law Review* 62 (1995): 1418.
27. Ibid.
28. Yury Kapgan, "Of Golf and Ghouls: The Prose Style of Antonin Scalia," *Legal Writing: The Journal of the Legal Writing Institute* 9 (2003): 101.
29. For a survey of these alternative means of rhetorical analysis, see Sonja K. Foss, *Rhetorical Criticism: Exploration and* Practice, 5th ed. (Long Grove, IL: Waveland Press, 2018) and Jim A. Kuypers, ed., *Rhetorical Criticism: Perspectives in* Action, 2nd ed. (Lanham, MD: Rowman & Littlefield, 2016). For discussions of modern rhetoric in a legal context, see Barbara P. Blumenfeld, "Rhetoric, Referential Communication and the Novice Writer," *Journal of the Association of Legal Writing Directors* 9 (2012): 207; Linda L. Berger, "Applying New Rhetoric to Legal Discourse: The Ebb and Flow of Reader and Writer, Text and Context," *Journal of Legal Education* 49 (1999): 155; Theresa Godwin Phelps, "The New Legal Rhetoric," *Southwestern Law Journal* 40 (1986): 1089; and James Boyd White, "Law as Rhetoric, Rhetoric as Law: The Arts of Cultural and Communal Life," *University of Chicago Law Review* 52 (Summer 1985): 684.
30. Kristen Konrad Tiscione, *Rhetoric for Legal Writers*, 2nd ed. (St. Paul, MN: West Academic Publishing, 2016), 47–48.
31. Benjamin N. Cardozo, "Law and Literature," in Margaret E. Hall, ed., *Selected Writings of Benjamin Nathan Cardozo* (Albany, NY: Matthew Bender, 1947), 342.
32. Aldisert, *Opinion Writing*, 3rd ed., 239.
33. Brett Rappaport, "Using the Elements of Rhythm, Flow, and Tone to Create a More Effective and Persuasive Acoustic Experience in Legal Writing," *Legal Writing: The Journal of the Legal Writing Institute* 16 (2010): 65.
34. Ibid., 78.
35. Ibid.
36. Griffin Bell, "Style in Judicial Writing," *Journal of Public Law* 15 (1966): 214.
37. Barack Obama, "Remarks at the 50th Anniversary of the Selma Marches," Selma, Alabama, March 7, 2015, accessed May 25, 2019, http://millercenter.org/the-presidency/presidential-speeches/march-7-2015-r.
38. Corbett and Connors, *Classical Rhetoric for the Modern Student*, 4th ed., 382.
39. Ibid., 390.
40. Ibid., 391.
41. Ibid., 392.
42. Ernest Hemingway, *For Whom the Bell Tolls* (New York: Charles Scribner's Sons, 1968), 17, quoted in Bret Rappaport, "Using the Elements of Rhythm, Flow, and Tone to Create a More Effective and Persuasive Acoustic Experience in Legal Writing," *Legal Writing: The Journal of the Legal Writing Institute* 16 (2010): 84.
43. Ibid., 88.
44. Ibid., 85.
45. Willa Cather, *My Antonia* (New York: Penguin Classics 2014), 49.
46. William Zinsser, *On Writing Well: The Classic Guide to Writing Nonfiction* (New York: HarperCollins, 2006), 9.
47. Corbett and Connors, *Classical Rhetoric for the Modern Student*, 4th ed., 398.
48. Corbett and Connors, *Classical Rhetoric for the Modern* Student, 4th ed., 394. John Wooden's famous saying appears in Swen Nater and Ronald Gallimore, *You Haven't Taught Until They Have Learned: John Wooden's Teaching Principles and Practices* (Morgantown, WV: Fitness Information Technology, 2010), 67.
49. Corbett and Connors, *Classical Rhetoric for the Modern Student*, 4th ed., 389.
50. 344 U.S. 443, 476 (1953).
51. Ibid., 540.
52. Corbett and Connors, *Classical Rhetoric for the Modern Student*, 4th ed., 383.
53. Aristotle, *On Rhetoric*, Bk. 1, Ch. 2, p. 105.

54. Linda Edwards, *Readings in Persuasion*, 36
55. Ibid.
56. BCE, which stands for "before the common era," is equivalent to "before Christ," albeit without the explicit religious reference. The traditional counterpart to BC was AD, or anno domini ("the year of our Lord"), referring to the period after the birth of Christ, whereas the more modern equivalent is CE ("common era"), which again lacks a religious reference. I have chosen to use BCE and CE in this book because the most recent sources I have consulted while researching this book use those terms.
57. Nater and Gallimore, *You Haven't Taught Until They Have Learned*, 61.

Chapter Two

The Rhetorical Roots of Persuasive Legal Writing

A. Rhetoric: A Brief Introduction

"Persuasion is what rhetoric is all about," notes a prominent textbook on the subject.[1] From its inception in the fifth century, BCE, rhetoric has been "the art of persuasive speech," designed to influence an audience to think or act in a certain way.[2] Aristotle believed that what people did instinctively in argument they could do more effectively if exposed to formal training in the art of persuasion.[3] Reflecting this view, he observed: "Rhetoric is the faculty of discovering in the particular case what are the available means of persuasion. This is not the function of any other art."[4] Aristotle sought to derive "fundamental principles from the practice of oratory" in an effort to show that rhetoric was not—as his teacher, Plato, argued—a mere "knack," but was instead a systematic discipline that could be taught and practiced toward constructive ends.[5]

Plato demeaned and distrusted rhetoric. In his view, rhetoricians, like poets, were more interested in opinions, appearances, and even persuasive lies than in the philosopher's transcendental truth. That is, rhetoricians sought to dazzle an audience rather than to teach it.[6] Plato viewed logic as the process by which one *acquired* knowledge; for him, rhetoric was merely the process by which one *expressed* knowledge (e.g., style and delivery).[7] Aristotle wrote his famous treatise, *Rhetoric*, in part to counter Plato's persistent criticisms of the persuasive art.[8] For Aristotle, logic and rhetoric were parallel processes; logic produced *certain* knowledge, whereas rhetoric produced *probable* knowledge. Both processes used the canons of invention and arrangement.[9]

Plato's distrust of rhetoric derived from his belief that, at best, it could produce only probable truth, not the universal truth that formal logic could produce. In short, Plato believed that rhetoric lacked intellectual substance. To be sure, Plato's method for obtaining knowledge was different from Aristotle's; Plato used the dialogue he had learned from Socrates because he believed that the only way to discover truth was to exchange ideas with another scholar. Rhetoric, on the other hand, was about persuasion, not the pursuit of truth, so Plato thought rhetoric was largely a waste of time.[10] The rhetorician's ability to argue for opposing positions (think moot court competitions) and on the basis of probability (think "preponderance-of-the-evidence") instead of certainty made rhetoric, in Plato's view, deeply flawed and unsatisfying.[11]

Plato's critique drew from a deep well of belief among Athenians that absolute truths existed and that the purpose of an Athenian's life was to pursue those truths, which pursuit was difficult but worthwhile because it would result in a virtuous life.[12] He advanced that critique in the voice of his former teacher, Socrates, in a series of dialogues. Speaking through Socrates in his famous dialogue, *Gorgias*, Plato charges that rhetoric "is not an art at all, in my opinion."[13] Equating rhetoric to cooking and cosmetics, he observes that rhetoric is "an experience in producing a sort of delight and gratification."[14] Like cooking and cosmetics, rhetoric is "a flattery."[15]

Admittedly, rhetoric and logic are distinct from each other. Rhetoric is found in a continuous discourse, whereas logic exists in a question-and-answer debate.[16] Rhetoric usually addresses a large audience, and the speaker must pay attention to the reactions of listeners, whereas logic usually features one-to-one argument and explicit agreement or refutation.[17] Rhetoric is typically applied to practical or specific questions, but logic usually concerns philosophical or at least general questions.[18] Finally, rhetoric is popular and expansive, but logic is rigorous and constructs chains of argument.[19]

Today, though, rhetoricians and philosophers generally believe that all truth is subjective, so the acquisition of truth occurs as part of the rhetorical process. According to this view, all knowledge results from persuasion; hence, it is probable, not certain.[20] Law professor James Boyd White expressed this idea when he wrote that rhetoric "is the art of establishing the probable by arguing from our sense of the probable."[21] Therefore, rhetoric creates knowledge as well as expressing it. A prominent example is the Constitutional Convention, which used probable knowledge and persuasion to build a new political community rooted in the rule of law.[22] Law, in turn, is rooted in rhetoric.[23]

Whatever its shortcomings might be, though, rhetoric—"the study and production of persuasion"—formed the core of education in the humanities for more than two thousand years and linked the humanities to the public life of the ordinary citizen.[24] Indeed, rhetoric made the humanities relevant to the political and religious life of society because it taught citizens how to communicate effectively in the public arena. Today, when humanities education no longer emphasizes rhetoric, perhaps it is not coincidental that the humanities have lost their former allure to undergraduates and would-be professors. "Possibly the single most telling reason for the decline of the humanities in the twentieth century," claims rhetoric scholar James L. Kinneavy, was "the alienation of rhetoric from the humanities."[25]

Although rhetoric has undergone something of a renaissance since the last third of the twentieth century, including the publication of many books and articles and the establishment of several journals on the subject, it is no longer the cornerstone of a liberal arts education. Consequently, many educated Americans, including lawyers, are ignorant of its importance to persuasion. Indeed, they may only refer to "rhetoric" in a pejorative sense, to suggest unfulfilled promises. They therefore ignore the importance of rhetoric to persuasion and the importance of persuasion to democracy. As James Boyd White has noted, "[t]he ultimate subjects of rhetoric are always justice, ethics, and politics in the best sense of that term."[26] In other words, the connections between rhetoric, persuasion, and democracy are as significant in the contemporary United States as they were in ancient Athens.

B. Rejection and Resurgence: A Short History of Rhetoric

The history of classical rhetoric spans more than two thousand years, from the fifth century BCE until the first quarter of the nineteenth century.[27] Two parallel developments in fifth century Athens—increased literacy and the rise of democracy—created the need for rhetoric and permitted it to flourish. Rhetoric had its roots in Sicily, where, in 466 BCE, the citizens revolted against a tyrannical ruler named Thrasybulus and sought to recover land he had stolen from them. To meet the citizens' need to represent themselves in court, a Greek scholar named Corax of Syracuse taught them how to use rhetoric to plead their respective cases.[28] Thus began rhetoric's storied association with the law because it was developed specifically to teach advocacy, the traditional mainstay of the legal profession.[29] Corax's signature contribution to the development of rhetoric was his outline for a courtroom argument, which included a "proem" (introduction); a "narration" (statement of facts); an "argument" (presenting one's own position and anticipating counter arguments); and a "peroration" (conclusion).[30] This arrangement of the elements of a "discourse" became a fixture of all subsequent rhetorical theory, as applied to discourses both oral and, later, written.[31]

Nowhere was rhetoric more important to civic life during antiquity, though, than in Athens, where, beginning in 461 BCE, a general named Pericles presided over not only a vast military empire, but also the maturation of a democracy and the blossoming of the arts and sciences.[32] On Pericles's watch, Athens became "the crossroads of the world," a fertile seedbed for ideas and discussion where citizens flocked to the Agora—the marketplace and center of the city—to attend court sessions, legislative assemblies, sporting events, and festivals.[33] Throughout the "Age of Pericles" (461–429 BCE) and for one hundred years after his death in 429, Athenians studied rhetoric, and rhetoric was central to Athenian social and political life. Popular assemblies were responsible for reviewing and instituting laws every year, and proposed laws were posted in the marketplace, discussed among the citizens, and debated in the councils of government.[34]

In this intellectual hothouse, courts soon became the social center of Athenian life, creating the need for training in rhetoric, as a citizen's success at protecting his freedom and property could depend on his ability to defend both by speaking persuasively in court.[35] Indeed, the most important ideal that emerged in Athens from the Age of Pericles was freedom of expression. Athenians were taught that the greatest power a culture can possess is the power of persuasion, which must not be stifled.[36]

Perhaps the foremost beneficiary of the democratic culture that Pericles championed in Athens was Aristotle, who was born in Stagira, a northern Greek city that bordered on Macedonia, in 384 BCE, less than fifty years after Pericles's death from the plague in 429.[37] Aristotle went to Athens in 367 to study at Plato's Academy and remained a member of the Academy for twenty years. He left Athens shortly before Plato's death in 347 and did not return until 335, when, following in Plato's footsteps, he opened a school, where he taught until 323, the year before his death.[38] Aristotle became, and remains, the foremost theorist of classical rhetoric.

A philosopher, scientist, logician, and teacher, Aristotle was also the author of *Rhetoric*, a manual that influenced all the rhetoricians who followed him, including Romans Cicero and Quintilian.[39] A basic assumption underlies Aristotle's view of rhetoric, namely, that it is to be used in a humanistic society based on skepticism, in which probability, not certainty, is the highest level of knowledge that can be applied to decide political and moral questions.[40] Unlike Plato, Aristotle saw value in "best truths" as well as in certain truth.[41] In Aristotle's view, best truths served justice because the clash of opposing views leads to truth, even if that truth is uncertain.[42] Therein is the philosophical foundation of Anglo-American jurisprudence.

Aristotle identified three general means or processes by which rhetoric persuades—*logos*, *pathos*, and *ethos*—which are foundational to his theory of rhetoric.[43] All three derive from invention—the process by which the speaker chooses particular arguments—because they are means of persuading audience members of the wisdom of those arguments. Logos is "[p]ersuasion through logic and rational argument"; pathos is persuasion through an appeal to the audience's emotions; and ethos is persuasion through the establishment of the speaker's (or writer's) credibility in the eyes of the audience.[44] Even though Aristotle and other Greek rhetoricians (and their Roman successors) grasped the importance of logic to persuasion, they also appreciated that judges and juries sometimes decide disputes based on nonrational factors, such as the sympathetic nature of certain persons or circumstances or the perceived integrity of a particular advocate.[45]

A pathos-based legal argument is one in which the advocate states, either explicitly or implicitly, that the values at stake in the matter at hand compel a decision for the advocate's client.[46] Pathos is especially valuable to the advocate whose argument cannot carry the day by logic alone; conversely, a logically compelling argument may not need pathos to be persuasive.[47]

Like pathos, ethos is influential because logos cannot always close the deal with the audience. As Professor Michael Smith notes, "Arguments based on the logical application of legal authorities rarely point to a single clear conclusion."[48] Therefore, the decision maker faced with a choice between two logical arguments may well be influenced by the perception that one advocate's credibility exceeds that of the other.[49] This observation mirrors Aristotle's recognition that for advocates to be persuasive, the audience must like and respect them. They must be knowledgeable and must possess integrity, because if they are not credible, the audience will likely reject their arguments out of hand.[50] In Aristotle's view, credibility must flow from what the advocate says, not from the advocate's reputation.[51] Said Aristotle: "We believe good men more readily than others: this is true generally whatever the question is, and absolutely true when exact certainty is impossible and opinions are divided."[52]

Throughout the Age of Pericles and for a century thereafter, which includes the lifetime of Aristotle, rhetoric was the defining characteristic of life in Athens. Oratorical training and practice continued until the Athenian Empire fell in 322 BCE, which was also the year that Aristotle died.[53]

Two centuries passed between Aristotle's death and the appearance of the first major Roman rhetorical treatises in approximately 90 BCE. During those two centuries, evidently, the most important developments in classical rhetoric were "codification and schematization" because the Roman rhetoric that appeared around 90 BCE was fully formed.[54] The identities of the architects of Roman rhetoric are unknown; indeed, the famous treatise *Rhetorica ad Herennium*, which was likely written at about that date, was the work of an anonymous author, even though it is the oldest complete rhetorical textbook written in Latin.[55] The earliest Roman rhetoricians showed the way to Rome's most famous rhetoricians, Marcus Tullius Cicero (109–43 BCE) and Marcus Fabius Quintilianus (35–95 CE), better known as Quintilian, who, along with Aristotle, rank as the foremost scholars of classical rhetoric.

Cicero was a politician, legal orator, scholar, Roman consul, and author who produced several books on rhetoric, most notably *De Oratore* (On the

Orator), which has been described as "a multi-volume comprehensive examination of rhetoric and its place in the world of practical affairs."[56] Quintilian was a legal orator, too, although he was primarily a teacher. He wrote *Institutio Oratoria* (Institutes of Oratory), which describes the principles of legal rhetoric along with Roman educational principles.[57]

Classical rhetoricians like Cicero and Quintilian have been dubbed "the first practical psychologists" for their emphasis on arguments that were clear, interesting, and memorable. Argumentative strategy was as important to the ancients as was logical, consistent reasoning, perhaps because the decision makers in legal disputes in ancient times were amateurs for whom emotional arguments and the credibility of individual advocates were often more persuasive than logical arguments.[58]

Unfortunately for the cause of rhetoric, though, Rome eventually experienced the same fate as Athens, with the same attendant decline in rhetorical instruction and practice. Indeed, even by the time Quintilian published his *Institutio Oratoria* in 95 CE, the book was an anachronism because Rome had ceased to be a haven for free speech and had become an authoritarian state, run by a series of twelve emperors, from Tiberius in 14 CE to Trajan in 95 CE.[59] The Roman Senate, the site of much rhetorical skill in previous eras, shrank in power even though the emperors maintained it and other outward forms of the old republican government. Various emperors reigned for another three centuries, until Rome fell in 410 CE.[60] In this atmosphere, rhetoric was dangerous instead of empowering because freedom of speech was a major casualty of autocratic rule, as insulting the emperor became a capital crime, and a network of secret police monitored the statements of his subjects.[61] The dark skies and chill winds of authoritarian rule that prevailed across Europe in the time of the emperors would alter the aims and emphases of rhetoric for centuries to come.

The fall of the Roman Empire marked the end of a virtually unbroken one-thousand-year history of the Greco-Roman rhetorical tradition. In succeeding centuries, rhetoric's fortunes alternately rose and fell in the wake of social and political changes. The eighteenth century was the last full century in which classical rhetoric would occupy a prominent position in academic curricula.[62] Still, at the end of the nineteenth century, rhetoric was down but not out. Indeed, professors Corbett and Connors have observed that "even when [rhetoric] has been singularly inactive for a long period of time, it always stages a comeback."[63]

In jurisprudence, by the dawn of the twentieth century, Plato's search for absolute truth was obsolete; truth had become not only relative, but the product of a plainly rhetorical process.[64] The foremost exponent of this relativistic view was Oliver Wendell Holmes, Jr., who rejected the notion of a "science of law," espoused by Christopher Columbus Langdell, who had been dean of the Harvard Law School between 1870 and 1895. Langdell, who pioneered the case (or Socratic) method of teaching law, claimed that one could approach cases scientifically to discern objectively correct answers to the questions they posed. He rejected all "nonrational" methods of persuasion and influences on judicial decisions.[65] In Langdell's "scientific" universe, rhetoric could play no useful role.[66] Holmes countered that judges decide cases by choosing between competing and relative interests, and that this process necessarily involves subjective judgment.[67] As the Holmesian view of judicial decision making became increasingly prominent among lawyers and judges in the twentieth century, opportunities arose for legal scholars to work at the intersection of law and rhetoric.

A renewed interest in rhetoric arose in American universities during the 1960s and eventually migrated to the law schools. "The New Rhetoric" (to be called "modern rhetoric" here because it is no longer "new") had a major impact on legal education in the last decades of the twentieth century. Law schools had added legal writing courses and faculty by the 1980s, having reached the conclusion that clear, concise, and persuasive writing can be taught. Modern rhetoricians teach that rhetoric creates knowledge as much as philosophy does because knowledge does not reside in the external or the internal world, but rather, is the product of the interaction of a speaker, the audience, and the speaker's message.[68] In other words, modern rhetoric teaches that instead of being merely a device for transmitting knowledge acquired by other means, rhetoric is itself a means of creating and acquiring knowledge. Law professor Kristen Tiscione writes:

> Today, we understand that the act of writing is far more complicated than putting fully formed thoughts on paper. Often, ideas are not really clear to the writer until she writes them.[69]

Rhetoric creates knowledge during writing and editing because, even within that ostensibly solitary exercise, the writer is conducting an internal dialogue as well as a dialogue with the intended audience for the final product. According to Professor Linda Berger, the "inside reader's eye" predominates as the writer reads various texts during research to interpret the information with which to work. The "inside writer's eye" takes over as the writer begins to develop ideas, plans, and goals for the written product and reviews the writing in progress to determine if the text matches the intent that spawned it. The "outside reader's eye" moves to the forefront when the writer's attention shifts to considering whether the developing text meets the audience's needs. The "outside writer's eye" then grabs the baton to run the anchor leg when the writer concentrates on whether the completed text has the intended effect on an outside reader.[70,71]

Five major theses espoused by modern rhetoricians reflect the wisdom of the ancients:

1. Writing is a recursive, not a linear, process, meaning that the writer moves back and forth between prewriting, writing, and rewriting multiple times during the course of drafting a motion, memorandum, or brief;
2. Writing is rhetorically based, meaning that the audience, the purpose of the document, and the occasion that prompts its drafting all figure prominently in its creation;
3. The measures of the written product's quality are how well it fulfills the writer's intent and meets the audience's needs;
4. Writing can be analyzed and described; hence, contrary to previous belief, can be taught and learned; and
5. Linguistic research and research into the composing process inform the teaching of writing.

These principles form the foundation for the legal writing courses currently being taught in American law schools. Rhetoric, both in its classical and modern forms, is ascendant in law schools today because of its value in creating persuasive writers and persuasive writing. Although this book will concentrate on classical rhetoric, both forms recognize the centrality of subjective judgments to legal decisions; hence, the importance of persuasion and its dependence on the ability to convey ideas effectively.

C. Rhetoric and Persuasion in American Law

Recall from chapter 1 that since antiquity, the study of rhetoric has been comprised of five parts: (1) *Invention* (*inventio* in Latin, *heuresis* in Greek), (2) *Arrangement* (*dispositio* in Latin, *taxis* in Greek), (3) *Style* (*elocutio* in Latin, *lexis* in Greek), (4) *Memory* (*memoria* in Latin, *mneme* in Greek), and (5) *Delivery* (*pronuntiatio* in Latin, *hypokrisis* in Greek).[72] Invention concerns the creation or discovery of arguments, arrangement pertains to the effective and orderly organization of arguments, and style relates to the choice and placement of particular words.[73] Memory is about the memorization of a speech, and delivery is about how to deliver a speech effectively.[74] Because this book focuses on the use of rhetorical techniques in *written* advocacy, it will discuss invention, arrangement, and style exclusively.

1. *Invention*

Invention is a systematic method of identifying and producing arguments on particular subjects.[75] Starting with a thesis, the speaker or writer turns to what classical rhetoricians called "the topics" to suggest one or more possible lines of argument.[76] Consulting the topics enables one to devise arguments that derive from (1) definition; (2) comparison; (3) relationship; (4) circumstance; or (5) testimony.[77]

A definition-based argument enables the speaker or writer to identify behavior that is permissible or prohibited and to distinguish between seemingly similar objects or circumstances.[78] This topic, joined by the subtopic of *genus*, encompasses all arguments that focus on the nature of a thing, such as "This is treason," "This is an impeachable offense," or "This is negligence per se."[79] Another subtopic of a definition-based argument is *division*, which may identify the organization of an argument that follows, establish the grounds for an argument, or set up an argument by a process of elimination.[80]

In contrast, a comparison-based argument focuses on the similarities or the differences between two ideas, policies, or sets of circumstances. One such argument, the analogy, argues from the similarities of dissimilar things. It rests on the principle that two things that resemble one another in several respects resemble one another in an additional respect that cannot be confirmed. Therefore, analogy is a leap from the known into the unknown; it achieves probability, but not certainty.[81] Another comparison-based argument is the argument from degree, which may involve a choice between a greater and lesser good or a greater and lesser evil.[82]

Relationship-based arguments can be cause-and-effect arguments or antecedent-and-consequence arguments. One who makes a cause-and-effect argument must beware of the trap known as *post hoc ergo propter hoc*, or "after this, therefore because of this." To fall into this trap is to assume that just because one event followed another, the first necessarily caused the second. A more relaxed form of the cause-and-effect argument is the antecedent-and-consequence argument, such as "if Jane Smith was not the legal wife of John Smith when he died, then she is not entitled to inherit his possessions."[83] Relationship-based arguments can also argue from "contraries," such as opposite or incompatible things of the same kind, such as liberty and slavery, or from "contradictions," whereby the truth of one proposition establishes the falsity of another, or what might be called the "you can't have it both ways" argument.[84]

Circumstance-based arguments can focus on the possible and the impossible, encouraging or discouraging certain action by showing that its success is possible or impossible. Alternatively, the argument could focus on "past fact" (whether or not something has happened) or "future fact" (whether or not something would happen under certain conditions). Such an argument might claim that if the less probable of two events has occurred, the more probable is likely to have occurred too, or if the antecedents were present, then the natural consequences occurred (and the reverse), or if the means are available, the end will be accomplished.[85]

Finally, testimony-based arguments rely on informed opinion, such as that of experts, contracts, wills, public opinion polls, statistics, laws, maxims (aphorisms), and precedents (examples). Case precedents, of course, are often keys to legal arguments, but conflicting arguments will point to different precedents as controlling the case at hand. Similarly, the authenticity of wills and contracts and the meaning of statutes are subject to dispute,[86] and statistics are usually subject to challenges based on the methodology that produced them.[87]

Arguments derived from these topics will appear in the Supreme Court opinions presented in the remaining chapters. For now, though, the focus will be on President Obama's use of "the topics" to create arguments for his "Remarks at the 50th Anniversary of the Selma Marches." This speech is readily available online, and the reader may wish to review its full text before reading further in this book.[88]

Invention in President Obama's Speech

President Obama begins his speech with an appeal to ethos, responding to an audience member's "We love you President Obama" by saying, "Well, you know I love you back." Then he added, "It is a rare honor in this life to follow one of your heroes. And John Lewis is one of my heroes." As the first African American president, Obama may not have needed to build goodwill with the African Americans in the audience, but his remarks likely reinforced the goodwill he already enjoyed. And several Biblical references in the speech presumably did the same with many listeners, both black and white.

Later in the speech (paragraph 31) he would again appeal to ethos, this time reaching out beyond African Americans by acknowledging that despite remaining social challenges, America had become considerably more tolerant and inclusive since the Selma marches in 1965. "If you think nothing's changed in the past 50 years," he emphasized, "ask somebody who lived through the Selma or Chicago or Los Angeles of the 1950s." "Ask the female CEO who once might have been assigned to the secretarial pool if nothing's changed. Ask your gay friend if it's easier to be out and proud in America now than it was thirty years ago." Mr. Obama sought to build solidarity with and among Americans of all races by recognizing the sins of the past while espousing hope for the future.

Pathos also plays a role in the president's speech. Early on (paragraphs 2–4), he recalls poignantly a premarch meeting in a Selma church, where "[y]oung folks with bedrolls and backpacks were milling about" and "[v]eterans of the movement trained newcomers in the tactics of nonviolence. . . ." After the marchers sang a final hymn, the president continues, a young John Lewis—"his knapsack stocked with an apple, a toothbrush, and a book on government—all you need for a night behind bars"—led them out of the church "on a mission to change America." Mr. Obama later (paragraph 39) pays tribute to participants in the civil rights struggle who lost their lives to violence as a result of their participation. He lauds their embrace of "the imperative of citizenship"; that is, their willingness "to decide they loved this country so much that they'd risk everything to realize its promise."

President Obama's use of pathos here is masterly. He recognizes that the occasion of his speech is so filled with pathos that only a light touch from him is necessary. Then, as if commemorating war dead at Arlington National Cemetery, he reminds the young of their predecessors' contributions to human freedom and calls on them to contribute too.

But the principal feature of President Obama's speech is logos. After some preliminary remarks, he draws on the topic of definition and the subtopic of genus (paragraph 9) to note that because of the civil rights marches, Selma would forever be defined as a place where American history was made, and as a place that helped to define modern America. He asks, rhetorically, "What could be more American than what happened in this place? What could more profoundly vindicate the idea of America than plain and humble people—unsung, the downtrodden, the dreamers not of high station, not born to wealth or privilege, not of one religious tradition but many, coming together to shape their country's course?" The marchers' quest for freedom and dignity was, he notes, "the same instinct that drew immigrants from across oceans and the Rio Grande; the same instinct that led women to reach for the ballot, workers to organize against an unjust status quo; the same instinct that led us to plant a flag at Iwo Jima and on the surface of the Moon."

In defining the Selma marches as "one leg in our long journey toward freedom" (paragraph 18), President Obama defines America, too, as a place that "requires the occasional disruption, the willingness to speak out for what is right, to shake up the status quo." "That's America," he says, concluding the argument from definition. "That's what makes us unique."

Then, drawing on the topic of relationship and the subtopic of antecedent and consequence, he observes, "Because of campaigns like this, a Voting Rights Act was passed." "And the change these men and women wrought is visible here today in the presence of African Americans who run boardrooms, who sit on the bench, who serve in elected office from small towns to big cities; from the Congressional Black Caucus all the way to the Oval Office." Still, Mr. Obama emphasizes that the message of Selma is that the pursuit of freedom and human dignity never ends. "The American experiment in self-government gives work and purpose to each generation," he said.

Rallying the audience to that work and that purpose, the president uses the topic of circumstance and the subtopic of possible and impossible (beginning in paragraph 32), telling his listeners, "There's nothing America can't handle if we actually look squarely at the problem." We can find solutions for "unfair sentencing and overcrowded prisons," "make sure every child gets an education suitable to this new century," and "make sure every person willing to work has the dignity of a job . . ."

Continuing in this vein, President Obama closes the speech by noting that "our march is not yet finished, but we're getting closer." Exhorting the audience to draw strength from the inspiration of the Selma marchers, he concludes:

> We honor those who walked so we could run. We must run so our children soar. And we will not grow weary. For we believe in the power of an awesome God, and we believe in this country's sacred promise.

Thus, the rhetorical canon of invention is plainly evident in President Obama's Selma speech. He uses the topic of definition to frame a unifying, inspiring vision of the United States and to fit the Selma marches comfortably within that vision, the topic of relationship to show how the marches helped to make the United States a fairer society, and the topic of circumstance to spur Americans to continue the civil rights work that their predecessors began.

2. *Arrangement*

The legal writer who discovers, through careful research, an argument to make in a particular case, must organize the available sources necessary to commit the argument to paper. After selecting those primary and secondary sources that best illustrate the substantive points to be made, the writer must put them in a logical order, because without such order, even the most compelling and well-researched materials will be less persuasive than they could be.[89] In other words, the writer must determine sequence: what matter to take up first and, once that matter has been addressed, what should come next.[90]

Recall that in the fifth century BCE, Corax of Syracuse devised an outline for a courtroom argument, comprised of an introduction, a statement of facts, an argument, and a conclusion.[91] Corax's outline remains the model for briefs, motions, and memoranda filed in trial and appellate courts throughout the United States today. It also remains the model for judicial opinions. Still, the modern variant of Corax's outline reflects the contributions of his Roman successors, especially Cicero, Quintilian, and the anonymous author of *Rhetorica ad Herennium*, who added a fifth section, the Summary of the Argument, which precedes the full Argument. This five-part arrangement—Introduction (exordium), Statement of the Case (narratio), Argument Summary (partitio), Proof of the Case (confirmatio), and Conclusion (peroratio)—is precisely what the rules of the United States Supreme Court require in a contemporary appellate brief.[92]

Following the ancient recipe, briefs, motions, and memoranda typically begin with an Introduction. "*Introduction* means 'a leading into'" because the basic function of the introduction is to lead the audience or the reader into the discourse or document.[93] The introduction "prepares" the audience to absorb the discourse by (1) informing it of the goal of the discourse and (2) influencing it to be receptive to the message of the speaker or writer.[94] When the discourse is oral and the subject is not somber or alarming, information may be secondary to influence, so the speech may begin with "a joke, an apt quotation, an entertaining anecdote," or some other gesture designed to build rapport between speaker and audience.[95] Whether the discourse is written or oral, when the setting is legal, humor usually fails, but an apt quotation may both inform the court and dispose it favorably toward the writer. For example, I once began a brief to the Vermont Supreme Court, in which the issue was the maintenance of a common driveway, by stating: "Robert Frost wrote that good fences make good neighbors. Judging by this case, the same cannot be said for common driveways."[96] For both Corax and the modern lawyer or judge, then, the introduction identifies the question to be answered and, depending on whether the author is advocate or judge, recommends or announces the answer.

For both advocate and judge, the next step in the discourse is the statement of facts, in which the writer informs the readers about the circumstances they need to know concerning the matter at hand. In this connection, note Quintilian's admonition that a statement of facts must be "lucid, brief, and probable."[97] Similarly, legal writing professors advise students, and law-firm partners tell new associates to be clear, concise, and credible. To achieve this, the writer must set forth all the facts the reader needs to know, because excessive brevity surely sacrifices clarity. But the writer must omit unnecessary, tangential facts, because clutter also sacrifices clarity.[98]

One key to achieving both clarity and brevity is an orderly presentation of the facts. In law, statements of fact often will proceed in chronological order beginning with the events that prompted the dispute on which the litigation is based. But not all cases lend themselves to chronological fact statements, so the writer must be open to arranging facts "from the general to the particular or from the more familiar to the less familiar," if necessary.[99]

A valuable technique for achieving clarity is a device the Greeks called *enargeia*, meaning "vividness." In the legal context, fact statements usually involve the recollection of past events, which can come to life and firmly implant themselves in the minds of jurors or a panel of appellate judges if presented in words that "paint a word-picture" of the events described.[100] Consider, for example, *Jespersen v. Harrah's Operating Company, Inc.*, in which a female bartender at a casino sued her former employer for sex discrimination after she was fired for refusing to wear makeup at work.[101] Her brief used enargeia when it stated that she refused to "paint her face." An amicus curiae brief written on behalf of the casino went even farther, stating that it had to maintain grooming standards lest it have "employees who sport jewelry like Mr. T., wear makeup like Gene Simmons of [the rock band] "Kiss," dress like Dennis Rodman, have hair like Fabio or [have] beards like a member of ZZ Top."[102]

Finally, the fact statement must be credible. Although it may, even should, emphasize the facts that present one's client and case in the best possible light, it should not embellish or mischaracterize facts or try to argue one's case. Argument belongs in the section of the motion or brief reserved for argument, not in the statement of facts. Professors Corbett and Connors wrote for a general audience, but they might as well have been addressing lawyers when discussing the importance of credibility in a fact statement. They observed:

> Readers will believe that the situation is as it has been described if they trust the authority or the character of the writer. The ethical appeal, of course, is important in all parts of the discourse, but we must not minimize its importance in this part of the discourse, which is concerned with a bare recital of the facts.[103]

Later, they added:

> We can further enhance the credibility of our statement of fact by being careful not to say anything contrary to nature or to historical fact, by assigning believable causes or reasons for events, by trusting more to understatement than to hyperbole.[104]

The third component in Corax's classic model, which follows the Statement of Facts (and, nowadays, the Summary) is the Argument. If the Introduction and the Statement of Facts, notes Professor Corbett, "are regarded as the preliminaries," the Argument "then may be regarded as the core, the central part, the main body, of our discourse—the part in which we do what we set out to do, whether that be to explain or to persuade."[105] In the legal context, of course, the aim is usually to persuade by means of arguments derived from the invention process discussed earlier.

Toward the end of persuasion, lawyers and judges try to make legal reasoning seem as objective and certain as mathematics.[106] The tool they use for this purpose is the *syllogism*, a device that illustrates deductive reasoning, or reasoning from the general premise to the specific conclusion.[107] The syllogism, a creature of formal logic, includes a major premise, a minor premise, and a conclusion, as illustrated in the following example:

Major Premise: All men are mortal;
Minor Premise: Socrates is a man;
Conclusion: Socrates is mortal.[108]

To be valid, a syllogism must satisfy two requirements: each premise must be indisputably true, and the major premise must apply logically to the minor premise to produce a correct conclusion.[109]

As the ancients knew, though, logic may be graced with indisputable premises, but rhetoric—like modern legal reasoning—is not so fortunate; therefore, lawyers and judges must rely on the *enthymeme* instead of the syllogism. Whereas the syllogism, with its indisputable premises, can prove, the enthymeme—a modified form of syllogism whose premises are invariably debatable—can only persuade.[110] Still, a legal argument that is presented in syllogistic form can exert a strong psychological impact on its audience.[111] That is why lawyers and judges use a syllogistic format known to every first-year law student by its acronym, IRAC, whose letters stand for Introduction, Rule, Application, and Conclusion. The "rule" means the legal principles and authorities (cases, statutes, constitutional provisions, etc.) that govern the issue at hand, and the "application" means the way in which those principles and authorities affect the particular issue. In the IRAC format, the R is the major premise, the A is the minor premise, and the C is the conclusion.[112] Besides being a convenient organizational tool, IRAC lends a legal conclusion an appearance of certainty that belies its debatable premises.

Appearances aside, the Greco-Roman rhetoricians recognized that rhetoric was about persuasion, not proof, so they used enthymemes instead of syllogisms to advance legal arguments. The enthymeme is Aristotle's solution to two long-standing problems: first, how to reason logically with an audience (e.g., a jury) that may be unaccustomed to meticulous analysis, and second, how to reason logically absent indisputable major premises.[113] Like the syllogism, the enthymeme has a major premise, a minor premise, and a conclusion, but in the enthymeme, unlike in the syllogism, the major premise is left unstated or is understood.[114] Because the enthymeme is predicated on a presumption about what the audience already knows or believes, it can express its premises and conclusion in a condensed form.[115] Although the enthymeme looks much like a syllogism, it is simpler and more flexible because it lacks the syllogism's formal validity.[116] For example, a syllogism might state:

> All students register for courses.
> Bob is a student.
> Bob is registered for courses.

But an enthymeme on the same subject would state: Bob is a student; therefore, Bob is registered for courses. The enthymeme omits the major premise—all students register for courses—when everyone in the audience knows it. Enthymemes take advantage of audience knowledge.[117]

The essential difference between the syllogism and the enthymeme is that the former leads to a necessary conclusion from universally true premises, whereas the latter leads to a tentative conclusion from probable premises.[118] That difference means that an enthymeme would not become a syllogism if its major premise were stated, because a syllogism proceeds from proven premises, but an enthymeme proceeds from probable premises.[119]

Not all legal arguments are presented as enthymemes, though, because enthymemes reflect deductive reasoning, yet legal reasoning is sometimes inductive; that is, it may infer from one set of circumstances that under similar conditions, similar results will occur. Instances of inductive rhetorical reasoning are called *examples*.[120] They assume that "if something is true in specific cases, then it is true in general."[121] Aristotle provides the following illustration of an example in his *Rhetoric*:

> To prove that Dionysius is aiming at a tyranny, because he asks for a body-guard, one might say that Pisistratus before him and Theagenes of Magara did the same, and when they obtained what they asked for made themselves tyrants.[122]

Reasoning from example, then, begins from the premise that "we have seen this before," meaning that the adverse consequences that followed a particular decision in the past will result again if a similar decision is made today. Such inductive arguments are made in the halls of legislatures and on the pages of judicial opinions every day.

Ultimately, whether one's argument favors enthymemes, examples, or a mixture of both, it must yield to the Conclusion. Absent a "Conclusion," a legal document "strikes us as merely stopping rather than ending."[123] Aristotle taught that a conclusion should: (1) inspire the audience to look favorably on the speaker or writer, (2) amplify the force of points made in the discourse, (3) arouse the appropriate emotions in the audience, and (4) recapitulate the gist of the argument in summary fashion.[124] In the modern legal context, recapitulation is the most important of these aims, but it should be as brief as possible because the audience—usually judges—is too busy to read a lengthy reprise of arguments already digested. By the same token, a conclusion that says: "For the foregoing reasons, this Court should grant the Defendant's motion to dismiss," is a waste of time because it is too superficial to be persuasive.

The happy medium, then, between Aristotle and the modern, harried lawyer, is a short restatement, in one sentence per argument, of the two or three major arguments presented in the document, followed by a one-sentence request to the court for the relief sought (e.g., to grant or deny a motion, to affirm or reverse on appeal). Direct emotional appeals are also inappropriate, but, as the forthcoming discussion of style will show, the writer's word choices in a conclusion can affect the reader's emotions in an equally effective, albeit more subtle, way.[125]

ARRANGEMENT IN PRESIDENT OBAMA'S SPEECH

A discussion of arrangement should not end without presenting a preeminent illustration, preferably one more generally applicable than a legal document. President Obama's Selma speech reflects careful arrangement. The speech opens with a tribute to John Lewis for his leadership at Selma and throughout the Civil Rights Movement. Then, after greeting the assembled dignitaries and his "fellow Americans," President Obama addresses the first major theme in his speech: Selma's place in American history. Both the place and the event, he observes, belong in the pantheon of "places and moments in America where this nation's destiny has been decided." The reason is that the march "was part of a broader campaign that spanned generations; the leaders that day part of a long line of heroes" worthy of celebration. The marchers deserve to be honored because their brave actions "gave courage to millions" even though "their faith was questioned," "[t]heir lives were threatened," [and] "[t]heir patriotism [was] challenged."

Indeed, President Obama continues, the marchers wrote themselves into American history by participating in a uniquely American act—the pursuit of freedom—that would, in the years that followed, inspire young people to pursue freedom in countries as diverse as East Germany and South Africa, Tunisia and Ukraine. Here at home, the Selma marches would inspire groups such as "Asian Americans, gay Americans, and Americans with disabilities" to push for a more inclusive America. Thus, President Obama observes, the importance of Selma lay not only in the many examples of individual courage and commitment by the marchers, but also in the influence the events there had on the quest for freedom at home and abroad.

Midway through his speech (paragraph 32), President Obama shifts his focus from the importance of Selma in American history to Selma's lessons for America's future. The principal lesson he draws from the marches is that committed Americans, working together, can solve any problem that presents itself. Despite the celebratory nature of the occasion, he does not shy away from identifying the problems ahead, noting "unfair sentencing and overcrowded prisons, and the stunted circumstances that rob too many boys of the chance to become men. . . ." "With effort," he stresses, "we can roll back poverty and the roadblocks to opportunity" . . . and "[w]e can make sure every person willing to work has the dignity of a job, and a fair wage, and a real voice, and sturdier rungs on that ladder into the middle class."

In Mr. Obama's view, Selma teaches the importance of the word "We," which he calls "the single-most powerful word in our democracy," noting its prominence in "We The People," "We Shall Overcome," and in his own campaign slogan, "Yes We Can." "We" may also be the most important word in the Selma speech because it symbolizes President Obama's aim not just to celebrate the achievement of voting rights by African Americans, but also to show how the events in Selma inspired the pursuit of freedom by a wide array of socially and politically disadvantaged groups in the United States and abroad. The arrangement of the speech serves this dual purpose of commemoration and inspiration by honoring the voting-rights achievement of the Selma marchers, while linking Selma to other ongoing struggles for freedom here and around the world.

3. *Style*

Legal writers must not only arrange the points to be made in motions, briefs, and memoranda, but must also put them into words, which is the realm of style.[126] The components of a good writing style include grammatical competence, a rich vocabulary, clarity and precision of word usage, rhythm achieved through varying sentence lengths, paragraphs that reflect, yet develop from the topic sentence, and the timely use of figures of speech.[127]

Two alternative styles existed among the Greco-Roman classical rhetoricians. The "Asiatic" or high style developed among the Greeks in what later became the Roman province of Asia Minor. Exemplified by Cicero, it featured complex sentence structures, ornate language, and ample use of figures of speech. In contrast, the "Attic" or low style, which was the brainchild of rhetoricians from the Greek province of Attica who lived during the fourth and fifth centuries BCE, most notably Isocrates, featured shorter sentences, plain language, and few figures of speech.[128] Today, legal writers favor a "middle style" that rejects the formality and ornamentation of the Asiatic style, but nevertheless employs figures of speech regularly.[129] The middle style reflects the wisdom of the ancients, recognizing that style and substance are inseparable in an argument because style can aid persuasion by both clarification and inspiration.[130]

The stylistic focus of this book is "figures of speech," a generic term for "any artful deviation from the ordinary mode of speaking or writing."[131] The term encompasses *schemes*, which feature deviations from the customary order in which words appear, and *tropes*, which feature deviations from the customary meanings of particular words.[132] Both categories of rhetorical device can enhance persuasion by making language comprehensible, appealing, and memorable. Chapter 1 introduced examples of both categories; this chapter will discuss them in more detail, but only those appearing for the first time will be printed in italics. The schemes and tropes presented here, a fraction of the more than two hundred that rhetoricians have unearthed, are particularly suitable to and appear regularly in legal writing.[133]

Among the schemes, some are quite familiar, even if their names are unfamiliar. Parallelism (par-uh-le-liz-uhm)—a similarity of structure in a pair or a series of related words, phrases, or clauses—is evident in "He tried to make the law clear, precise, and equitable," because the three related words are all adjectives.[134] Parallelism reflects orderly thinking and is pleasing to the ear; both features aid persuasion.

When the parallel elements are not only similar in structure, but also have the same or nearly the same number of words (or syllables), the scheme is called isocolon (**ahy**-*suh*-koh-l*uh-n*), as in: "His purpose was to impress the ignorant, to perplex the dubious, and to confound the scrupulous."[135] When a series of three words, phrases, or clauses is arranged in parallel structure, the result is *tricolon* (*tri*- + koh-l*uh-n*), as in "life, liberty, and the pursuit of happiness," ends to which the drafters of the Declaration of Independence pledged "our lives, our fortunes, and our sacred honor," also an example of tricolon.[136]

Another familiar scheme is antithesis (an-*tith-uh*-sis)—the juxtaposition of contrasting ideas, often expressed in parallel structure—as illustrated in the statement that President Ronald Reagan made in 1987 in a speech delivered at the Brandenburg Gate (Berlin Wall), which separated East and West Germany.

> As long as this gate is closed, as long as this scar of a wall is permitted to stand, it is not the German question alone that remains open, but the question of freedom for all mankind. Yet I do not come here to lament. For I find in Berlin a message of hope, even in the shadow of this wall, a message of triumph.[137]

An everyday example occurs when a student seeks advice from a professor about a personal problem, and the professor thinks: How can I possibly help? I'm a historian, not a psychologist.

Alliteration (*uh*-lit-*uh-rey*-sh*uh* n), another familiar scheme, which repeats initial or medial consonants in two or more adjacent words, appears in the following sentence from President Kennedy's book, *Profiles in Courage*: "Already American vessels had been searched, seized, and sunk."[138] Alliteration's first cousin is *assonance* (*as-uh*-n*uh* ns), the repetition of similar vowel sounds, preceded and followed by different consonants, in the stressed syllables of adjacent words. Less useful than alliteration in legal writing, assonance most often appears in poetry, but it can also appear in prose, as in Samuel Johnson's *Life of Thomas Gray*, in which Johnson wrote: "Had Gray written often thus, it had been vain to blame and useless to praise him."[139] The vowel sound "A" repeats in Gray, vain, blame, and praise, illustrating assonance.

Still another familiar scheme is *anastrophe* (*uh-nas*-tr*uh*-fee), the inversion of the natural or usual word order in a sentence, as in: Gone are the days when I was young and strong.[140] Ordinarily, this sentence would read: The days when I was young and strong are gone.

Other schemes are less familiar, and often have tongue-twisting names that are hard to learn and even harder to remember. One of these, asyndeton (*uh-sin*-di-ton)—the deliberate omission of conjunctions between a series of related clauses—increases the pace of a sentence or clause. President Abraham Lincoln knew that when he promised, in the Gettysburg Address, "that government of the people, by the people, for the people, shall not perish from the earth."[141] Lincoln's fast cadence reflects the urgency of his desire to win the Civil War and rebuild the nation.

The opposite of asyndeton is *polysyndeton* (pol-ee-*sin*-di-ton), the deliberate use of many conjunctions, which slows the rhythm of the prose to produce a special emphasis or a solemn tone.[142] The latter aim is evident in the Bible's Book of Genesis, chapter 1, verse 25. It reads in part:

> And God made the beasts of the earth according to their kinds and the cattle according to their kinds and everything that creeps upon the ground according to its kind. And God saw that it was good.[143]

Easier to pronounce is anaphora (ə-ˈna-f(ə-)rə)—the repetition of the same word or group of words at the beginnings of successive clauses—as reflected in Prime Minister Winston Churchill's speech to the British House of Commons, early in World War II. Churchill famously said:

> We shall fight on the beaches, we shall fight on the landing-grounds, we shall fight in the fields, and in the streets, we shall fight in the hills.[144]

Another tongue-challenging, but useful scheme is *antimetabole* (an-tee-muh-*tab*-oh-lee), the repetition of words, in successive clauses, in reverse grammatical order, which the French playwright, Moliere, demonstrated (along with good judgment and antithesis) in stating: "One should eat to live, not live to eat."[145] A close relative of antimetabole is *chiasmus* (kahy-*az*-m*uh* s), the reversal of grammatical structures in successive phrases or clauses. The two schemes are similar in that both involve a reversal, but dissimilar in that chiasmus does not use the same words in two successive clauses. "It is hard to make money, but to spend it is easy" is an example of chiasmus.[146]

Polyptoton (päləpˈtōˌtän) is the repetition of words derived from the same root. President Franklin D. Roosevelt buoyed Americans' spirits during the Great Depression by stating, in his first inaugural address: "Let me assert my firm belief that the only thing we have to fear is fear itself." A more lighthearted example of polyptoton is the title of the Beatles' song, "Please, Please Me."[147]

Finally, anadiplosis (an-*uh*-di-*ploh*-sis)—the repetition of the last word of one clause at the beginning of the following clause—appears in international relations scholar Zbigniew Brzezinski's statement about totalitarian leadership: "Having power makes it isolated; isolation breeds insecurity; insecurity breeds suspicion and fear; suspicion and fear breed violence."[148]

Like schemes, tropes can aid persuasion, but by giving words unconventional meanings instead of by reordering them. One of the most familiar tropes is the metaphor (*met-uh*-fawr), the implied comparison between two things of unlike nature that occurs to us when liberal and conservative commentators appear on a news program to discuss an issue and we think, "This is going to be a food fight."[149] The metaphor, of course, depicts a figurative food fight, not a literal one.

Metaphors are popular and powerful because they "make[] the particular universal"; that is, they enable us "to see a larger truth in a specific set of circumstances."[150] For the same reason, they can be dangerously misleading, like the "domino theory" of Communist expansion that underlay the Vietnam War.[151] Of legal metaphors generally, Judge (later Justice) Benjamin Cardozo observed that "starting as devices to liberate thought, they often end by enslaving it."[152] Of one specific legal metaphor—the so-called wall of separation between church and state—Justice Stanley Reed wrote, in a dissent: "A rule of law should not be drawn from a figure of speech."[153]

Closely related to the metaphor is the *simile* (sim-*uh*-lee), an explicit comparison between two things of unlike nature that, nonetheless, have something in common.[154] Typically, the writer uses "like" or "as" to make the comparison explicit, thereby creating a simile instead of a metaphor. "In court, John behaved as if he were a pit bull" illustrates a simile. "Like an arrow, the prosecutor went directly to the point" does the same thing.[155]

A less familiar trope, despite its introduction in chapter 1, is synecdoche (sə-ˈnek-də-(ˌ)kē), in which a part stands for the whole, as in: "Washington and Moscow are at odds over the invasion of Crimea and the status of eastern Ukraine," which means the United States and Russia disagree about those subjects.[156]

A close relative of synecdoche is *metonymy* (mi-*ton-uh*-mee), the substitution of some attribute or evocative word for what is actually meant. Winston Churchill used metonymy when he told the British House of Commons on May 3, 1940: "I have nothing to offer but blood, toil, tears, and sweat."[157]

Another useful trope is *antanaclasis* (ant-an-*uh-klas*-is), the repetition of a word in two different senses. Founding Father Benjamin Franklin used this trope to memorable effect in the following examples: "If we don't hang together, we'll hang separately" and "Your argument is sound, nothing but sound."[158] In the initial example, "hang" means mutual support and assistance in the first clause, but severe punishment in the second clause.

Finally, *personification* (pər-ˌsä-nə-fə-ˈkā-shən) is useful too; it assigns human qualities or abilities to abstractions or inanimate objects. "The ground thirsts for rain" is an example of personification.[159] Justice John Marshall Harlan's dissent in *Plessy v. Ferguson*, in which the Court majority legalized racial segregation in public facilities, used personification to powerful effect, speaking to Americans' consciences, not their prejudices. He wrote: "Our Constitution is color-blind, and neither knows nor tolerates classes among citizens."[160]

STYLE IN PRESIDENT OBAMA'S SPEECH

The Selma speech features not only the effective use of invention and arrangement, but also an inspiring style, including a few well-chosen figures of speech. Early in the speech (paragraph 10), President Obama employs anaphora, isocolon, metonymy, and metaphor to recall the grit of the Selma marchers.

> We gather here to celebrate them. We gather here to honor the courage of ordinary Americans willing to endure billy clubs and the chastening rod; tear gas and the trampling hoof; men and women who despite the gush of blood and splintered bone would stay true to their North Star and keep marching toward justice.

Anaphora—the repeated use of "we gather here"—commands the attention of the audience, emphasizing the importance of the words to follow. "Billy clubs and the chastening rod" and "tear gas and the trampling hoof" illustrate the power of isocolon to give words a rhythm that makes them memorable. Those same clauses, along with "the gush of blood and splintered bone," reflect metonymy because the rough treatment they depict was just a part of the systemic resistance and gratuitous violence civil rights marchers faced in Selma and elsewhere. Metaphor lies in their determination, despite the obstacles they encountered, to "stay true to their North Star and keep marching toward justice."

Soon thereafter (paragraph 13), Mr. Obama uses antithesis to show that the Selma marchers were ordinary people who nonetheless accomplished something extraordinary.

> The Americans who crossed this bridge, they were not physically imposing. But they gave courage to millions. They held no elected office. But they led a nation.

In the next paragraph, again using antithesis to highlight his point, he predicts that "what they did here will reverberate throughout the ages, not because their victory was complete, but because they proved that nonviolent change is possible, that love and hope can conquer hate."

Still, the stylistic highlight of the Selma speech occurs almost three-quarters of the way through it (paragraph 42), when the president unveils a series of metaphors to show how the Selma marches reflect the American character.

> Look at our history. We are Lewis and Clark and Sacajawea, pioneers who braved the unfamiliar, followed by a stampede of farmers and miners, and entrepreneurs and hucksters. That's our spirit. That's who we are.
>
> We are Sojourner Truth and Fannie Lou Hamer, women who could do as much as any man and then some. And we're Susan B. Anthony, who shook the system until the law reflected that truth. That is our character.
>
> We're the immigrants who stowed away on ships to reach these shores, the huddled masses yearning to breathe free—Holocaust survivors, Soviet defectors, the Lost Boys of Sudan. We're the hopeful strivers who cross the Rio Grande because we want our kids to know a better life. That's how we came to be.

President Obama's "We are" metaphors stitched the Selma marches into the "crazy quilt" of American history, showing them to be as important to the American story as baseball and the Battle of Bunker Hill. All Americans can identify with them, and all Americans should commemorate them.

Still, soaring rhetoric of this type is less applicable to the legal context, so legal writers should apply to figures of speech the same rule that good taste applies to cosmetics and to the wearing of bright colors: a little bit goes a long way. An occasional figure of speech, like a sprinkle of scent or a splash of color, enhances, but just like too much scent or too many colors, too many figures of speech destroy the desired effect.

D. Conclusion: Classical Rhetoric and the Modern Supreme Court

In legal writing, invention and arrangement have not changed dramatically over time, but style has changed, especially as regards the tone of judicial opinions, including opinions written by members of the Supreme Court. "Tone" refers to the relationship between the judicial writer and the reader.[161] The detached, "magisterial" tone that Chief Justice John Marshall used in the early nineteenth century had its roots in religious writing and evinced a sort of clergyman-congregant relationship between writer and reader. The "technical and professional" tone that replaced it modified that relationship to teacher and student or expert and novice, but still reflected the writer's authority. In contrast to both its predecessors, today's "conversational" tone, which is increasingly evident in judicial opinions, shows the author communicating with readers as fellow members of a community, inviting them to participate in the author's resolution of the case.[162]

The first practitioner of the conversational tone on the Supreme Court was Oliver Wendell Holmes, Jr., who served from 1902 until 1932. Holmes had a distinct and influential legal philosophy, but he is equally admired for the tart, pithy language that peppers his opinions. Holmes combined informal writing with a "magisterial" tendency to mask his reasoning, so he is a bridge between traditional and modern styles of judicial writing. His life and work are the focus of chapter 3.

NOTES

1. Edward P. J. Corbett and Robert J. Connors, *Classical Rhetoric for the Modern Student*, 4th ed. (New York: Oxford University Press, 1999), 5.
2. Edward P. J. Corbett, *Classical Rhetoric for the Modern Student*, 2nd ed. (New York: Oxford University Press, 1971), 31–32.
3. Ibid., 41.
4. Aristotle, *Rhetoric*, trans. W. Rhys Roberts (New York: Barnes & Noble Classics, 2005), 105.
5. Corbett, *Classical Rhetoric for the Modern Student*, 2nd ed., 598.
6. Ibid.
7. Kristen Konrad Tiscione, *Rhetoric for Legal Writers: The Theory and Practice of Analysis and Persuasion*, 2nd ed. (St. Paul, MN: West Academic, 2016), 39.
8. Corbett, *Classical Rhetoric for the Modern Student*, 2nd ed., 598.
9. Tiscione, *Rhetoric for Legal Writers*, 2nd ed., 39.
10. Kristen Robbins-Tiscione, *Rhetoric for Legal Writers: The Theory and Practice of Analysis and Persuasion* (St. Paul, MN: West Publishing Company, 2009), 14.
11. Ibid., 15.
12. Ibid., 28.
13. *Essential Dialogues of Plato: Gorgias*, trans. Benjamin Jowett and rev. Pedro de Blas (New York: Barnes & Noble Books, 2005), 133–34.
14. Ibid., 134.
15. Ibid., 136–37.
16. George A. Kennedy, *Classical Rhetoric and Its Christian and Secular Tradition from Ancient to Modern Times*, 2nd ed. (Chapel Hill, NC: University of North Carolina Press, 1999), 80–81.
17. Ibid., 81.
18. Ibid.
19. Ibid.
20. Tiscione, *Rhetoric for Legal Writers*, 2nd ed., 39.
21. James Boyd White, "Law as Rhetoric, Rhetoric as Law: The Arts of Cultural and Communal Life," *University of Chicago Law Review* 52 (1985): 684.
22. Ibid., 694.
23. Tiscione, *Rhetoric for Legal Writers*, 2nd ed., 40.
24. James L. Kinneavy, "Restoring the Humanities: The Return of Rhetoric from Exile," in James J. Murphy, ed., *The Rhetorical Tradition and Modern Writing* (New York: Modern Language Association of America, 1982), 20.
25. Ibid., 19–20.
26. White, "Law as Rhetoric, Rhetoric as Law," 695.
27. Corbett and Connors, *Classical Rhetoric for the Modern Student*, 4th ed., 489.
28. Robbins-Tiscione, *Rhetoric for Legal Writers*, 9.
29. Ibid., 10.
30. Ibid.
31. Corbett and Connors, *Classical Rhetoric for the Modern Student*, 4th ed., 490.
32. James J. Murphy, Richard A. Kafula, Forbes I. Hill, and Donovan J. Oaks, *A Synoptic History of Classical Rhetoric*, 3rd ed. (Mahwah, NJ: Lawrence Erlbaum Associates, 2003), 12.
33. Ibid., 14.

34. Ibid., 22.
35. Ibid., 8.
36. Ibid., 18.
37. Kennedy, *Classical Rhetoric and Its Christian and Secular Tradition from Ancient to Modern Times*, 2nd ed., 74.
38. Ibid., 75.
39. Michael H. Frost, *Introduction to Classical Legal Rhetoric: A Lost Heritage* (Burlington, VT: Ashgate Publishing Company, 2005), 2.
40. Howard Streifford, "An Axiological Analysis of the Rhetorical Implications in Selected Supreme Court Decisions" (Unpublished Doctoral Dissertation, Southern Illinois University-Carbondale, 1967), 106.
41. Robbins-Tiscione, *Rhetoric for Legal Writers*, 17.
42. Ibid., 19.
43. Michael R. Smith, *Advanced Legal Writing: Theories and Strategies in Persuasive Writing,* 3rd ed. (New York: Wolters Kluwer, 2013), 12–15.
44. Ibid., 25.
45. Michael Frost, "Ethos, Pathos, and Legal Audience," *Dickinson Law Review* 99 (1994): 115.
46. Smith, *Advanced Legal Writing*, 2nd ed. (New York: Wolters Kluwer, 2008), 97.
47. Ibid., 105.
48. Ibid., 126.
49. Ibid.
50. Robbins-Tiscione, *Rhetoric for Legal Writers* (West, 2009), 122.
51. Kennedy, *Classical Rhetoric and Its Christian and Secular Tradition from Ancient to Modern Times*, 2nd ed., 82.
52. Aristotle, *Rhetoric*, 107.
53. Murphy et al., *A Synoptic History of Classical Rhetoric*, 3rd ed., 33.
54. Ibid., 127–28.
55. Ibid., 132.
56. Marcus Tullius Cicero, *On the Orator*, trans. E.W. Sutton and H. Rackham (Cambridge, MA: Harvard University Press, 1942); Frost, *Introduction to Classical Legal Rhetoric: A Lost Heritage*, 2–3.
57. Curtis Dozier and Lee H. Honeycutt, eds., Quintilian, *Institutes of Oratory,* trans. John Selby Watson (Published by the Editors, 2015).
58. Frost, *Introduction to Classical Rhetoric*, 35, 59.
59. Murphy et al., *A Synoptic History of Classical Rhetoric*, 3rd ed., 230.
60. Ibid.
61. Ibid.
62. Corbett and Connors, *Classical Rhetoric for the Modern Student*, 4th ed., 511.
63. Ibid., 543.
64. Kristen K. Robbins, "Philosophy v. Rhetoric in Legal Education: Understanding the Schism Between Doctrinal and Legal Writing Faculty," *Journal of the Association of Legal Writing Directors* 3 (2006): 108.
65. Linda Lavine and Kurt M. Saunders, "Thinking Like a Rhetor," *Journal of Legal Education* 43 (1993): 108.
66. Ibid., 111–13.
67. Robbins, "Philosophy v. Rhetoric in Legal Education," 124.
68. Robbins-Tiscione, *Rhetoric for Legal Writers* (2009), 78.
69. Tiscione, *Rhetoric for Legal Writers*, 2nd ed., 225.
70. Robbins-Tiscione, *Rhetoric for Legal Writers*, 82.
71. Theresa Godwin Phelps, "The New Legal Rhetoric," *Southwestern Law Journal* 40 (1986): 1089.
72. Corbett and Connors, *Classical Rhetoric for the Modern Student*, 4th ed., 17–22.
73. Robbins-Tiscione, *Rhetoric for Legal Writers*, 102.
74. Ibid.
75. Corbett and Connors, *Classical Rhetoric for the Modern Student*, 4th ed., 20.

76. Ibid., 29; see also Tiscione, *Rhetoric for Legal Writers*, 2nd ed., 69.
77. Corbett and Connors, *Classical Rhetoric for the Modern Student*, 2nd ed., 87.
78. Tiscione, *Rhetoric for Legal Writers*, 2nd ed., 69.
79. Corbett and Connors, *Classical Rhetoric for the Modern Student*, 2nd ed., 133.
80. Ibid., 91–92.
81. Ibid., 94.
82. Ibid., 97.
83. Ibid., 104.
84. Ibid., 105–7.
85. Ibid., 110–12.
86. Ibid., 118.
87. Ibid., 115.
88. Both audio and print versions of the speech are available through the Miller Center at the University of Virginia. See http://millercenter.org/the-presidency/presidential-speeches/march-7-2015-r . . .
89. Corbett and Connors, *Classical Rhetoric for the Modern Student*, 4th ed., 256.
90. Ibid., 277.
91. Ibid., 490.
92. Frost, *Introduction to Classical Legal Rhetoric*, 45, citing US Supreme Court rules 14 and 24.
93. Corbett and Connors, *Classical Rhetoric for the Modern* Student, 4th ed., 260.
94. Ibid.
95. Ibid.
96. The line comes from Frost's poem titled "Mending Wall." See Edward Connery Latham, ed., *The Poetry of Robert Frost* (New York: Holt, Rinehart & Winston, 1969), 33.
97. Dozier and Honeycutt, eds., Quintilian, *Institutes of Oratory*, trans. John Selby Watson, Bk. 4.2 (Published by the Editors, 2015), 198.
98. Corbett and Connors, *Classical Rhetoric for the Modern Student*, 4th ed., 274.
99. Ibid.
100. Ibid., 275.
101. 444 F.3d 1104 (9th Cir. 2006).
102. Linda Edwards, *Readings in Persuasion: Briefs That Changed the World* (New York: Wolters Kluwer 2012), 75. An amicus curiae brief is the work of a third party, often a nonprofit organization with a policy interest in a particular case, that presents a court—usually an appellate court—with legal and policy reasons why it should decide a particular case in favor of one side or the other. The organization does not represent the party it supports; it is an independent "friend of the court," as the name "amicus curiae" suggests.
103. Corbett and Connors, *Classical Rhetoric for the Modern Student*, 4th ed., 276.
104. Ibid.
105. Ibid.
106. Lucille A. Jewel, "Old School Rhetoric and New-School Cognitive Science: The Enduring Power of Logocentric Categories," *Legal Communications & Rhetoric: Journal of the Association of Legal Writing Directors* 13 (Fall 2016): 39.
107. Ibid; See also Kristen K. Robbins, "Paradigm Lost: Recapturing Classical Rhetoric to Validate Legal Reasoning," *Vermont Law Review* 27 (2003): 483.
108. Robbins, "Paradigm Lost,"493.
109. Ibid.
110. Ibid., 496.
111. Ibid., 497.
112. Jewell, "Old-School Rhetoric and New-School Cognitive Science," 59, n. 125.
113. Robert J. Connors, Lisa S. Ede, and Andrea A. Lunsford, *Essays on Classical Rhetoric and Modern Discourse* (Carbondale, IL: Southern Illinois University Press, 1984), 144.
114. Frost, *Introduction to Classical Legal Rhetoric*, 32.
115. Connors, Ede, and Lunsford, *Essays on Classical Rhetoric and Modern Discourse*, 144.
116. William M. Keith and Christian O. Lundberg, *The Essential Guide to Rhetoric* (Boston: Bedford/St. Martin's, 2008) 37.

117. Ibid.
118. Corbett and Connors, *Classical Rhetoric for the Modern Student*, 4th ed., 53.
119. Connors, Ede, and Lunsford, *Essays on Classical Rhetoric and Modern Discourse*, 144.
120. Ibid., 146.
121. Keith and Lundberg, *The Essential Guide to Rhetoric*, 37–38.
122. Aristotle, *Rhetoric*, trans. W. Rhys Roberts, Bk. 1 (New York: Barnes & Noble Books, 2005), 117.
123. Corbett and Connors, *Classical Rhetoric for the Modern Student*, 4th ed., 283.
124. Ibid., 284.
125. Ibid., 290.
126. Corbett and Connors, *Classical Rhetoric for the Modern Student*, 4th ed., 337.
127. Ibid., 339–59.
128. Tiscione, *Rhetoric for Legal Writers*, 131–32.
129. Ibid., 133.
130. Frost, *Introduction to Classical Legal Rhetoric*, 4, 12–13.
131. Corbett and Connors, *Classical Rhetoric for the Modern Student*, 4th ed., 379.
132. Ibid.
133. Ibid., 378–79.
134. Ibid., 381.
135. Corbett and Connors, *Classical Rhetoric for the Modern Student*, 4th ed., 382.
136. Edwards, *Readings in Persuasion*, 77.
137. Address from the Brandenburg Gate (Berlin Wall) of President Ronald Reagan, June 12, 1987, accessed May 25, 2019, http://millercenter.org/the-presidency/presidential-speeches/june-12-1987-a . . .
138. Corbett and Connors, *Classical Rhetoric for the Modern Student*, 4th ed., 389.
139. Ibid.
140. Ibid., 383–84.
141. Ibid., 387.
142. Ibid., 388.
143. American Bible Society, *The Bible*, Revised Standard Version, Genesis 1:25 (New York 1970).
144. Corbett and Connors., *Classical Rhetoric for the Modern Student*, 4th ed., 390.
145. Ibid., 394.
146. Ibid., 395.
147. Ibid.
148. Ibid., 393.
149. Ibid., 396.
150. Haig A. Bosmajian, *Metaphor and Reason in Judicial Opinions* (Carbondale, IL: Southern Illinois University Press, 1992), 45.
151. The domino theory argued that if the United States permitted a Communist government to unify and govern Vietnam, then other countries in Asia would soon fall to Communism, like a succession of dominoes. It precipitated the long and costly American military involvement in Vietnam. Gordon M. Goldstein, *Lessons in Disaster: McGeorge Bundy and the Path to War in Vietnam* (New York: Henry Holt, 2008), 44–45.
152. *Berkey v. Third Avenue Railway Company*, 155 N.E. 58, 61 (1926).
153. *McCollum v. Board of Education*, 333 U.S. 203, 247 (1948).
154. Corbett and Connors, *Classical Rhetoric for the Modern Student*, 4th ed., 396.
155. Ibid.
156. Ibid., 397.
157. Ibid., 398.
158. Ibid., 399.
159. Ibid., 402.
160. 163 U.S. 537, 559 (1896).
161. William D. Popkin, *Evolution of the Judicial Opinion: Institutional and Individual Styles* (New York: NYU Press, 2007), 3.
162. Ibid., 143–47, 154.

Chapter Three

Oliver Wendell Holmes, Jr.

Literary Lion

A. Beginnings

Harvard Law Professor (and later Justice) Felix Frankfurter said of his friend Justice Holmes: "No judge of the Supreme Court has done more to establish it in the consciousness of the people. Mr. Justice Holmes is built into the structure of our national life and has written himself into the slender volume of the literature of all time."[1] "Literature" is the operative word in that observation because Holmes's talent as a writer was crucial to his influence in American law. Holmes "had the ability to convey ideas concisely, vividly, and poignantly, often articulating with blinding clarity what many others vaguely felt."[2]

Both nature and nurture contributed to Holmes's literary legacy. Born in Boston in 1841, Wendell, as he was known in his youth, was the namesake of Oliver Wendell Holmes, Sr., a leading physician and author known for both his prose and his poetry. Besides writing the famous poem "Old Ironsides," which helped to save a Revolutionary War–era ship from a planned destruction, Dr. Holmes penned a series of essays called "The Autocrat of the Breakfast Table" in the *Atlantic Monthly*, a literary magazine of which he was a founder. "The Autocrat," along with Dr. Holmes's poetry, other prose, and editorship of the *Atlantic Monthly*, had made him one of the best-known American writers of the nineteenth century by the time of his death in 1894.[3]

As for nurture's role in Wendell's intellectual development, he was fortunate to have grown up in Boston. Beginning in about 1815, with the founding of the *North American Review* by a group of Harvard professors and reaching its peak in 1857, with the establishment of the *Atlantic Monthly*, Boston was the center of literary life in America. Because of Dr. Holmes's prominence as an author, leading literary lights Ralph Waldo Emerson, Henry Wadsworth Longfellow, and James Russell Lowell were family friends and visitors to the Doctor's home.[4]

Nourished by this environment, young Wendell took a keen interest in literature and philosophy and showed a flair for writing at Harvard College, which he entered in 1857 at age sixteen. Overall, he was an indifferent student, but writing captivated him. Beginning in 1858, he wrote for the *Harvard Magazine*, producing book reviews and editorials, and was selected to be one of its editors in July 1860.[5] During the summer of 1860, which preceded his senior year, he wrote an essay on Plato for the *University Quarterly*, an intercollegiate magazine published in New Haven, Connecticut. His essay was judged the best one written by an undergraduate that year, and he was awarded the twenty-dollar first prize.[6]

For Wendell, though, the twilight of the undergraduate years coincided with the dawn of the Civil War. At graduation, in June 1861, he shared the annual prize for Greek prose composition.[7] Afterward he sought a role in the Civil War. In late July, 1861, a few weeks after graduation, he succeeded, with the help of his cousin, an aide to the governor of Massachusetts, in obtaining a commission as a first lieutenant in the Massachusetts Twentieth Volunteer Infantry.[8]

The Civil War experience would shape Wendell as much as growing up in Dr. Holmes's house and attending Harvard College had. For the next three years, he was either, in biographer Liva Baker's words, "suffering the dangers and discomforts of the battlefield or recovering from wounds."[9] The wounds, of course, reflected the dangers; the discomforts—vermin, disease, mud, hunger, thirst, and fatigue—were less dreaded, but ever-present.[10]

Holmes traveled south with his regiment in early September 1861; in late October, he saw combat at the Battle of Ball's Bluff, near Leesburg, Virginia. Receiving the order to attack while lying in a grassy field, Holmes rose to advance, but a spent bullet hit him in the stomach, knocking the wind out of him. Two fellow soldiers helped him to his feet, and one, a colonel, ordered him to the rear, but Holmes soon returned to the fray when he discovered he was not wounded. Upon his return, a second bullet struck him in the chest almost immediately, and he fell.[11] Although the wound proved not to be life-threatening, it warranted six months of recuperation. After spending a week at a friend's house in Philadelphia, Holmes returned by train to Boston, where he enjoyed a hero's welcome, complete with flowers, ice cream, and a steady stream of visitors.[12]

Holmes rejoined his regiment in the spring of 1862, now a captain. In mid-September, at the Battle of Antietam, near Sharpsburg, Maryland, he was wounded again, one of ten thousand Union soldiers who suffered that fate. Following orders to retreat on the run as the enemy fired from the flank,

Holmes was shot in the back of the neck.[13] The bullet emerged from his throat to the left of his windpipe, leaving a gaping hole, but not affecting his ability to walk, breath, or speak.[14] Once again, Holmes returned to Boston to recuperate; after recovering completely, he returned to his regiment in November 1862.

Holmes would be wounded one more time during his military service, in May 1863, at Chancellorsville, Virginia, where he was shot in the heel. The wound did not cost Holmes his foot, but it sent him back to Boston for another six months of convalescence and kept him out of the Battle of Gettysburg in July, where his regiment lost half of its enlisted men and ten of its thirteen officers.[15]

Now experiencing battle fatigue, Holmes took a staff position as an aide to a general, away from the front lines, when he returned to duty in January 1864. But his war weariness continued. Therefore, when the Twentieth Massachusetts Infantry dissolved in June 1864, at the end of its three-year tour, having lost most of its officers and seen its ranks reduced to a mere fraction of its former strength, Holmes felt his duty was done. He mustered out of the Army on July 17, 1864, and returned to Boston.[16] Soon he would be expected to choose his life's work.

B. Professional Life

Despite his philosophical bent, Holmes was not interested in a life of pure introspection because the war experience had spawned in him a thirst for action. That thirst would be evident many years later in a famous quote from his Memorial Day Address in 1884.

> I think that, as life is action and passion, it is required of a man that he should share the passion and action of his time at peril of being judged not to have lived.[17]

But neither was he interested in amassing great wealth, so becoming a banker or a railroad baron was out too.[18] Instead, in October 1864, Holmes enrolled at the Harvard Law School, which had no stringent requirements for admission in those days; one merely had to be at least nineteen years of age, able to afford the fifty-dollar tuition, and able to "produce testimonials of [one's] good moral character."[19] No course was required, and nobody took attendance at lectures.[20] One could take one's courses in any order; although prerequisites were suggested, they were not required.[21] And one received an L.L.B. after two years of study—a year and a half in exceptional cases—even if the course of study was circuitous and haphazard.[22]

Holmes's legal education was haphazard, but Harvard nonetheless conferred the L.L.B. on him in the summer of 1866, despite his not having completed the prescribed program.[23] Holmes had quickly tired of sitting passively listening to his professors, so before completing his third semester of lectures, he had gone to work as a clerk in the small law office of his cousin, Robert Morse, copying documents, running errands, and doing research.[24]

After graduation and a five-week sojourn in Europe, Holmes returned to Boston and joined the law firm of Shattuck, Bradley, and Thayer, where he was a somewhat reluctant lawyer who disliked law practice "apart from arguing cases."[25] A more exciting professional opportunity presented itself in the winter of 1869–1870, when Holmes's senior colleague at the law firm, James Bradley Thayer, accepted an invitation to update Chancellor James Kent's famous legal treatise, *Commentaries on American Law*, whose first edition dated back to 1830.[26] Thayer asked Holmes to assist, whereupon the younger man threw himself into the work, largely ignoring his law practice and his friends for the next two years and expanding the modest task he had been offered into something much more significant.[27] Instead of just adding new cases and their holdings, Holmes wrote short summaries of how the law had developed since Kent's day and essays that assessed the influence of modern legal scholars on that development.[28] Between his compensation for his work on the *Commentaries* and part-time teaching at Harvard, Holmes was able to earn a living during this time.[29]

After completing Kent's *Commentaries*, Holmes, now just shy of his thirty-fifth birthday, returned to law practice in the new firm of Shattuck, Holmes, and Munroe. As a practicing lawyer, he argued thirty-two cases before the Massachusetts Supreme Judicial Court between 1867 and 1881, and in 1879 joined George Shattuck as counsel for one of the parties in a business dispute before the US Supreme Court; the record does not indicate which man argued for the client.[30] Holmes could not avoid the scholarly life for long, though; indeed, between 1876 and 1881, he pushed nearly all his other interests aside to devote himself to uncovering foundational legal principles on which he hoped to erect an overarching theory of law.[31] He continued to practice law by day, but after hours he could usually be found at Boston's venerable Social Law Library reading and making notes until 9 p.m., when the building closed.[32] Holmes would then unwind before heading home by walking around Boston Common for an hour with a colleague.[33]

The result of Holmes's after-hours scholarship was *The Common Law*, published in 1881 by Boston's Little, Brown and Company, just five days before Holmes's fortieth birthday.[34] The book has been called the greatest work of legal thought in American history.[35] Holmes's work departed dramatically from the governing legal paradigm of the day, which was that our law derived from natural law, reflected divine will, and, as explained by the great English jurist William Blackstone and his American counterpart, Chancellor Kent, was immutable and eternal.[36] According to this view, to resolve cases, judges had only to discover the relevant eternal principle and apply it. In this environment, Holmes's opening words in *The Common Law* seemed to dance on the gravestones of the ancients. He famously wrote:

> The life of the law has not been logic; it has been experience. The felt necessities of the time, the prevalent moral and political theories, institutions of public policy, avowed or unconscious, even the prejudices which judges share with their fellow men, have had a good deal more to do than the syllogism in determining the rules by which men should be governed. The law embodies the story of a nation's development through many centuries, and it cannot be dealt with as if it contained only the axioms and corollaries of a book of mathematics.[37]

Put simply, policy and politics were substantially more important to the resolution of cases and the development of law than the logical reasoning in which they were clothed and expressed. That is taken for granted today, but not so in 1881.

The publication of *The Common Law* gave Holmes a new scholarly gravitas, which enabled him to shed the unwelcome demands of law practice in favor of a professorship at the Harvard Law School.[38] But Holmes did not linger in the groves of academe long enough to smell the flowers; indeed, he did not even complete the first term, instead resigning abruptly in December 1882 when Governor John Long appointed him to the Massachusetts Supreme Judicial Court.[39] The prospect of a judgeship was irresistible to Holmes because it offered a chance for both action and scholarship.[40]

Holmes's ascension to the Massachusetts Court coincided with the appearance on the docket of new issues that reflected the increasingly urban and industrial nature of Massachusetts.[41] In responding to these issues, Holmes exhibited a tolerance for legislative experimentation that would later characterize his constitutional jurisprudence on the United States Supreme Court. For example, in *Commonwealth v. Perry* in 1891, the majority of the Massachusetts Court invalidated a state law that prohibited employers from firing or withholding wages from weavers in textile mills whose work was less than perfect.[42] Holmes, in dissent, deferred to the judgment of the state legislature, which had sought to protect employees from such punitive practices.[43]

Similarly, Holmes wrote a solo dissent in *Vegelahn v. Guntner* in 1896.[44] In that case, Holmes's colleagues upheld an injunction that prohibited striking upholsterers from picketing in front of their employer's factory.[45] Holmes dissented because he thought workers should be permitted to strike for higher wages, just as a new business is permitted to supplant an established one if it can.[46] Holmes harbored serious doubts about the wisdom of unions and socialism, but he preferred that labor-management disputes be resolved by arguments in the courts instead of by violence in the streets.[47]

His abiding skepticism that either labor or management had the "right answer" enabled him to remain above the fray.

In July 1899, after serving nearly seventeen years on the Massachusetts Court, Holmes became chief justice when his predecessor died in office. Three years later, when Justice Horace Gray, a Massachusetts native, retired from the US Supreme Court, President Theodore Roosevelt appointed Holmes to succeed Gray.[48] The Senate confirmed Holmes unanimously and without debate on December 4, 1902.[49] He and his wife Fanny, both aged sixty-one, would move away from Boston for the first time.[50]

C. On the Court

The Supreme Court that Holmes joined was largely united on the dominant issue it faced: governmental regulation of business. Outside the Court, the world had changed rapidly and dramatically during the last quarter of the nineteenth century.[51] Economic change had brought unprecedented wealth for captains of industry, but for many workers, "it meant living in sunless, airless tenements, working in sunless, airless factories, back-breaking hours, wage slavery, disease, dirt, and, often, premature death."[52] Yet Holmes's colleagues remained anchored in a bygone era, consistently interpreting the "liberty" guaranteed by the Fourteenth Amendment to mean "liberty of contract," a strict prohibition on governmental regulation of the employer-employee relationship. But Holmes's deep skepticism led him to question the Court's capacity to decide what was good for society and persuaded him that courts should allow the people to make such choices.[53]

His most memorable rejection of liberty of contract came in *Lochner v. New York*, in which the majority invalidated a New York statute that limited bakers' hours.[54] Holmes dissented, arguing that the constitutionality of a statute should not turn on whether five justices thought it was a good idea, based on their devotion to free-market economics.[55] Holmes dissented again in *Hammer v. Dagenhart*, in which the majority invalidated a federal statute that prohibited interstate commerce in goods made by child labor. He thought that Congress, not the Court, should determine, under its power over interstate commerce, whether to prohibit such goods from entering the commercial stream.[56]

Besides social welfare legislation, the major constitutional issue of Holmes's day was the freedom of speech, and "[h]istory has judged Holmes right and most of his Court wrong" on both.[57] World War I tested the limits of free speech in the United States. In *Schenck v. United States*, the Supreme Court, with Holmes writing for the majority, upheld convictions for publishing leaflets that urged opposition to conscription. Holmes observed that government could surely punish speech that intentionally interfered with conscription during wartime, despite the First Amendment's guarantee of free speech.[58] To Holmes, "The question in every case is whether the words used are used in such circumstances and are of such a nature as to create a clear and present danger that they will bring about the substantive evils that Congress has a right to prevent."[59]

Some thoughtful voices that Holmes respected disagreed with his opinion in *Schenck* and made their disagreements known. For example, Zechariah Chafee, a professor at the Harvard Law School, published a critical analysis of *Schenck* and another Holmes free speech opinion—*Debs v. United States*—in the *Harvard Law Review*.[60] Fortuitously, when Holmes returned to Massachusetts for the summer, the justice and the professor discussed the matter over tea.[61]

Chafee apparently persuaded Holmes to use the clear-and-present-danger test to protect speech more broadly, that is, by judging its imminent risk of harm. In *Abrams v. United States*, which followed their meeting, Holmes dissented from a decision to affirm convictions under the Espionage Act of several persons who had published leaflets critical of President Wilson for sending American troops to Russia after the 1917 Russian Revolution. In that dissent, which mirrored Chafee's article in several respects, Holmes famously wrote that "the ultimate good desired is better reached by free trade in ideas" and that "the best test of truth is the power of the thought to get itself accepted in the competition of the market. . . ."[62]

In the wake of his *Abrams* dissent, Holmes finally received the recognition he had long desired. In 1924 he received the Roosevelt (now Presidential) Medal of Freedom, in 1926, he was the subject of a profile in *The New Republic*, and in 1929 and 1931, respectively, journalist Alfred Lief published two books about Holmes: *The Dissenting Opinions of Mr. Justice Holmes* and *Representative Opinions of Mr. Justice Holmes*. His dissents in *Lochner* and *Abrams* still influence American law. They became majority views on the Court after Holmes's death in 1935. Today, in Holmesian fashion, courts usually defer to legislative judgments regarding economic regulation, but not to legislative judgments about personal freedom, especially the freedom of speech.[63] Thus, Holmes's prominence is deserved because his service on the Court fundamentally changed American law.

D. Holmes the Writer

Legal scholars disagree about the nature of, the influences on, and the wisdom of Oliver Wendell Holmes's jurisprudence, but, writes Professor Thomas Grey, "[o]ne of the few points on which all commentators agree is Holmes' greatness as a prose stylist."[64] Indeed, legal scholar and former judge Richard Posner contends that Holmes's true greatness [was not achieved] as a lawyer, judge, or legal theorist," but instead, as a "writer-philosopher" for having infused "literary skill and philosophical insight into his legal work."[65] Elaborating on this theme, Posner noted,

> His majority and dissenting opinions alike are remarkable not only for the poet's gift of metaphor that is their principal stylistic distinction, but also for their brevity, freshness, and freedom from legal jargon; a directness bordering on the colloquial; a lightness of touch foreign to the legal temperament; and an insistence on being concrete rather than legalistic—on identifying values and policies rather than intoning formulas.[66]

Holmes strived for literary quality in his opinions. "To arrange the thoughts so that one springs naturally from one that precedes it," he observed, "and to express them with a singing variety is the devil and all."[67]

The remainder of this chapter will highlight the cases in which Holmes made his most important contributions to American law, which cases also illustrate his effective use of rhetorical techniques. The cases, and the contributions they represent, include *Lochner* and *Hammer* (judicial restraint); *Schenck* and *Abrams* (freedom of speech); and *Frank v. Mangum*[68] and *Moore v. Dempsey* (due process).[69]

1. *Lochner v. New York*

In *Lochner*, a bakery owner was convicted of violating a New York statute that prohibited him from either requiring or permitting an employee to work more than sixty hours in one week.[70] Emphasizing that the statute prohibited employees of bakeries and confectionary shops from working beyond sixty hours in a week even if they wished to, Justice Rufus Peckham's majority opinion concluded that the New York law interfered with the right of employers and employees to contract for their mutual benefit. "The general right to make a contract in relation to his business is part of the liberty of the individual protected by the 14th Amendment of the Federal Constitution," Peckham wrote.[71] "Of course," he added, "the liberty of contract relating to labor includes both parties to it. The one has as much right to purchase as the other to sell labor."[72] Because neither public health nor any other basis existed for interfering with liberty of contract in this case, the challenged statute was unconstitutional.

Holmes's dissent is brief (under two pages), but powerful. It derives from the rhetorical topic of "comparison," in particular the argument based on "difference," which asserts that one case should not be treated like another.[73] In this case, according to Holmes, the crucial "difference" is between the economic theory of laissez faire—minimal government regulation of economic activity—and the constitutional principle of "liberty," which embraces no particular economic theory. Consistent with that difference, the opening paragraph reflects Holmes's "judicial restraint," or deference to legislative judgments, in economic matters. Holmes writes:

> This case is decided upon an economic theory which a large part of the country does not entertain. If it were a question whether I agreed with that theory, I should desire to study it further and long before making up my mind. But I do not conceive that to be my duty, because I strongly believe that my agreement or disagreement has nothing to do with the right of a majority to embody their opinions in law.[74]

The opening paragraph also reflects Holmes's rhetorical skill. The vividness of the first sentence, presented in an aphorism, forces the reader to face the possibility of an illegitimate decision by the majority based not on a fair reading of the Commerce Clause, but instead, on the majority's favored economic policy. That vividness—which derives from directness and brevity—makes the sentence memorable. Judge Posner suggests that it would not have been so memorable if Holmes had written a conventional judicial sentence, such as: "I respectfully but earnestly dissent from the majority's unwarranted substitution of its own views of public policy for the more flexible mandate of the Constitution."[75]

The second sentence in the opening paragraph is rhetorically significant for its appeal to ethos. Holmes makes the reader confident that his dissent does not simply reflect distaste for the majority's economic philosophy; on the contrary, he stresses, if taking a position on that philosophy were necessary, he would study it in good faith. But such study is unnecessary, he continues, because whatever one thinks of free-market economics, the Court has no right to base a constitutional decision on it.[76]

Later in the same paragraph, Holmes further demonstrates his rhetorical skill by employing a now-famous *aphorism* to show that "liberty of contract" is not included in the language of the Constitution. Referring to a leading nineteenth-century tract that championed free-market economics, Holmes writes, "The 14th Amendment does not enact Mr. Herbert Spencer's Social Statics."[77] Aphorisms, or *maxims*, as the ancients called them, are "general statements about human affairs."[78] They serve as either the premises or the conclusions of enthymemes—rhetoric's probabilistic counterparts to logic's syllogisms—and they become complete enthymemes when a reason or conclusion is added.[79] For example, as Aristotle explains, an aphorism might state: "There is no man in all things prosperous." When a reason is added, such as: "for all are slaves of money or of chance," an enthymeme results.[80] The reference to *Social Statics* also illustrates synecdoche because the book is just one part of a larger economic philosophy that Holmes uses the book to symbolize.

Aphorisms are effective rhetorical devices because they state as a general rule widely held opinions about certain subjects and because they foster ethos by showing the writer making a public declaration of moral principles.[81] Justice Holmes uses them to great effect in *Lochner* and other opinions; absent the reference to Spencer's book, for example, Holmes's *Lochner* dissent would likely be less enduring than it has been. After commanding the reader's attention with the aphorism, Holmes reminds his colleagues that the Court has upheld a wide array of laws that regulated economic activity (e.g., compulsory vaccinations, sales of securities, and an eight-hour day for miners) because the Constitution does not embody any particular economic theory that fits the facts of every case.[82]

In conveying that reminder, Holmes once again draws from the topic of comparison, but now to show the similarity, not the difference, between two cases. He explains that no great leap of logic is required to uphold a law that limits the working hours of bakers because the Court has upheld the regulations on vaccinations, securities, and miners' working hours. Then, as if to underscore that point, Holmes offers another aphorism: "General propositions [e.g., liberty of contract] do not decide concrete cases."[83]

Toward the end of his dissent, Holmes uses a third aphorism—"[e]very opinion tends to become a law"—to begin a passage that explains his trademark deference to legislative enactments of dominant opinions in economic affairs. In support of that deference, he returns to the argument based on difference to distinguish the constitutional principle of liberty from the economic philosophy of laissez faire. Holmes writes:

> I think that the word "liberty," in the Fourteenth Amendment, is perverted when it is held to prevent the natural outcome of a dominant opinion, unless it can be said that a rational and fair man necessarily would admit that the statute proposed would infringe fundamental principles as they have been understood by the traditions of our people and our law.[84]

Because a rational person could view the New York law as "a proper measure on the score of health," Holmes concludes that it should stand.[85]

Thus, Holmes's *Lochner* opinion employs several memorable aphorisms in support of his judicial philosophy of deference to legislative judgment in economic matters. Such deference derived from deep skepticism about the wisdom of one policy choice over another, leading Holmes to support Congress's choice as long as the Constitution did not prohibit it. His *Lochner* opinion qualifies as legal literature because it "can be detached from the setting in which [it was] created"; in other words, *Social Statics* is long forgotten, but Holmes's rejection of it as constitutional doctrine lives on in the power of his rhetoric.[86]

2. *Hammer v. Dagenhart*

Hammer featured a father who, on his own behalf and as best friend of his two minor sons, sought to enjoin the enforcement of a federal statute that prohibited interstate commerce in products made by child labor.[87] To limit the reach of Congress's power under the Commerce Clause, Justice William Day's majority opinion distinguished between "commerce," which he conceded Congress could regulate, and "production," which he insisted Congress could not regulate. He wrote:

> Commerce "consists of intercourse and traffic . . . and includes the transportation of persons and property, as well as the purchase, sale and exchange of commodities." The making of goods and the mining of coal are not commerce, nor does the fact that these things are to be afterwards shipped, or used in interstate commerce, make their production a part thereof.[88]

Thus, the aim of the Commerce Clause was to give Congress authority to regulate the interstate transportation of goods, but not to "control the states in their exercise of the police power over local trade and manufacture."[89]

The challenged statute, Justice Day concluded, exceeded Congress's authority by, in effect, enabling it to "regulate the hours of labor of children in factories and mines within the state, a purely state authority."[90] If Congress could regulate production, he concluded in a bit of apocalyptic hyperbole, "all freedom of commerce will be at an end, and the power of the states over local matters may be eliminated, and thus our system of government be practically destroyed."[91]

Holmes, in a dissent joined by Justices Joseph McKenna, Louis Brandeis, and John Clarke, envisioned no such apocalypse. The dissent begins with an argument derived from the topic of "definition," which is useful to distinguish between permissible and impermissible behavior.[92] In this instance, the proper definition of Congress's power to "regulate" interstate commerce, according to Holmes, allows Congress to exclude from that commerce items it believes harm society.

Holmes then expresses his argument in a flashy display of rhetorical style, observing:

> It would not be argued today that the power to regulate does not include the power to prohibit. Regulation means the prohibition of something, and when interstate commerce is the matter to be regulated, I cannot doubt that the regulation may prohibit any part of such commerce that Congress sees fit to forbid.[93]

A legal writing professor could balk at the double negative, which obscures not only an otherwise effective aphorism—the power to regulate is the power to prohibit—but also polyptoton (the repetition of "power" in two successive clauses) and isocolon (two clauses with an equal number of syllables). Holmes mitigates any damage caused by the double negative, though, by beginning the second sentence with another aphorism that is abundantly clear: "Regulation means the prohibition of something." Therefore, his expression of judicial restraint in economic matters is clear and comprehensible. Regulation includes prohibition; hence, Congress's power to regulate interstate commerce necessarily implies power to exclude from that commerce goods that Congress deems harmful.

Then, in a manner reminiscent of his *Lochner* dissent, Holmes uses the topic of comparison, this time calling on an argument from "similarity" to equate Congress's exclusion from interstate commerce of products of child labor with other items whose exclusion the Court has blessed, such as lottery tickets and colored oleomargarine. If interstate traffic in these items can be prohibited, Holmes continues, so can such traffic in the products of child labor, because "the evil of premature and excessive child labor" is a matter "upon which civilized countries have agreed far more unanimously" than on others.[94] Employing parallelism and analogy, Holmes writes, "It is not for this Court to pronounce when prohibition is necessary to regulation if it ever may be necessary—to say that it is permissible as against strong drink but not as against the product of ruined lives."[95] Parallelism lies in the two "as against" clauses, and the analogy compares liquor to products made by children, both of which Congress barred from interstate commerce.

If "ruined lives" sounds hyperbolic, note that *hyperbole* (the use of exaggerated terms for the purpose of emphasis or heightened effect) is a recognized trope in classical rhetoric, albeit one that legal writers rarely use.[96] The reference to ruined lives is also an appeal to pathos—at a time when child labor was a major social ill in the United States—by a justice known more for reason than empathy. Holmes employs it to assert that if Congress could pass a bill the previous year to outlaw the manufacture and sale of liquor (which would become the Eighteenth Amendment in 1919), Congress could surely pass a bill to outlaw interstate shipments of products made by children. To Holmes and the dissenters, the law was constitutional. A century later, Holmes's words give *Hammer* an enduring resonance, which results chiefly from his designation of the prohibited cargo as the product of "ruined lives," not "child labor." The latter is a historical relic in the United States, but adverse social conditions continue to produce hardships for children and debates about remedies, so, like his *Lochner* dissent, Holmes's dissent in *Hammer* is still meaningful for readers today.

3. *Schenck v. United States*

In *Schenck*, Holmes wrote for a unanimous Court about the freedom of speech in wartime. Joseph Schenck and Elizabeth Baer stood convicted of violating the Espionage Act of 1917 by conspiring to cause insubordination in the Armed Forces and to obstruct recruiting of soldiers for service in World War I, and of using the mails toward those ends.[97] The leaflets they produced and mailed, in Holmes's words, "intimated that conscription was despotism in its worst form and a monstrous wrong against humanity in the interest of Wall Street's chosen few."[98]

For Holmes, the wartime context in which the defendants' "circular" was produced deprived it of any First Amendment protection it might otherwise enjoy. As befits his emphasis on context, Holmes's argument originates in the topic of comparison, specifically the argument from "degree," here suggesting that speech that might be unwelcome, but permissible, in peacetime can be impermissible in wartime.[99] In a passage that ends with one of his most memorable metaphors, Holmes observes:

> We admit that in many places and in ordinary times the defendants in saying all that was said in the circular would have been within their constitutional rights. But the character of every act depends upon the circumstances in which it is done. The most stringent protection of free speech would not protect a man in falsely shouting fire in a theatre and causing a panic.[100]

The vivid metaphor of one falsely shouting fire in a theater is still invoked in discussions of free speech today, making it a teaching tool for the ages. Presumably, if Holmes had written that "the most stringent protection of free speech does not permit one to say whatever he wishes at any time or place," his words would not be so iconic and their message not so readily repeated today.

In the Aristotelian tradition, Holmes uses the fire metaphor to give "names to nameless things."[101] His metaphor instructs because it is visceral; it "originate[s] in the world of the senses" because the effects of smoke, fire, and panic "are as physiological as they are logical."[102] Put another way, the metaphor educates by "superimposing a known structure [panic in a theater] onto a new concept" [the protection of speech].[103]

Building on the previous passage, Holmes uses his literary skill to announce a mechanism for judging wartime speech. Again focused on "degree," he writes:

> The question in every case is whether the words used are used in such circumstances and are of such a nature as to create a clear and present danger that they will bring about the substantive evils that Congress has a right to prevent. It is a question of proximity and degree. When a nation is at war many things that might be said in time of peace are such a hindrance to its effort that their utterance will not be endured so long as men fight and that no Court could regard them as protected by any constitutional right.[104]

Thus was born of Holmes's literary skill the "clear and present danger" test—a pithy and concise formulation, in parallel structure, that evoked the destabilizing speech the Court thought Congress could justifiably punish in wartime. According to Professor David Currie, Holmes seemed to be saying that "[t]hose who wrote the [first] amendment . . . were too reasonable to have disabled society from protecting itself against speech that all would agree ought to be prohibited."[105] In any event, the clear and present danger test, albeit in a form more protective of speech than it was in 1919, would become in 1937, after Holmes's death, the governing standard in American jurisprudence concerning political free speech.[106]

Less memorable, but also rhetorically effective, was his use of parallelism in characterizing the tension between free speech and national security as "a question of proximity and degree."[107] Other rhetorically noteworthy features of the passage are Holmes's vivid phrase "so long as men fight" to depict wartime and his variation of sentence lengths to inject rhythm. Regarding rhythm, note the separation of two long, explanatory sentences by a short, more dramatic sentence. The latter states: "It is a question of proximity and degree." Remarkably, Holmes's unforgettable passages graced an opinion that was only four pages long.

4. Abrams v. United States

The Supreme Court decided *Schenck* in March of 1919. In November, just eight months later, the Court decided *Abrams*, which raised the same issue as *Schenck*, but produced a dramatically different opinion—a powerful dissent—from Justice Holmes. Like the *Schenck* defendants, the *Abrams* defendants were convicted of conspiring to violate the Espionage Act by inciting and encouraging resistance to American involvement in World War I.[108] Jacob Abrams and four compatriots had published and hurled from an open factory window on the Upper East Side of Manhattan, several thousand circulars critical of President Woodrow Wilson's conduct of the war. Their particular target was Wilson's decision to send American troops to Vladivostok in the Russian Far East, which decision the defendants, avowed anarchists, saw as a threat to the Russian Revolution.[109]

Based on his *Schenck* opinion, Holmes might well have reached a similar decision in *Abrams*, but he did not and the likely reason for the change of position was the influence of his visit with Professor Chafee during the previous summer (see p. 51). In a June 1919 article critical of *Schenck*, Chafee had argued that the solution to his criticism was to apply the clear-and-present-danger test in a way that was more protective of the abstract advocacy in which Mr. Schenck had engaged.[110] Holmes and Chafee discussed the article, after which Chafee left the meeting believing that he had failed to persuade Holmes, although the opposite was true. Holmes had come to appreciate Chafee's position: the Court should establish a line between protected and unprotected speech, under the clear-and-present-danger test, that emphasized society's compelling interest in free speech.[111]

Justice John Clarke wrote the majority opinion in *Abrams* for himself and six colleagues. He observed that the Russian-born defendants had published leaflets critical of the US government, intending to bring the United States "into contempt," encourage resistance to American participation in World War I, and promote curtailment of the domestic production of war materials.[112] He added that they had denounced President Wilson as a hypocrite and a coward for having sent American troops to Russia.[113] Their purpose, Clarke emphasized, was to defeat American war plans by paralyzing the country through a general strike and stopping the production of munitions necessary to the war effort.[114] Because of that purpose, their convictions must stand.

Professor G. Edward White has argued that Holmes's dissent, in which Justice Brandeis concurred, "gave his 'clear and present danger' test for speech cases much more bite" than it had in his majority opinion in *Schenck*.[115] The "bite" lay in the principle he adopted for protecting society's interest in the freedom of speech, as advocated by Professor Chafee: free trade in ideas.[116]

To express that principle, Holmes relied again on the topic of comparison, more precisely an argument based on the difference between the charges the defendants faced and their actual conduct. The charges included conspiracy to: (1) "publish[ ] "abusive language about the form of government of the United States"; (2) "publish language intended to bring the [American] form of government into contempt"; (3) "encourage resistance to the United States [military effort in World War I] by publishing leaflets"; and (4) "incite curtailment of production of things necessary to the prosecution of the war ...."[117] Then, after quoting the leaflets, which mainly criticized President Wilson's decision to send American troops to Russia, Holmes wrote that "these pronunciamentos in no way attack the government of the United States . . ."; hence, "they do not support the first two counts."[118] Note the sarcastic tone reflected in Holmes's use of the word "pronunciamentos." His word choice suggests that the leaflets may have puffed up their authors a bit, but they stood no chance of achieving their objective; hence, the federal government had grossly overestimated the danger they posed.

The third count was not satisfied either, in Holmes's view, because the mere publication and circulation of leaflets did not evince "some forcible act of opposition to some proceeding of the United States in pursuance of the war."[119] As to the fourth count, Holmes writes that although one of the leaflets did "urge curtailment of production of things necessary to the prosecution of the war . . ." the defendants' actions did not reflect an intent "to cripple or hinder the United States in the prosecution of the war," as the statute required.[120] Finally, regarding the substance of the leaflets, Holmes observes, "Now nobody can suppose that the surreptitious publishing of a silly leaflet by an unknown man, without more, would present any immediate danger that its opinions would hinder the success of the government arms or have any appreciable tendency to do so."[121] Again, Holmes's tone, as expressed in his reference to "the surreptitious publishing of a silly leaflet by an unknown man," reflects his conclusion that the defendants' action posed no threat to the American war effort.

Therein lay the "bite" in the principle of free trade in ideas.[122] Using his trademark conversational style, Holmes writes:

> Persecution for the expression of opinions seems to me perfectly logical. If you have no doubt of your premises or your power and want a certain result with all your heart you naturally express your wishes in law and sweep away all opposition. To allow opposition by speech seems to indicate that you think the speech impotent, as when a man says that he has squared the circle, or that you do not care whole heartedly for the result, or that you doubt either your power or your premises.[123]

The metaphor of "sweeping away" opposition shows the swift and certain way in which the autocrat who is sure he has (and is) the right answer to society's ills quashes opposing points of view. An underlying certainty suppresses dissent; after all, why allow expression of opposing views if they are wrong and yours are right?

But the ever-skeptical Holmes, who doubted everyone's premises, including his own, would place his bet on the airing of opposing views, not their suppression. He writes:

> [W]hen men have realized that time has upset many fighting faiths, they may come to believe even more than they believe the very foundations of their own conduct that the ultimate good desired is better reached by free trade in ideas—that the best test of truth is the power of the thought to get itself accepted in the competition of the market, and that truth is the only ground upon which their wishes safely can be carried out. That at any rate is the theory of our Constitution. It is an experiment, as all life is an experiment.[124]

This passage is memorable not only for its defense of freedom of speech, but also for its eloquence, to which several rhetorical techniques contribute. The alliteration of "fighting faiths" stays with the reader, as does the polyptoton in the use of "believe" twice in the same sentence. So does the personification in "the power of the thought to get itself accepted," as if the thought were a person seeking social acceptance or customers for a new product or service. Still, the most important rhetorical techniques in this passage are the metaphors—"free trade in ideas" and "the competition of the market," which underpin Holmes's free-speech jurisprudence. Every metaphor is, by definition, an analogy, and these metaphors analogize the freedom of speech to an idea almost all Americans held dear in 1919: free enterprise. By analogizing a controversial idea—freedom of speech in wartime—to a popular one—capitalism—Holmes legitimized the former.[125] Yet another metaphor—the Constitution and life itself as experiments—wrapped in an aphorism, adds to the power of Holmes's words.

To preserve free trade in ideas, Holmes concludes, opinions like those of Abrams and his cohorts should be protected unless they pose an imminent threat to the rule of law. To remove that protection is to abandon our constitutional experiment and shutter the laboratory.

5. *Frank v. Mangum*

At issue in *Frank* was the availability of habeas corpus relief for state prisoners who were convicted in unconstitutional proceedings. Leo Frank was convicted of murder in a Georgia court after a disorderly trial that a mob outside the courthouse threatened to disrupt. In a habeas corpus petition, Frank challenged both the conditions under which the trial was conducted and the trial judge's decision to bar Frank and his attorney from the courtroom when the verdict was read for fear that the mob would attack them. He charged that the former amounted to mob domination and "dissolution" of the court and that the latter denied him due process of law under the Fourteenth Amendment.[126]

Justice Mahlon Pitney, writing for the majority, acknowledged that when a mob dominates a trial, subject to no correction by the state, and the state then renders a judgment of death or imprisonment based on a verdict tainted by mob domination, "the state deprives the accused of his life or liberty without due process of law."[127] But, he noted, the precedents show that such disorder is not a "dissolution of the court" that robs it of jurisdiction and bars further proceedings.[128] Instead, a new trial was the customary remedy, but the Georgia courts had denied Frank a new trial "because they found his charges untrue save in a few minor particulars . . . and not prejudicial to the accused."[129]

Neither, in Pitney's view, did Frank's absence from the courtroom when the verdict was rendered violate due process. Frank's counsel had waived his client's right to be present, but without Frank's knowledge or consent. Justice Pitney, affirming the district court's denial of Frank's habeas corpus petition, reasoned that the prisoner's presence at the reading of the verdict was not so essential that a rule permitting him to waive it, and binding him to the waiver, denied due process.

Holmes, in dissent along with Justice Hughes, began his opinion by noting the unusual circumstances of Frank's trial. He described a courtroom "packed with spectators and surrounded by a crowd outside, all strongly hostile to the petitioner."[130] When the trial resumed on a Monday morning after a weekend hiatus, and the prosecutor entered the courtroom, Holmes recounted, "he was greeted with applause, stamping of feet and clapping of hands," which prompted the trial judge to suggest to Frank's lawyer a waiver of Frank's right to attend the reading of the verdict.[131]

After setting the trial scene, Holmes establishes the legal context for the case—habeas corpus—in an opinion rich in rhetorical devices. The opinion draws from the topic of "relationship" and employs an argument based on "contraries," here the fundamental incompatibility between mob rule and due process of law.[132] It also makes an ethical appeal for the importance of the rule of law as an alternative to anarchy.

Habeas corpus, Holmes writes metaphorically, "cuts through all forms and goes to the very tissue of the structure."[133] "It comes in from the outside," he continues, "not in subordination to the proceedings, and although every form may have been preserved, opens the inquiry whether they have been more than an empty shell."[134] Holmes's metaphors display the power of habeas corpus to find the core of a legal proceeding and determine if form supplanted substance. Perhaps no metaphor can suggest the triumph of form over substance as clearly as the "empty shell."

Cutting through the forms in this case meant determining whether mob rule had deprived Frank of due process. Despite disagreements about the scope of that concept, Holmes observes, "there can be no doubt that it embraces the fundamental conception of a fair trial, with opportunity to be heard."[135] Then, in an aphorism that underscores the inherent conflict between a mob and due process, Holmes writes that "[m]ob law does not become due process of law by securing the assent of a terrorized jury."[136] And when mob law subverts the cause of justice by denying due process, a district court is authorized to issue a writ of habeas corpus.

But Holmes's rhetorical flourishes are not finished; in a later passage, he uses alliteration, personification, and metaphor to assess the likelihood that the mob had influenced the jury at Frank's trial. "This is not a matter for polite presumptions," he writes; "we must look facts in the face. Any judge who has sat with juries knows that, in spite of forms, they are extremely likely to be impregnated by the environing atmosphere."[137] "Polite presumptions" embodies alliteration, looking facts "in the face" illustrates personification, and the reference to juries "impregnated" by public attitudes is, of course, metaphorical, even hyperbolic, considering the candor of the word "impregnated" in 1915. Taken together, these devices force the reader to confront the gravity of the due process violation in this case. Mr. Frank's jury capitulated to public pressure, as reflected in the trial judge's fear that the verdict would precipitate mob vengeance.

In such a rhetorically rich opinion, it is fitting that the concluding sentence would feature alliteration, analogy, isocolon, and parallelism. Holmes writes that his Court is duty-bound "to declare lynch law as little valid when practiced by a regularly drawn jury as when administered by one elected by a mob intent on death."[138] "Lynch law" illustrates alliteration, the comparison of a jury to a mob is an analogy, and the phrases "practiced by a regularly drawn jury" and "administered by a mob intent on death" demonstrate parallelism ("practiced by" and "administered by") and isocolon (equivalent numbers of syllables). In *Frank*, Holmes concludes, the jury did the mob's bidding, producing, in effect, an indoor lynching; thus, the Court should have vacated the verdict and granted the writ. Holmes's figures of speech underscore his dissent's appeal to ethos, specifically the rule of law.

6. *Moore v. Dempsey*

Moore also featured a habeas corpus petition, but in *Moore*, decided eight years

after *Frank*, Holmes writes for the Court's majority, enshrining his view of habeas corpus into law.[139] The start of his opinion describes a hauntingly familiar historical scenario in which five black men who were convicted of first-degree murder sought a writ of habeas corpus, alleging that mob pressure had hastened their convictions and their death sentences. A federal district court in Arkansas had denied their petition for habeas corpus.[140]

The instigators of violence were white men who attacked and fired on a group of blacks assembled in a church; a white man was killed in the ensuing melee. A report of that killing led to more violence, including the death of a second white man, for whose murder the petitioners were indicted.

Their trial raced along on fast forward, as Holmes recounted, noting that their counsel did not seek a delay or a change of venue despite community hostility to the accused parties, nor challenge a member of the jury, nor ask for separate trials for the respective defendants. Neither did counsel consult with the defendants before trial, call defense witnesses, or call any of the defendants to the witness stand. The trial lasted forty-five minutes, and in less than five minutes, the jury returned a verdict of first-degree murder against each defendant.[141]

Largely in one paragraph, Holmes explains the circumstances, like those that had been present in *Frank*, under which habeas corpus is warranted. Here, just as in *Frank*, his argument derives from the topic of relationship and the subtopic of contraries—mob rule and due process. And here, as in *Frank*, the argument makes an ethical appeal in favor of the rule of law in general and habeas corpus in particular, this time with the support of the Court majority.

Using metaphor (legal procedure as a "mask" and a "wave" of public passion) and assonance (repeated vowel sounds in "perfection" and "correction"), he depicts the legal facade that triggers the need for habeas corpus.

> It certainly is true that mere mistakes of law in the course of a trial are not to be corrected [by habeas corpus]. But if the case is that the whole proceeding is a mask—that counsel, jury and judge were swept to the fatal end by an irresistible wave of public passion, and that the State Courts failed to correct the wrong, neither perfection in the machinery for correction nor the possibility that the trial court and counsel saw no other way of avoiding an immediate outbreak of the mob can prevent this Court from securing the petitioners their constitutional rights.[142]

In this case, Holmes concludes, trial formalities obscured the jury's surrender to public passion, warranting habeas corpus review. The Court reversed and remanded for that review, establishing that state prisoners convicted in violation of the Constitution could obtain a remedy through federal habeas corpus proceedings.[143]

Thus, in *Moore*, Holmes used rhetoric to achieve what he was unable to achieve in *Frank*: a successful appeal to ethos. His reference to judge and jury being "swept to the fatal end by an irresistible wave of public passion" employs metaphor (the wave analogy) and isocolon (equal numbers of words in "an irresistible wave" and "of public passion") to depict events occurring rapidly, overwhelming individuals and skewing their judgments. The judge and jury in the court below allowed public passion about the trial to deter them from following the rule of law. Thanks, at least in part, to Holmes's rhetorical skill, the majority supported his reasoning, and the rule of law prevailed in *Moore*.

E. Conclusion

Oliver Wendell Holmes's colossal influence on American law flows from his magnificent intellect and exquisite prose. Even without the literary flair, his philosophy of judicial restraint in economic matters and broad protection for the freedom of speech may well have become prominent, even dominant on the Supreme Court after his death. But absent that flair, his ideas (including the need to protect the intellectual "marketplace," while still punishing the person who falsely shouts "fire" in a theater) would probably not have endured as they do among modern Americans. If any person ever embodied Aristotle's aphorism that how you say it is as important as what you say, that person was Justice Holmes.

NOTES

1. Sheldon M. Novick, *Honorable Justice: The Life of Oliver Wendell Holmes* (Boston: Little, Brown, and Co., 1989), xv.
2. Matthias Reimann, "Why Holmes,?" *Michigan Law Review* 88 (1990): 1913.
3. Novick, *Honorable Justice*, 9.

4. Liva Baker, *The Justice from Beacon Hill: The Life and Times of Oliver Wendell Holmes* (New York: Harper Collins, 1991), 69–70.
5. Ibid., 86–87.
6. Ibid., 89–90.
7. Ibid., 99.
8. Ibid., 101.
9. Ibid., 105–6.
10. Ibid., 106.
11. Ibid., 116.
12. Ibid., 120.
13. Novick, *Honorable Justice*, 66.
14. Ibid.
15. Baker, *The Justice from Beacon Hill*, 143.
16. Novick, *Honorable Justice*, 88; Baker, *The Justice from Beacon Hill*, 152.
17. Mark DeWolfe Howe, ed., *The Occasional Speeches of Justice Oliver Wendell Holmes* (Cambridge, MA: Harvard University Press, 1962), 6–7. See also Mark Tushnet, "The Logic of Experience: Oliver Wendell Holmes on the Supreme Judicial Court," *Virginia Law Review* 63 (1977): 1006.
18. Baker, *The Justice from Beacon Hill*, 163–64.
19. Ibid., 167.
20. Ibid., 169.
21. Ibid.
22. Ibid., 170.
23. Ibid., 177.
24. Novick, *Honorable Justice*, 102.
25. Baker, *The Justice from Beacon Hill*, 190.
26. Ibid., 209; Novick, *Honorable Justice*, 121.
27. Baker, *The Justice from Beacon Hill*, 209; Novick, *Honorable Justice,* 121.
28. Baker, *The Justice from Beacon Hill*, 216.
29. Novick, *Honorable Justice*, 122.
30. Baker, *The Justice from Beacon Hill*, 243–44.
31. Ibid., 246.
32. Ibid.
33. Ibid.
34. Ibid., 253; Novick, *Honorable Justice*, 159.
35. Novick, *Honorable Justice*, xv.
36. Baker, *The Justice from Beacon Hill*, 249, 257.
37. Oliver Wendell Holmes, Jr., *The Common Law* (Boston: Little, Brown, and Co. 1881, 1923), 1.
38. Novick, *Honorable Justice*, 166; Baker, *The Justice from Beacon Hill*, 264.
39. Baker, *The Justice from Beacon Hill*, 265; Novick, *Honorable Justice*, 168.
40. Baker, *The Justice from Beacon Hill*, 269–70.
41. Ibid., 275–76.
42. 155 Mass. 117.
43. Baker, *The Justice From Beacon Hill*, 298.
44. 167 Mass. 92.
45. Baker, *The Justice From Beacon Hill*, 318.
46. Tushnet, "The Logic of Experience: Oliver Wendell Holmes on the Supreme Judicial Court," 1038.
47. Novick, *Honorable Justice*, 203.
48. Ibid., 234–36.
49. Baker, *The Justice From Beacon Hill*, 356.
50. Novick, *Honorable Justice*, 237.
51. Baker, *The Justice From Beacon Hill*, 366.
52. Ibid.
53. Reimann, "Why Holmes?," *Michigan Law Review* 88 (1990): 1919.

54. 198 U.S. 45 (1905).
55. Ibid.
56. 247 U.S. 251 (1918).
57. Albert W. Alschuler, *Law Without Values: The Life, Work, and Legacy of Justice Holmes* (Chicago: University of Chicago Press, 2000), 181.
58. 249 U.S. 47 (1919).
59. Ibid., 52.
60. 249 U.S. 211 (1919); Zechariah Chafee, "Freedom of Speech in Wartime," *Harvard Law Review* 32 (1919): 932.
61. Patrick J. Kelley, "The Life of Oliver Wendell Holmes, Jr.," *Washington University Law Quarterly* 68 (1990): 477.
62. 250 U.S. 616 (1919).
63. Richard A. Posner, ed., *The Essential Holmes: Selections From the Letters, Speeches, Judicial Opinions, and Other Writings of Oliver Wendell Holmes, Jr.* (Chicago: University of Chicago Press, 1992), xii–xiii.
64. Thomas C. Grey, "Holmes and Legal Pragmatism," *Stanford Law Review* 41 (1989): 787.
65. Posner, *The Essential Holmes*, xvi.
66. Ibid., xiii.
67. Robert A. Ferguson, "Holmes and the Judicial Figure," *University of Chicago Law Review* 55 (1988), 522.
68. 237 U.S. 309 (1915).
69. 261 U.S. 86 (1923).
70. 198 U.S. 45 (1905).
71. Ibid., 53.
72. Ibid., 56.
73. Tiscione, *Rhetoric for Legal Writers*, 2nd ed., 70.
74. 198 U.S. at 75.
75. Richard A. Posner, *Law and Literature*, 3rd ed. (Cambridge, MA: Harvard University Press, 2009), 343.
76. Ibid., 343–44.
77. 198 U.S. at 75.
78. James J. Murphy, Richard A. Katula, Forbes I. Hill, and Donovan J. Ochs, *A Synoptic History of Classical Rhetoric*, 3rd ed. (Mahwah, NJ: Lawrence Erlbaum Associates, 2003), 101.
79. Ibid.
80. Aristotle, *Rhetoric*, Bk. II, 341.
81. Murphy, Katula, Hiil, and Ochs, *A Synoptic History of Classical Rhetoric*, 3rd ed., 102.
82. 198 U.S. at 75.
83. Ibid., 76.
84. Ibid.
85. Ibid.
86. Posner, *Law and Literature*, 3rd ed., 333.
87. 247 U.S. 251 (1918).
88. Ibid., 272.
89. Ibid., 273–74.
90. Ibid., 276.
91. Ibid.
92. Tiscione, *Rhetoric for Legal Writers*, 2nd ed., 70.
93. 247 U.S. at 277–78.
94. Ibid., 280.
95. Ibid.
96. Edward P. J. Corbett and Robert J. Connors, *Classical Rhetoric for the Modern Student*, 4th ed. (New York: Oxford University Press, 1999), 403.
97. 249 U.S. 47 (1919).
98. Ibid., 51.

99. Corbett and Connors, *Classical Rhetoric for the Modern Student*, 4th ed., 97.
100. 249 U.S. at 52.
101. Michael Frost, "Greco-Roman Analysis of Metaphoric Reasoning," *Legal Writing: Journal of the Legal Writing Institute* 2 (1996): 138.
102. Ibid., 137.
103. Linda L. Berger, "What Is the Sound of a Corporation Speaking? How the Cognitive Theory of Metaphor Can Help Lawyers Shape the Law," *Journal of the Association of Legal Writing Directors* 8 (2004), 169.
104. 249 U.S. at 52.
105. David P. Currie, "The Constitution in the Supreme Court: 1910–1921," *Duke Law Journal* 34 (1985): 1148.
106. White, *Oliver Wendell Holmes, Jr.*, 112.
107. 249 U.S. at 52.
108. 250 U.S. 616 (1919).
109. Baker, *The Justice from Beacon Hill*, 536.
110. Kelley, "The Life of Oliver Wendell Holmes, Jr.," 475–76; Chafee, "Freedom of Speech in Wartime," 967–68.
111. White, *Oliver Wendell Holmes, Jr.*, 108.
112. 250 U.S. at 617.
113. Ibid., 619.
114. Ibid., 622.
115. White, *Oliver Wendell Holmes, Jr.*, 110.
116. Ibid.
117. 250 U.S. at 624–25.
118. Ibid., 626.
119. Ibid., 629.
120. Ibid., 626.
121. Ibid., 628.
122. Ibid., 630.
123. Ibid.
124. Ibid.
125. Michael R. Smith, "Levels of Metaphor in Persuasive Legal Writing," *Mercer Law Review* 58 (2007): 935–36.
126. 237 U.S. 309 (1915).
127. Ibid., 335.
128. Ibid., 337.
129. Ibid., 338.
130. Ibid., 345.
131. Ibid., 346.
132. Corbett and Connors, *Classical Rhetoric for the Modern Student*, 4th ed., 105.
133. 237 U.S. at 346.
134. Ibid.
135. Ibid., 347.
136. Ibid.
137. Ibid., 349.
138. Ibid., 350.
139. 261 U.S. 86 (1923).
140. Ibid., 87.
141. Ibid., 89.
142. Ibid., 91.
143. Posner, ed., *The Essential Holmes*, xiii.

Chapter Four

Robert H. Jackson

Country Lawyer with a Golden Pen

A. Beginnings

Like Oliver Wendell Holmes, Jr., Robert Jackson possessed a remarkable facility for self-expression. Unlike Holmes, though, Jackson discovered and nourished his literary bent in a public high school in small-town western New York State. If Holmes was bred for success like a prize colt is bred for racing, Jackson galloped to the front of the pack with considerably less breeding by virtue of natural talent, hard work, and a knack for cultivating mentors.[1]

Robert Jackson began life in 1892 in the old Jackson family farmhouse at Spring Creek, Pennsylvania, where both his father and grandfather had been born.[2] Previous generations of Jacksons had been farmers, but Robert's father—William—was more interested in business than farming. Therefore, when William's father retired from farming, the family moved twenty-five miles north to Frewsburg, New York, where William bought and managed a hotel and a livery stable.[3] Justice Jackson later recalled that pre–World War I Frewsburg "was made up of farmers, of family size farms, small tradespeople, with no capitalist and no servant class."[4] "Everybody was expected to work."[5]

Robert demonstrated his ear for language and his talent for debate at Frewsburg High School, where he was elected president of the literary society. Judge Harley N. Crosby of Falconer, New York, witnessed Robert's debating skill in high school and recalled that experience years later.

> As a (then) young lawyer, I was called to Frewsburg, his home town, to sit on a board of judges in a high school debate between Frewsburg and Sinclairville.

> The debate was going very well indeed for Sinclairville until the last speaker from Frewsburg burst into song. He was a mere strippling of a boy, wore knee pants, I recall, and was not more than fourteen years old. Holy Moses! You should have heard that boy debate. I was astonished.[6]

After graduating from Frewsburg High School in 1910, Robert enrolled for a one-year postgraduate course at the public high school in the nearby small city of Jamestown, where he became a protégé of Mary Willard, an English teacher and Shakespeare aficionado who encouraged him to study law.[7] Robert did just that after completing his course at Jamestown High School, where he honed the debating skills developed earlier and gave the class oration at commencement. Attorney Frank Mott of Jamestown was related to Robert's mother by marriage and agreed to take Robert into his law practice as an apprentice in 1911.[8] The unlikely adventure that was Robert Jackson's professional life was about to begin.

B. Professional Life

In Jackson's day, law school was not required for an applicant to take the bar exam in New York; a three-year apprenticeship in a law office, or some combination of an apprenticeship and law school, would qualify one to take the bar exam.[9] Jackson spent the first year of his legal training in the Mott law office, where Mott himself was not as dedicated to the practice as he might have been, but his law partner, Benjamin Dean, was industrious, scholarly, and a gifted writer, making him an ideal mentor for a young apprentice.[10] Dean directed Jackson's reading of Blackstone's *Commentaries*, James Kent's *Commentaries*, and other fundamental legal writings, and then discussed with Jackson at length the readings and the ideas and questions they raised for him.[11] He also taught Jackson how to research the law.[12]

After one year of apprenticeship, Robert Jackson decided that because he had not attended college, he should attend law school, at least for a year. His father, who disliked and distrusted lawyers, would not give Robert money for law school, so he borrowed money from his mother's brother to enroll at Albany Law School.[13] Albany admitted him in 1911 to its one-year course for "law office men," who had apprenticed for a year before enrolling. It offered a curriculum that emphasized civil and criminal procedure and evidence to prepare these students for the bar exam.[14] Alternatively, a two-year course of study was available for students who had not done an apprenticeship beforehand.[15] Because he received one year of credit for his law-office work, Jackson completed the necessary two-year law school program after just one year at Albany. He was still just twenty years old, though—too young to take the bar exam—so the law school awarded him a diploma of graduation in 1912 instead of a law degree.[16] Albany was good to Robert Jackson personally too, as he met his future wife, Irene Gerhart, while he was a student there.[17] In 1916 they were married in Albany and settled in Jamestown, where they raised a son and a daughter.[18]

In the summer of 1913, while Jackson was serving his last year as an apprentice to Frank Mott, the older man was appointed Secretary of the New York State Public Service Commission, which required him to move to Albany.[19] He left his law practice to Jackson, who passed the bar exam later that year and was admitted to practice in November.[20] As a lawyer, Jackson started small, frequently participating in trials before justices of the peace, who were usually not lawyers, in makeshift "courtrooms" located in schools, churches, the dance hall of a Masonic temple, wherever space was available.[21] On one occasion, Jackson later recalled, the J.P. lacked room in his house for the trial, so "we put up some oil lanterns, put some boards across potato crates for people to sit on, and we tried the case in the barn."[22]

But Jackson's law practice did not remain small time. Instead, it grew along with the industrialization of Upstate New York. He practiced alone at first, but later as a named partner in Jackson, Manley, and Herrick in 1923, which became Jackson, Herrick, Durkin, and Leet in 1927, which it remained until 1933, shortly before Jackson left Jamestown for Washington, D.C.[23] He acquired a diverse mix of clients, including the Jamestown Telephone Corporation, the Jamestown Street Railway, the Central Labor Council, and the Bank of Jamestown.[24] The practice was so successful that Jackson amassed a substantial personal fortune, which enabled him to keep a thirty-foot boat on Lake Chautauqua and take his family on vacations to Cuba, Florida, Bermuda, California, and Arizona during the Great Depression.[25]

Despite a commitment to his law practice, Jackson increasingly made time for other professional activities. In 1930, Franklin Roosevelt, who by then was governor of New York, appointed him to a commission to investigate the administration of justice in the state, which brought him into Roosevelt's orbit.[26] In 1933, he accepted an invitation from Democratic National Committee chair James Farley to tour New York State with Farley ahead of the 1934 elections so as to encourage the election of Democrats to the state legislature who would support Governor Herbert Lehman, who succeeded FDR in Albany.[27] Later, Farley asked Jackson if he would like a job in FDR's new administration in Washington; initially, Jackson declined, but in 1934, at age forty-two, he accepted a position as counsel to the Bureau of the Internal Revenue.[28] From this modest beginning, Jackson would ascend rapidly during the next six years to become a close friend of FDR, assistant attorney general, solicitor general, attorney general, and associate justice of the Supreme Court.[29]

Jackson became an intimate of FDR, which accounts for Jackson's meteoric rise, by making himself indispensible to the administration. For example, as the ranking assistant attorney general in the Justice Department, Jackson came to FDR's aid regarding the president's ill-advised and ultimately ill-fated "Court-packing plan." The plan authorized the president to nominate a new federal judge—including a Supreme Court justice—for every sitting judge over age seventy. The bill that he sent to Congress in February, 1937, provided for presidential appointment of an additional judge for each one who had served for ten years or more, but failed to retire within six months after reaching age seventy.[30] At that time, six justices were over age seventy, so if the proposal passed, it would enable FDR to gain majority support on the Court for his New Deal economic programs, which featured unprecedented government intervention in the economy.[31]

Despite FDR's popularity, his plan proved to be a tough sell. Congressional leaders were upset that he had failed to consult them before announcing it, and the legislation scared many liberals—the president's usual supporters—because they feared its future use by a conservative administration.[32] Jackson made five speeches in support of FDR's proposal and delivered what generally was considered the most effective testimony to the Senate in favor of it.[33] He cast aside the administration's stated reason for the plan—the Court's inability to keep up with its work—and argued instead that the majority's penchant for invalidating Congressional legislation had given the Court a veto that Congress could not override.[34] The Court had also, in Jackson's view, impaired the states' rights under the Tenth Amendment by denying them the flexibility to devise potential legislative remedies for social and economic problems.[35] Finally, the serious internal divisions among the justices, often reflected in 5–4 decisions, demanded the addition of new members to improve the Court's functioning and restore its prestige.[36] No evidence indicates that Jackson's speeches or Senate testimony changed any minds, but those efforts nevertheless "marked him as a loyal, able, and indefatigable proponent of the administration's case."[37]

In the end, though, FDR got the result he wanted without having to add justices to the Court. Beginning in the spring of 1937, Chief Justice Charles Evans Hughes and Associate Justice Owen Roberts voted consistently with the Court's liberal bloc to uphold economic and social legislation, including the State of Washington's minimum wage law, the National Labor Relations Act, and the Social Security Act, respectively.[38] The Court-packing plan died in the Senate in July 1937, but by then, FDR had achieved the result he sought without it.[39]

Jackson proved to be indispensible to FDR as attorney general, too. In 1940, in response to British Prime Minister Winston Churchill's request for naval destroyers for the Royal Navy, FDR decided to ask Britain to lease its naval bases in the Atlantic and the Caribbean to the United States in exchange for receiving the destroyers.[40] But earlier that year, FDR had signed legislation stating that no war materiel could be sold that was "essential to the defense of the United States." Thus, a question arose whether FDR could execute his plan to aid the British without violating American law.[41]

Attorney General Jackson persuaded the chief of naval operations to certify that the destroyers were not essential to American defenses. He issued an opinion that authorized the destroyers-for-bases transaction, without Congressional approval, his major achievement as attorney general.[42] To critics who charged that this arrangement violated the traditional definition of neutrality by aiding one of the belligerents, Jackson replied that aiding Britain was not an act of war against Germany because Germany had itself violated international law by engaging in "aggressive war."[43] Germany's aggression against its European neighbors was an attack on the entire international community, he reasoned, which permitted us to give as much aid as we chose to countries trying to defend themselves against Germany.[44]

Jackson would remain attorney general for just a year and a half, though, because change was afoot at the Supreme Court in the early summer of 1941. Chief Justice Hughes announced his retirement, and FDR responded by appointing Associate Justice Harlan Fiske Stone to replace Hughes and Attorney General Robert H. Jackson to take Stone's old seat.[45] Jackson would be the last appointee to the Court who had learned his law primarily as an apprentice, and perhaps the Court's last link to that icon of American legal lore, the "generalist country lawyer."[46]

C. On the Court

Robert Jackson was the seventh of FDR's eight appointees to the Supreme Court; by the time of his appointment, only Harlan Stone and Owen Roberts remained from the Court that had repeatedly rejected New Deal legislation in the early years of the Roosevelt administration.[47] A metaphor for Jackson's temperament was the framed 1919 *Life* magazine photograph that hung in his chambers at the Court, just as it had hung in his Jamestown law office years before, which depicted a man working alone. Quoting "The Winners" in *The Story of the Gadsbys*, written in 1888 by English poet Rudyard Kipling, the photo's caption read: "He travels fastest who travels alone." Jackson lived by that motto.[48]

FDR's appointees quickly split into two rival ideological camps. Hugo Black, William Douglas, Frank Murphy, and Wiley Rutledge were a consistently liberal, or activist, bloc, whereas Felix Frankfurter, Stanley Reed, and Jackson were conservative, that is, inclined toward restraint.[49] In time, these blocs would fragment further, with various justices expressing their individual views much more often than their predecessors had done.[50] The number of concurrences and dissents rose dramatically in the Roosevelt Court, compared to prior Courts, as individualistic justices regularly wrote separately "to distinguish or qualify their opinions or to reject the opinions of their colleagues."[51]

For his part, Jackson remained true to the motto on his office wall: he "traveled" alone. Despite siding more often with the Frankfurter bloc than the Black/Douglas bloc, Jackson did not adhere to Frankfurter's reliance on majoritarian democracy—notably, the legislative process—to resolve all social problems. He was more willing to use judicial power to restrain majorities; indeed, for Jackson, the Court played a key role in overseeing and sometimes adjusting the constitutional balance between majority rule and minority rights.[52] Jackson also rejected the absolutism of Black and Douglas in civil liberties, especially First Amendment, cases because he believed strongly in balancing individual rights against governmental authority.[53] He was likely to see both sides of an issue, weigh them against each other, and choose what he considered to be a practical resolution in each case, often by shedding unaccustomed light on unexamined assumptions.[54] In the words of one Jackson scholar, his decision making process was "a dialectical enterprise which required a constant accommodation of opposing principles—of order and liberty, of majoritarian preference and minority right, of law and politics."[55] The line-drawing in each case "was never a simple matter; it demanded a careful examination of the facts of each case and a pragmatic assessment of alternative outcomes."[56]

Jackson rejected the libertarian activism of Black and Douglas in part because he believed strongly in the separation of powers and was keen to the limits of judicial power. He was a proponent of federalism, favoring the rights of states to experiment with legislative solutions to social and economic problems. In civil liberties cases, he often defended the rights of communities to enforce their standards against disruptive conduct by individuals. But his vote in any particular case was not easy to predict; never doctrinaire, he periodically voted counter to his customary position on questions of federalism and civil liberties.[57]

Jackson's support for freedom of conscience was reflected in his majority opinion in *West Virginia State Board of Education v. Barnette*, which invalidated the compulsory flag salute in public schools.[58] But that support did not necessarily extend to the conduct that one's conscience prompted. In this regard, he seemed to be influenced by his unique and historic experience as the chief prosecutor at the trial of accused Nazi war criminals at Nuremberg, Germany in 1945–1946, the first international criminal trial in history.[59] Jackson's Nuremberg experience had made him sympathetic to the efforts of local officials to combat social conflict and aggressive expressions of dissent. Specifically, he drew from the rise of the Nazis the lesson that government must curb radical organizations in their early stages, and he even argued that the Court should resort to the controversial doctrine of conspiracy toward that end.

Jackson's concern for protecting social order led him to dissent in *Terminiello v. Chicago*, in which the majority reversed the conviction of a speaker who had been found guilty of disorderly conduct after his anti-Semitic, anti-Communist rant precipitated a "breach of the peace" inside and outside the hall where he spoke.[60] Jackson emphasized that such conduct was not immune from prosecution just because it was verbal.[61]

Jackson's pragmatism likely deprived him of the judicial legacy warranted by his original thinking and powerful writing. He lacked the predictability that flows from a clear ideology and that helps a justice attract influential supporters who can burnish a reputation after retirement or death.[62] Personal factors likely contributed too, including his premature death in 1954 at age sixty-two and, especially, a bitter dispute with Hugo Black that arose from Black's participation in a case in which his former law partner argued for the winning litigant in a 5–4 decision.[63] Jackson believed that Black should have recused himself, and when the losing party sought a rehearing, Jackson attached a separate statement to the Court's order denying the request, which implied just that.[64] Black took great offense, exacerbating existing divisions within the Court and persuading President Truman not to nominate Jackson for chief justice in the spring of 1946, when Harlan Fiske Stone died.[65] Jackson made matters worse by sending to President Truman from Germany a caustic cable that attacked Black's conduct in the case, forwarding it to the House and Senate Judiciary Committees, and even holding a press conference.[66] Silence burnished Black's reputation during this dispute, while unrestrained anger tarnished Jackson's.[67]

Jackson's stock has risen of late, though, because of his considerable contribution in the always-important realm of executive power and because scholars now appreciate what an exemplary literary stylist he was.

D. Jackson the Writer

In a sentence that seems to have been composed with this book in mind, Jackson biographer Eugene Gerhart wrote, "It would profit us all to study the words with which Robert Jackson clothed his thought."[68] "They were rather clear and simple Anglo-Saxon words," Gerhart added, "arranged frequently in an epigrammatic form but always chosen to bring to light the truth he feared might otherwise lie hidden."[69] Most importantly, "[t]hey were the words best designed to strip from logic its dullness and make it exciting and memorable."[70]

Jackson's words were rarely dull and frequently memorable. Indeed, observed Potter Stewart, who was appointed to the Supreme Court several years after Jackson's death, because Jackson could express himself so clearly and powerfully, "there shines through the pages of his writing not just his intellect, but the whole power of his personality."[71] Despite Jackson's natural ear for language, noted his former law clerk, James Marsh, "the smoothness of his opinions c[ame] as much from working over as from his natural style and ability."[72] "We would often go through 4 or 5 typewritten and hand-corrected drafts before sending anything to the printer," Marsh recalled—and then three or four versions were printed before we circulated anything to the Brethren. . . ."[73]

Both Jackson's literary skill and his hard work will be evident in the remaining paragraphs of this chapter, which will address his two areas of greatest influence: the First Amendment and executive power. The featured cases include *West Virginia State Board of Education v. Barnette*,[74] *Terminiello v. Chicago*,[75] *American Communication Association v. Douds*,[76] *Korematsu v. United States*,[77] *Johnson v. United States*,[78] and *Youngstown Sheet and Tube Co. v. Sawyer*.[79]

1. *West Virginia State Board of Education v. Barnette*

Barnette was a rarity because it directly overruled an existing Supreme Court precedent, and just three years after the earlier case was decided.[80] In *Minersville School District v. Gobitis*, the Court had upheld a compulsory flag salute rule for public school students against a challenge by parents who were Jehovah's Witnesses. They claimed that the rule—mandated by a local school board in Pennsylvania—deprived them of liberty without due process.[81] In the wake of *Gobitis*, the State Board of Education in West Virginia adopted the same requirement, under penalty of expulsion for refusing to comply. West Virginia's state rule, like the local rule in *Gobitis*, collided with the Jehovah's Witnesses' literal reading of Exodus, chapter 20, verses 4 and 5, which admonish not to bow down to or serve a "graven image," including—in the Witnesses' view—the American flag. Writing for the majority, Justice Jackson notes that officials had threatened to send the expelled children to "reformatories maintained for criminally inclined juveniles" and that the parents of the expelled children "have been prosecuted and are threatened with prosecutions for causing delinquency."[82] This language is an appeal to pathos designed to arouse the reader's sympathy for children and parents who faced draconian punishments just for silently adhering to their religious faith.

Barnette was an ideal vehicle for Jackson to demonstrate his commitment to freedom of conscience. The children's religious freedom claim does not conflict with rights asserted by anyone else; "[t]he sole conflict," Jackson observes, is "between authority and rights of the individual."[83] His opinion draws on the rhetorical topic of relationship and the subtopic of contraries, specifically, the fundamental incompatibility between a compulsory flag-salute law and an individual's freedom of conscience.

Noting that "the flag salute is a form of utterance," Jackson explains that flags and other symbols can communicate ideas that attract us and ideas that repel us. He writes:

> Symbolism is a primitive but effective way of communicating ideas. The use of an emblem or flag to symbolize some system, idea, institution, or personality, is a short cut from mind to mind. Causes and nations, political parties, lodges and ecclesiastical groups seek to knit the loyalty of their followings to a flag or banner, a color or design. The State announces rank, function, and authority through crowns and maces, uniforms and black robes; the church speaks through the Cross, the Crucifix, the altar and shrine, and clerical raiment. Symbols of State often convey political ideas just as religious symbols come to convey theological ones. Associated with many of these symbols are appropriate gestures of acceptance or respect: a salute, a bowed or bared head, a bended knee. A person gets from a symbol the meaning he puts into it, and what is one man's comfort and inspiration is another's jest and scorn.[84]

Several rhetorical techniques give this passage a pleasant rhythm and make it memorable. Parallelism ("system, idea, institution, or personality"; "rank, function, and authority"; "crowns and maces, uniforms and black robes"; "the Cross, the Crucifix, etc."; "a salute, a bowed head, a bended knee") establishes a rhythm that grabs the reader's attention, and two metaphors ("a short cut from mind to mind" and "knit the loyalty of their followings") hold that attention. Two aphorisms—"a person gets from a symbol the meaning he puts into it" and "one man's comfort and inspiration is another's jest and scorn"—along with the isocolon present in "comfort and inspiration" and "jest and scorn," end the passage dramatically, illustrating the folly of forced utterance divorced from belief.

Jackson then responds to specific rationales the Court had advanced in *Gobitis* for upholding the compulsory flag salute. First, he answers the *Gobitis* Court's statement that public school authorities are authorized to impose the flag-salute on schoolchildren generally. In a now-famous defense of individual liberty, Jackson observes:

> The very purpose of a Bill of Rights was to withdraw certain subjects from the vicissitudes of political controversy, to place them beyond the reach of majorities and officials and to establish them as legal principles to be applied by the courts. One's right to life, liberty, and property, to free speech, a free press, freedom of worship and assembly, and other fundamental rights may not be submitted to vote; they depend on the outcome of no elections.[85]

This passage is less dependent for its power on figures of speech than on its choice of words and phrases such as "withdraw," "beyond the reach of majorities and officials," and "may not be submitted to vote," which, taken together, make clear that unlike tax policy and economic policy, our fundamental freedoms are not beholden to majority rule. Still, the parallelism of "life, liberty, and property" and "free speech, a free press, freedom of worship and assembly, and other fundamental rights," contributes a pleasing rhythm that complements the word choices on which the passage relies.

Jackson also responds to the statement in the *Gobitis* opinion that courts should uphold the compulsory flag salute because it promotes national unity, which is the basis for national security, and public officials are entitled to select appropriate means of achieving that security. Part of that response appears below.

> Those who begin coercive elimination of dissent soon find themselves eliminating dissenters. Compulsory unification of opinion achieves only the unanimity of the graveyard.[86]

This short passage highlights two figures of speech. The use of "elimination" and "eliminating" and of "dissent" and "dissenters" in the first sentence illustrates polyptoton, which is the repetition of words derived from the same root. Polyptoton is also present in the second sentence in the form of "unification" and "unanimity." And "graveyard" can be viewed as a metaphor for the death of democratic values.

Viewed as a whole, the passage depicts a fatal progression that begins with the outlawing of dissent, followed by the silencing of dissenters, and concludes in a freedom-crushing totalitarianism. Note how the passage ends with the graveyard metaphor, which is not coincidental. "Good advocates," explains Michael Frost, "do not just hope that an apt metaphor will occur to them; instead, they consciously seek or create the proper metaphor to achieve a specific rhetorical effect."[87] No better metaphor exists for Jackson's suggestion that punishing beliefs will result in the death of democracy than "the graveyard."

In the same vein, Jackson offers the tart aphorism that "freedom to differ is not limited to things that do not matter much."[88] Also in this vein, he closes the opinion with what may be its most memorable language.

> If there is any fixed star in our constitutional constellation, it is that no official, high or petty, can prescribe what shall be orthodox in politics, nationalism, religion, or other matters of opinion or force citizens to confess by word or act their faith therein. If there are any circumstances which permit an exception, they do not now occur to us.[89]

The opening dependent clause in the first sentence features both an astronomical metaphor and the alliteration of "constitutional constellation." Freedom of conscience is the "fixed star" in that constellation; government cannot be permitted to prescribe spiritual or intellectual orthodoxy. Put another way, in a free society, one expresses one's religious or political faith only voluntarily.

The rest of the first sentence includes the parallelism of "politics, nationalism, religion, or other matters of opinion," which gives it rhythm, and the metaphor of "confessing faith" outside a religious setting, which raises the specter of compelled speech. And the passage closes with humble words that enhance the ethos of the opinion by suggesting that if an exception exists to this rule, the Court's careful search has not revealed it. The persnickety legal writing professor could quibble about the improper use of "which" (instead of "that") in a restrictive clause, but quibbling in the face of such elegance would be tasteless. The professor would be wiser to emphasize Jackson's *Barnette* opinion as rhetorical mastery in the service of freedom of conscience.

2. Terminiello v. Chicago

A municipal court in Chicago found Arthur Terminiello, a Catholic priest whose superiors had suspended him from ministry, guilty of violating a local ordinance against disorderly conduct by giving a speech that denigrated Jews and Communists, whom the speech equated.[90] In a 5–4 decision, the Court reversed the conviction, with Justice William Douglas writing for the majority that the ordinance violated the freedom of speech by permitting a conviction if one's speech stirred people to anger, invited public dispute, or brought about unrest.[91]

Jackson's dissent reflects the distinction he drew in First Amendment cases between beliefs, which he sought to protect, and conduct, which he was prone to punish when it threatened violence and disorder. *Terminiello* followed Jackson's Nuremberg experience, which left him acutely aware of how the Nazi Party had sprouted in Germany and fearful that overly tolerant judicial attitudes toward free speech could seed a comparable outcome in the United States. His argument is derived from the topic of comparison and the subtopic of difference, here the difference, in Jackson's eyes, between beliefs, for which First Amendment protection was absolute, and conduct, for which it was not.

Jackson's frustration with the majority's reasoning is evident from the beginning of his dissent. He writes:

> The Court reverses this conviction by reiterating generalized approbations of freedom of speech with which, in the abstract, no one will disagree. Doubts as to their applicability are lulled by avoidance of more than passing reference to the circumstances of Terminiello's speech and judging it as if he had spoken to persons as dispassionate as empty benches, or like a modern Demosthenes practicing his Philippics on a lonely seashore.[92]

Jackson thought the majority was dangerously naive about the potential for violence by both proponents and opponents of speeches like the one Terminiello had made. Although the phrase "avoidance of more than passing reference" is indirect and wordy, Jackson's use of the verb "lulled" is crucial to his point that the majority trivialized the threat to social cohesion posed by

Terminiello's conduct. And the similes in the second sentence ("persons as dispassionate as empty benches" and "like a modern Demosthenes") join with a literary allusion to emphasize Jackson's point that the majority failed to see Terminiello's speech for what it was: an incitement to violence and social discord.

To buttress that point, Jackson recounts in detail the facts of the case, noting the disorderly behavior that the speech prompted both inside and outside the hall. Outside, he explains, "[b]ricks were thrown through the windowpanes before and during the speaking" and "[a]bout 28 windows were broken."[93] "Police were unable to control the mob," which [besides breaking windows at the meeting hall], persisted in "drowning out the speaker's voice at times and breaking through the backdoor of the auditorium."[94] Inside, some listeners audibly supported Terminiello's viewpoint, whereas others shouted insults at him.[95] As Jackson observes, the speech "stirred the audience not only to cheer and applaud, but [also] to expressions of immediate anger, unrest and alarm."[96]

Drawing on his Nuremberg experience, he continues: "We need not resort to speculation as to the purposes for which these tactics are calculated nor as to their consequences. Recent European history demonstrates both."[97] He even quotes a statement by Adolph Hitler attesting to the value of mass street demonstrations as a means of building the Nazi movement.[98] In referring to Hitler and the Nazis, Jackson assumes the role of a 1940s Paul Revere, sounding the alarm that "it can happen here too," especially if the United States was slow to respond to antidemocratic movements, as Germany had been in the 1930s.

Then, using antithesis, isocolon, and metaphor, Jackson pens his most memorable language in *Terminiello*. He writes:

> This Court has gone far toward accepting the doctrine that civil liberty means the removal of all restraints from these crowds and that all local attempts to maintain order are impairments of the liberty of the citizen. The choice is not between order and liberty. It is between liberty with order and anarchy without either. There is danger that, if the Court does not temper its doctrinaire logic with a little practical wisdom, it will convert the constitutional Bill of Rights into a suicide pact.[99]

The variation in lengths between the first and second sentences injects rhythm into the passage and highlights the false choice between "order and liberty" that Jackson thinks the majority opinion presents. The second and third sentences use antithesis to underscore what Jackson sees as the choice that faces the Court in *Terminiello*, a dramatically more stark choice than, in his view, the majority was willing to acknowledge.

In juxtaposing "order and liberty," "liberty with order," and "anarchy without either"—phrases of equal length—Jackson adds isocolon to the pot to produce a heartier rhetorical stew. The reference to "anarchy without either" warns that the United States will sacrifice both law and order if it continues to allow speech that incites violence to go unpunished. Finally, to make the warning bell louder, he adds a metaphor (and hyperbole, too) suggesting the Court majority seemed hell bent to make the Bill of Rights "a suicide pact."[100] Jackson, whose opinion Justice Harold Burton joined, would have affirmed Terminiello's conviction.

3. *American Communications Association v. Douds*

No case better reflects the distinction that Robert Jackson drew between beliefs and conduct in First Amendment cases than *Douds*.[101] At issue was the constitutionality of Section 9(h) of the Labor Management Relations Act of 1947, known as the "non-Communist affidavit provision."[102] The Court majority upheld that provision, which conditioned the formal recognition of a labor union by the National Labor Relations Board on the filing of affidavits by the union's officers that they did not belong to the Communist Party and did not believe in the overthrow of the US government by force.[103]

As befit his distinction between beliefs and conduct, Jackson concurred in part and dissented in part in *Douds*. He concurred with the majority that union officers could be compelled to file affidavits stating that they did not belong to the Communist Party. "Congress could rationally conclude," he wrote," that "behind its political party façade, the Communist Party is a conspiratorial and revolutionary junta, organized to reach ends and to use methods which are incompatible with our constitutional system."[104] In light of the party's aims, violent methods of obtaining power overseas, and infiltration of American unions, Jackson reasoned, Congress could "require labor union officers to disclose their membership in or affiliation with the Communist Party."[105]

But to Jackson, beliefs were distinct from affirmative acts, such as joining the Communist Party. Regarding beliefs, he wrote, the issue was "whether Congress has power to proscribe any opinion or belief which has not manifested itself in any overt act."[106] He concluded that Congress had no such power. Thus, Jackson's argument reflects both the similarity and difference subcategories of the topic of comparison. It reflects similarity because Jackson finds the required certification of nonmembership in the Communist Party compatible with the First Amendment. But it also reflects difference because, in Jackson's view, the required certification of nonbelief in the forceful overthrow of the US government violates the First Amendment.

The most enduring language in Jackson's *Douds* opinion, which appears below, uses an aphorism, polyptoton, metaphor, and parallelism to make that point.

> Progress generally begins in skepticism about accepted truths. Intellectual freedom means the right to re-examine much that has long been taken for granted. A free man must be a reasoning man, and he must dare to doubt what a legislative or electoral majority may most passionately assert. The danger that citizens will think wrongly is serious, but less dangerous than atrophy from not thinking at all. Our Constitution relies on our electorate's complete ideological freedom to nourish independent and responsible intelligence and preserve our democracy from that submissiveness, timidity and herd-mindedness of the masses which would foster a tyranny of mediocrity. The priceless heritage of our society is the unrestricted constitutional right of each member to think as he will. Thought control is a copyright of totalitarianism, and we have no claim to it. It is not the function of our Government to keep the citizen from falling into error; it is the function of the citizen to keep the Government from falling into error. We could justify any censorship only when the censors are better shielded against error than the censored.[107]

The first sentence is a potent aphorism, and the second sentence includes one of its own: "a free man must be a reasoning man." The alliteration in "dare to doubt" also enhances that sentence. Polyptoton, namely, the use of "think" and "thinking," adorns the fourth sentence. The fifth sentence features the parallelism of "submissiveness, timidity, and herd-mindedness," and the metaphor equating mediocrity with tyranny when freedom of conscience is suppressed.

In the seventh sentence, a stunning metaphor—"thought control is a *copyright* of totalitarianism"—reminds the reader that freedom of conscience lies at the core of American democracy. This metaphor comports with author William Domnarski's description of Jackson's prose as "a muscular, concrete, tactile prose that in its purest expressions startles the reader with its vigor, edge, and essence."[108] It also confers all of the benefits an author can reap from using an original metaphor. In the present example, these include: (1) providing an analogy that clarifies the substance of Jackson's point; (2) establishing Jackson as a credible and knowledgeable source of information; (3) evoking positive emotions in the reader; and (4) drawing attention to Jackson's message.[109] Furthermore, because Jackson created a metaphor here instead of borrowing one from the archives, he enhanced his credibility in the reader's eyes more than he would have by appropriating an established metaphor.[110]

The penultimate sentence in the quoted passage uses antithesis and antimetabole to reinforce the point that freedom of conscience is the foundation of democracy. In a democracy, the people check the government's power, not vice versa. Antithesis lies in the distinction between what is and is not the government's function, and antimetabole lies in the reversed order of the words "government" and "citizen" in the two clauses of that sentence. The final sentence uses polyptoton—here, three variations of the word "censor"—to seal the passage's argument against punishing beliefs. The inevitable fallibility of the censors renders censorship of the citizenry unacceptable.

Thus, Jackson concludes that Congress can compel union officers to disclose membership in the Communist Party, but it cannot compel them to swear that they harbored no belief in the violent overthrow of the US government. "I think," he writes, "that under our system, it is time enough for the law to lay hold of the citizen when he acts illegally, or in some rare circumstances when his thoughts are given illegal utterance."[111] "I think that we must let his mind alone."[112]

4. Korematsu v. United States

The first casualty of wartime is often personal freedom. Nobody knew that better than Fred Korematsu. An American citizen, he was convicted of remaining in a portion of a military area from which persons of Japanese ancestry were excluded in 1942, for fear they would aid a Japanese military attack on the West Coast.[113] The exclusion order, issued by the commanding general of the Western Command, resulted from a statute and an executive order, respectively, each of which authorized such military orders designed to prevent espionage and sabotage.[114] A six-member Court majority, speaking through Justice Black, upheld Korematsu's conviction, stating: "We are unable to conclude that it was beyond the war power of Congress and the Executive to exclude those of Japanese ancestry from the West Coast war area at the time they did."[115] Black emphasized that the exclusion order was reasonable when issued because "[t]here was evidence of disloyalty on the part of some, the military authorities considered that the need for action was great, and time was short."[116] Therefore, hindsight should not dictate a contrary judgment just because the threat perceived earlier no longer existed.[117]

Jackson's dissent reflected his inclination to weigh both sides of an issue carefully before resolving it. Here, that weighing led him to conclude that the commanding general was authorized to issue the exclusion order, but the Court should not bestow constitutional legitimacy on the order by affirming Korematsu's conviction. His opinion flows from the topic of relationship and the subcategory of "antecedent and consequence"; here the consequence for Fred Korematsu of his Japanese ancestry was a denial of constitutional rights that he would have enjoyed had his parents not been born in Japan. Jackson writes:

> Much is said of the danger to liberty from the Army program for deporting and detaining these citizens of Japanese extraction. But a judicial construction of the due process clause that will sustain this order is a far more subtle blow to liberty than the promulgation of the order itself. A military order, however unconstitutional, is not apt to last longer than the military emergency. Even

> during that period a succeeding commander may revoke it all. But once a judicial opinion rationalizes such an order to show that it conforms to the Constitution, or rather rationalizes the Constitution to show that the Constitution sanctions such an order, the Court for all time has validated the principle of transplanting American citizens. The principle then lies about like a loaded weapon ready for the hand of any authority that can bring forward a plausible claim of an urgent need.[118]

Jackson's use of figures of speech here is sparing; he holds his rhetorical fire until the last sentence. But the simile of an errant constitutional principle that "lies about like a loaded weapon," an invitation to abuse by an unprincipled or overzealous leader, underlines the danger that Jackson fears. And the isocolon reflected in "a plausible claim" and "an urgent need" adds a pleasing cadence to the sentence.

Thus, Jackson's nuanced reasoning would have left the military commander free to issue the exclusion order, presumably still subjecting Fred Korematsu and other Japanese Americans to exclusion and relocation to internment camps, but would have denied the order a constitutional seal of approval, which the majority gave it. His conclusion appears below.

> My duties as a justice as I see them do not require me to make a military judgment as to whether General DeWitt's evacuation and detention program was a reasonable military necessity. I do not suggest that the courts should have attempted to interfere with the Army in carrying out its task. But I do not think they may be asked to execute a military expedient that has no place in law under the Constitution. I would reverse the judgment and discharge the prisoner.[119]

This paragraph has several rhetorical virtues. First, it has a conversational tone, evident in the use of "I" and "my," as if Jackson were explaining his thinking to a Jamestown jury. Second, it makes his distinction between allowing such military orders to be issued and enshrining them in the Constitution as clear as possible. Finally, it concludes with a pleasing, rhythmic example of isocolon—"reverse the judgment" and "discharge the prisoner." The rhythmic language at the end of the passage conveys resignation and a desire for finality. In Jackson's view, the exclusion order has done its harm; the Court should accept that result, but should not make matters worse by validating the order.

5. *Johnson v. United States*

If the Nuremberg experience made Justice Jackson a less libertarian defender of the freedom of speech than colleagues such as Hugo Black and William Douglas, it did not diminish, and may even have augmented, his appreciation for constitutional protections such as the Fourth Amendment freedom from unreasonable searches and seizures. A case in point is *Johnson v. United States*.[120]

The petitioner, Anne Johnson, who lived in a hotel in Seattle, was convicted on four counts charging violations of federal narcotics laws. At issue before the Supreme Court was whether a police officer, who lacked a search warrant, had acted lawfully in arresting her and searching her living quarters.[121] Based on an informant's tip, the officer went to Johnson's door, where he smelled opium; he knocked on the door, and Johnson let him in. His subsequent search revealed opium and materials for smoking it.[122] After the trial court denied her motion to suppress and convicted her, the appellate court affirmed.[123] In the Supreme Court, Johnson challenged the search on Fourth Amendment grounds, but the government countered that the search was incident to a lawful arrest, therefore constitutional.[124]

Jackson, writing for a five-member majority, emphasized the centrality of neutral magistrates to lawful searches and seizures under the Fourth Amendment. "When the right of privacy must reasonably yield to the right of search is," he stressed, "as a rule, to be decided by a judicial officer, not by a policeman or Government enforcement agent."[125] The sentence's use of antithesis highlights the preeminence of judges, rather than police officers, in evaluating the lawfulness of police-conducted searches. Accordingly, Jackson's reasoning is based on the topic of comparison and the subtopic of difference, in particular the difference between allowing a police officer to determine probable cause and requiring a neutral magistrate to do so.

The government conceded that the officer lacked probable cause to arrest until he had entered Johnson's room and found her alone. Only after gaining entry to her room, based on their police authority, and then searching the room did they obtain the evidence on which the arrest was predicated.[126] In Jackson's view, this scenario did not create probable cause. He wrote:

> Thus the Government is obliged to justify the arrest by the search and at the same time to justify the search by the arrest. This will not do. An officer gaining access to private living quarters under color of his office and of the law which he personifies must then have some valid basis in law for the intrusion. Any other rule would undermine "the right of the people to be secure in their persons, houses, papers and effects," and would obliterate one of the most fundamental distinctions between our form of government, where officers are under the law, and the police-state where they are the law.[127]

The opening sentence stresses the circularity of the government's reasoning by using antimetabole to "justify the arrest by the search," then to "justify the search by the arrest." If the government's position is confusing, Jackson's conclusion is abundantly clear: "This"—meaning the government's circular reasoning—"will not do." The short second sentence is direct and unmistakable in its meaning when viewed in conjunction with the much longer opening sentence. Taken together, the two sentences give the passage rhythm, and the second sentence answers the conundrum posed by the first.

The final sentence notes the importance of the Fourth Amendment to a democracy, using antithesis and isocolon to distinguish between societies in which "officers are under the law" and those where "they are the law." Because the United States is among the former, the Court reversed Johnson's conviction.

6. *Youngstown Sheet & Tube Co. v. Sawyer*

If wartime restricts civil liberties, as *Korematsu* showed, it also tests the bounds of executive power, as *Youngstown* shows. The *Youngstown* Court considered the constitutionality of President Truman's order to his commerce secretary to seize control of most of the Nation's steel mills and keep them operating despite a threatened strike, so as to ensure a steady supply of steel for the Korean War effort.[128] The mill owners challenged the order as an exercise in lawmaking, a legislative function that the Constitution assigns to Congress, not the president.[129]

Writing for the majority, Justice Black reasoned that if the president had the authority to issue the order, then that authority must derive from "some provisions of the Constitution."[130] The government did not argue that express constitutional language granted such authority, but rather, that it was implicit in provisions of Article II stating that "the executive Power shall be vested in a President" . . . ; that "he shall take Care that the Laws be faithfully executed"; and that he "shall be Commander in Chief of the Army and Navy of the United States."[131]

Black rejected the argument that the order was a proper exercise of the president's powers as Commander-in-Chief of the Armed Forces. In his view, those powers were not so broad as to enable the president to "take possession of private property in order to keep labor disputes from stopping production."[132] "This is a job for the Nation's lawmakers, not for its military authorities."[133] Black also rejected the argument that the seizure authority derived from several constitutional provisions that grant the president executive power. He noted that the president is to execute laws, not make them. "And," in his words, "the Constitution is neither silent nor equivocal about who shall make laws which the President is to execute."[134] Thus, the Court affirmed a district court decision that restrained the commerce secretary from continuing to seize and possess American steel mills.[135]

Justice Jackson's concurrence in *Youngstown* has probably had more enduring influence on American jurisprudence than any other opinion he wrote during his tenure on the Court because it is a thorough and prescriptive treatise on the proper parameters of executive power. Therefore, it merits a detailed discussion both substantively and rhetorically. It draws on the topic of "definition" and the subtopic of "division," separating presidential behavior into more or less constitutionally defensible categories, depending on the degree of congressional authorization on which the president acts.

Jackson begins the opinion by lamenting the lack of "really useful and unambiguous authority" available to judges faced with "concrete problems of executive power."[136] To highlight this point, he employs a simile and a biblical allusion in the next sentence, offering that "[j]ust what our forefathers did envision, or would have envisioned had they foreseen modern conditions, must be divined from materials almost as enigmatic as the dreams Joseph was called upon to interpret for Pharoah."[137]

Having captured the reader's attention, Jackson unfurls his tripartite conception of the constitutional limits of presidential power. "When the President acts pursuant to an express or implied authorization of Congress," Jackson observes, "his authority is at its maximum, for it includes all that he possesses in his own right plus all that Congress can delegate."[138] Under such circumstances, the president "may . . . be said (for what it may be worth) to personify the federal sovereignty."[139] Thus, a seizure the president executed according to a federal statute "would be supported by the strongest of presumptions and the widest latitude of judicial interpretation, and the burden of persuasion would rest heavily upon any who might attack it."[140]

When, however, the president acts absent either a congressional grant or denial of authority, "he can only rely upon his own independent powers, but there is a zone of twilight in which he and Congress may have concurrent authority, or in which its distribution is uncertain."[141] Note Jackson's use of the metaphor "zone of twilight" to depict the murky region at the border between congressional and presidential authority. "In this area," Jackson explains, "any actual test of power is likely to depend on the imperatives of events and contemporary imponderables rather than on abstract theories of law."[142]

In the third and final presidential power scenario, in which "the President takes measures incompatible with the expressed or implied will of Congress," Jackson argues that "his power is at its lowest ebb, for then he can rely only upon his own constitutional powers minus any constitutional powers of Congress over the matter."[143] Under such circumstances, "[c]ourts can sustain exclusive Presidential control . . . only by disabling the Congress from acting upon the subject."[144] And courts should examine such presidential claims of power with great care, Jackson warns, "for what is at stake is the equilibrium established by our constitutional system."[145]

In *Youngstown*, according to Jackson, neither of the first two scenarios applies. Therefore, the presidential seizure of the steel mills is subject to "the severe tests under the third grouping," meaning that it is defensible only as an exercise of whatever executive power survives after eliminating Congress's power over the matter.[146] "In short," according to Jackson, "we can sustain the President only by holding that seizure of such strike-bound industries is within his domain and beyond control by Congress."[147]

For Jackson, that was a bridge too far. He writes:

> The purpose of lodging dual titles [President and Commander-in-Chief of the Armed Forces] in one man was to insure that the civilian would control the military, not to enable the military to subordinate the presidential office. No penance would ever expiate the sin against free government of holding that a President can escape control of executive powers by law through assuming his military role. What the power of command may include I do not try to envision, but I think it is not a military prerogative, without support of law, to seize persons or property because they are important or even essential for the military and naval establishment.[148]

This passage conveys an important constitutional principle: the Commander-in-Chief power is not a backdoor route to the exercise of powers that the Constitution neither expressly nor implicitly confers on the president, including power to seize persons or property. Part of the passage's power, though, lies in its use of antithesis, chiasmus, metaphor, alliteration, and isocolon to achieve rhythm and force. The distinction drawn in the first sentence between civilian control of the military and vice versa illustrates antithesis. It also illustrates chiasmus, which is "the reversal of grammatical structures in successive phrases or clauses."[149] "[T]o insure that the civilian would control the military, not to enable the military to subordinate the presidential office" is an example of chiasmus (not antimetabole) because although it includes a reversal of grammatical structures between two phrases, the second phrase does not repeat the words of the first.[150]

The second sentence's reference to "penance" and "sin" offers a vivid metaphor, especially for members of some Christian sects. It intimates that for the Court to hold that a president could use the Commander-in-Chief power to evade limits on executive authority would be a grave jurisprudential error. The inverted word order in the third sentence ("what the power of command may include I do not try to envision") is an example of anastrophe. Jackson uses it to stress that seizing persons or property for military purposes is not part of the Commander-in-Chief power under the Constitution. The rhetorical devices in the final sentence are more subtle, but effective nonetheless, because they inject a pleasing rhythm attributable to the alliteration in "persons or property" and the isocolon in "a military prerogative," "without support of law," "seize persons or property," "important or even essential," and "the military and naval establishment."[151]

Similarly, low-key rhetorical tools grace the closing passages of Jackson's concurrence. "With all its defects, delays and inconveniences," he wrote, "men have discovered no technique for long preserving free government except that the Executive be under the law, and that the law be made by parliamentary deliberations."[152] Note the use of alliteration and parallelism in the first clause ("defects, delays, and inconveniences") and polyptoton (the repetition of "law") in the second. The final, two-sentence, paragraph in the opinion states: "Such institutions may be destined to pass away. But it is the duty of the Court to be last, not first, to give them up." Antithesis figures prominently here, as Jackson underscores the Court's role as the guardian of the constitutional separation of powers.

Out of concern for that role, Jackson joined the six-member majority that invalidated President Truman's order to seize the steel mills. In so doing, he left an indispensable chart to future navigators of separated power under the Constitution.

E. Conclusion

Judge Ruggero Aldisert has observed that Robert Jackson "wrote with a golden pen."[153] The praise is appropriate, but the prose was golden too. Key to the beauty and power of Jackson's prose was its creative and assertive use of rhetorical devices, particularly figures of speech. The literature of Supreme Court opinions is immensely richer for his contribution.

NOTES

1. I am indebted for the horseracing metaphor to one of Holmes's biographers, Liva Baker, who used it on page 47 of *The Justice from Beacon Hill.*
2. Eugene C. Gerhart, *Robert H. Jackson: Country Lawyer, Supreme Court Justice, America's Advocate* (Buffalo, NY: William S. Hein & Co., 2003), 25.
3. Harlan Phillips, ed., *The Reminiscences of Robert H. Jackson* (New York: Columbia University Oral History Research Office, 1955), 40.
4. Ibid, 37.
5. Ibid.
6. Gerhart, *Robert H. Jackson*, 32.
7. John Q. Barrett, "Albany in the Life Trajectory of Robert H. Jackson," *Albany Law Review* 68 (2005): 517.
8. Phillips, ed., *Reminiscences*, 65.
9. Noah Feldman, *Scorpions: The Battles and Triumphs of FDR's Great Supreme Court Justices* (New York: Twelve, Hatchett Book Group, Inc., 2010), 42.
10. Barrett, "Albany in the Life Trajectory of Robert H. Jackson," 518.
11. Ibid.
12. Ibid.
13. Ibid., 520.
14. Ibid., 521.
15. Ibid.
16. Ibid., 529. If Albany Law School can be accused of discrimination based on age in refusing to award Jackson a law degree in 1912, it surely cannot be accused of sex discrimination. Two other recipients of a diploma of graduation in his class were the Pritchard sisters—twins from Tivoli, New York named Clara and Clarissa—who were just nineteen. Ibid.
17. Ibid., 525–26.
18. Ibid., 529.
19. Gerhart, *Robert H. Jackson*, 35–36.

20. Ibid., 36.
21. Phillips, ed., *Reminiscences*, 76.
22. Ibid., 80.
23. Gerhart, *Robert H. Jackson*, 36–37.
24. Ibid., 41.
25. Feldman, *Scorpions*, 46–47.
26. Gerhart, *Robert H. Jackson*, 58.
27. Ibid., 64.
28. Feldman, *Scorpions*, 50; Stephen R. Alton, "Loyal Lieutenant, Able Advocate: The Role of Robert H. Jackson in Franklin D. Roosevelt's Battle with the Supreme Court," *William & Mary Bill of Rights Journal* 5 (1997): 528.
29. Feldman, *Scorpions*, 50.
30. Alton, "Loyal Lieutenant, Able Advocate," 548.
31. Feldman, *Scorpions*, 107–8.
32. Alton, "Loyal Lieutenant, Able Advocate," 551–52.
33. Ibid., 530.
34. Ibid., 571–72.
35. Ibid., 572.
36. Ibid., 572–73.
37. Ibid., 594.
38. Ibid., 595–98.
39. Ibid., 609.
40. Feldman, *Scorpions*, 196.
41. Ibid., 197.
42. Ibid., 199–200.
43. Ibid., 200.
44. Ibid.
45. Gerhart, *Robert H. Jackson*, 230–31.
46. Jeffrey D. Hockett, *New Deal Justice: The Constitutional Jurisprudence of Hugo L. Black, Felix Frankfurter and Robert H. Jackson* (Lanham, MD: Rowman & Littlefield Publishers, 1996), 215.
47. David M. O'Brien, *Justice Robert Jackson's Unpublished Opinion in Brown v. Board: Conflict, Compromise, and Constitutional Interpretation* (Lawrence, KS: University Press of Kansas, 2017), 26; Louis L. Jaffe, "Mr. Justice Jackson," *Harvard Law Review* 68 (1955): 942.
48. O'Brien, *Justice Robert Jackson's Unpublished Opinion in Brown v. Board*, 7.
49. Ibid., 30.
50. Ibid.
51. Laura Krugman Ray, "Judicial Personality: Rhetoric and Emotion in Supreme Court Opinions," *Washington & Lee Law Review* 59 (2002): 196.
52. O'Brien, *Justice Robert H. Jackson's Unwritten Opinion in Brown v. Board*, 24.
53. Ibid., 23.
54. Ray, "Judicial Personality," 209.
55. Laura Krugman Ray, "A Law Clerk and His Justice: What William Rehnquist Did Not Learn from Robert Jackson," *Indiana Law Review* 29 (1996): 591.
56. Ibid.
57. Ibid., 560.
58. 319 U.S. 624 (1943).
59. Robert H. Jackson, "Final Report to the President Concerning the Nurnberg War Crimes Trial," *Temple Law Quarterly* (1946): 338.
60. 337 U.S. 1 (1949).
61. Paul Freund, "Individual and Commonwealth in the Thought of Mr. Justice Jackson," in Paul Freund, *On Law and Justice* (Cambridge, MA: Harvard University Press, 1968), 174.
62. Feldman, *Scorpions*, 413.
63. *Jewell Ridge Coal Corp. v. United Mineworkers of America Local 6167*, 325 U.S. 161 (1945).
64. Feldman, *Scorpions*, 270.

65. Ibid., 293–96.
66. Ray, "A Law Clerk and His Justice," 542.
67. Ibid.
68. Gerhart, *Robert H. Jackson*, 302.
69. Ibid., 303.
70. Ibid.
71. Potter Stewart, "Robert H. Jackson's Influence on Federal-State Relationships," in Charles S. Desmond, Paul A. Freud, Potter Stewart, and Lord Shawcross, *Mr. Justice Jackson: Four Lectures in His Honor* (New York: Columbia University Press, 1969), 63.
72. O'Brien, *Justice Robert H. Jackson's Unpublished Opinion in Brown v. Board*, 59.
73. Ibid.
74. 319 U.S. 624 (1943).
75. 337 U.S. 1 (1949).
76. 339 U.S. 382 (1950).
77. 323 U.S. 214 (1944).
78. 333 U.S. 10 (1948).
79. 343 U.S. 579 (1952).
80. 319 U.S. 624 (1943).
81. 310 U.S. 586 (1940).
82. 319 U.S. at 630.
83. Ibid.
84. Ibid., 632–33.
85. Ibid., 638.
86. Ibid., 641.
87. Frost, "Greco-Roman Analysis of Metaphoric Reasoning," *Legal Writing: Journal of the Legal Writing Institute* 2 (1996): 126.
88. 319 U.S. at 642.
89. Ibid.
90. 337 U.S. 1 (1949).
91. Ibid., 5.
92. Ibid., 13.
93. Ibid., 16.
94. Ibid.
95. Ibid., 22.
96. Ibid.
97. Ibid., 23.
98. Ibid., 23–24.
99. Ibid., 37.
100. Ibid.
101. 339 U.S. 382 (1950).
102. Ibid., 413.
103. Ibid., 415.
104. Ibid., 424.
105. Ibid., 435.
106. Ibid., 436.
107. Ibid., 442–43.
108. William Domnarski, *The Great Justices 1941–1954: Black, Douglas, Frankfurter, and Jackson in Chambers* (Ann Arbor: University of Michigan Press, 2006), 41.
109. Michael R. Smith, "Levels of Metaphor in Persuasive Legal Writing," *Mercer Law Review* 58 (2007): 940.
110. Ibid.
111. 339 U.S. at 444.
112. Ibid.
113. 323 U.S. 214 (1944).
114. Ibid., 217.
115. Ibid., 217–18.

116. Ibid., 223–24.
117. Ibid.
118. Ibid., 245–46.
119. Ibid., 248.
120. 333 U.S. 10 (1948).
121. Ibid., 11.
122. Ibid., 12.
123. Ibid.
124. Ibid., 12–13.
125. Ibid., 14.
126. Ibid., 16.
127. Ibid., 16–17.
128. 343 U.S. 579 (1952).
129. Ibid., 582.
130. Ibid., 587.
131. Ibid.
132. Ibid.
133. Ibid.
134. Ibid.
135. Ibid., 589.
136. Ibid., 634.
137. Ibid.
138. Ibid., 635.
139. Ibid., 636.
140. Ibid., 637.
141. Ibid.
142. Ibid.
143. Ibid.
144. Ibid., 637–38.
145. Ibid., 638.
146. Ibid., 640.
147. Ibid.
148. Ibid., 646.
149. Corbett and Connors, *Classical Rhetoric for the Modern Student*, 4th ed., 394.
150. Ibid., 395. Had Jackson written instead that the purpose of lodging dual titles in the same person was to insure "that the civilian would control the military, not that the military would control the civilian," he would have employed antimetabole rather than chiasmus.
151. 343 U.S. at 646.
152. Ibid., 655.
153. Ruggero Aldisert, *Opinion Writing*, 3rd ed. (Durham, NC: Carolina Academic Press, 2012), 247.

Chapter Five

Hugo Black

Master of Simplicity

A. Beginnings

A biographer described Hugo Black as "a dedicated and purposeful champion of the underdog."[1] He surely began life as an underdog, born in 1886 among the scrubby pine trees and clay hills of east-central Alabama in Ashland, sixty miles east of Birmingham.[2] His ancestors had been in the United States since 1800, when they left Ireland as fugitives from a failed rebellion and settled in South Carolina.[3]

Hugo's response to the periodic alcoholic episodes of his father, a country storekeeper and farmer, was to draw closer to his mother and become more serious and introspective. He spent long hours reading Sir Walter Scott, Charles Dickens, Victor Hugo, and much history, along with standard boyhood fare such as detective and sports stories.[4] His mother's love and emotional support gave him a confidence that would enable him to take on and overcome daunting challenges later in life.[5]

Still, the path to a legal career was bumpy and circuitous. The fifteen-year-old Hugo intervened when a teacher punished his sister for whispering in class, resulting in his dismissal from high school.[6] One unsatisfying year at Birmingham Medical College followed, persuading him to abandon plans for a medical career.[7] In September 1904, Black, then eighteen years old, arrived in Tuscaloosa, home of the University of Alabama, where he sought to enroll in the sophomore class based on his high school and medical school courses.[8] But to be admitted with "advanced standing," he would have to take an exam, an admissions office requirement that the president of the university refused to waive.[9] Unwilling to take the exam to become a sophomore undergraduate, Black entered the law school, which did not require a bachelor's degree for admission.[10]

B. Professional Life

Black's academic training before law school may have been suspect, but his performance during law school was outstanding; indeed, he did not receive a grade lower than A during the two-year course.[11] Establishing what would become a lifelong pattern, Black identified what he needed to know and doggedly set about learning it. He took advantage of rules that allowed him to enroll in courses outside the law school and studied history, political economy, literature, and rhetoric. In May 1906, he graduated with highest honors and, as many law school graduates before and since have done, he went home to "hang out a shingle" and begin practicing law among his childhood friends and neighbors.[12]

Back in Ashland, Black rented two rooms over a grocery store in a corner of the town square and, while waiting in vain for clients, began to study subjects he had not studied in Tuscaloosa and to read textbooks on rhetoric, grammar, and writing.[13] He earned a small income by preparing credit reports at fifty cents apiece on insurance applicants for the Atlanta-based Retail Credit Corporation, which represented several large insurers, and he collected old debts still owed to his father's estate.[14] But Black's dreams of practicing law in his hometown went up in smoke in February of 1907, when the building that housed his office and library was destroyed in a fire.[15]

Several months later, eager to start anew, Black left Ashland for Birmingham, carrying less than ten dollars in his pocket and walking part of the way to reduce the train fare.[16] In Birmingham, Black shared a room in a boarding house with three other men and rented desk space for seven dollars a month, cash in advance, in a building full of lawyers located across the street from the county courthouse.[17] He continued to investigate the credit of insurance applicants for the Retail Credit Corporation, at fifty cents per investigation. For a time, the fifty dollars or so per month that he earned from this work was his only source of income.[18]

Black's talents did not go unnoticed for long, though. His greatest early success was his representation of Willie Norton, an African American convict whose sentence had lasted twenty-two days past its proper conclusion because the sheriff's office had leased him to a steel company to work under Alabama's notorious convict-leasing system.[19] Norton sued for damages, and Black, in his first jury trial, persuaded an all-white jury of the justice of his client's cause, which resulted in a damage award of $150, of which Black and the lawyer who had referred the case to him each took $37.50.[20] The twenty-five-year-old Black's trial performance so impressed the company's lawyer that he offered Black a position in his firm, which the young man from Ashland turned down, preferring to represent working people instead of corporations.[21] The trial judge was impressed, too, and in 1911 he arranged for Black to be appointed to the part-time post of police judge, a municipal judgeship.[22]

For a year and a half, Black juggled his judgeship and his private practice, eventually resigning the former to pursue the latter full time because it was now thriving.[23] In 1914, he made his first run for public office, seeking to become Jefferson County Solicitor, the county's prosecutor.[24] In his trademark high-energy fashion, Black began his campaign six months before any of his opponents, and on Election Day he defeated his nearest rival by more than two thousand votes. He was twenty-eight years old.[25] Three years later, Black resigned when critics who resented his efforts to speed up the processing of cases began to challenge Black's authority in court. The courtroom challenges soon became an argument about whether Black could hire his own assistants, which went to the Alabama Supreme Court for resolution. When the Court decided against Black, he quit, stating publicly that if he could no longer hire his own assistants, he could not perform his duties effectively.[26]

The year he resigned, 1917, saw the United States enter World War I. At thirty-one, Black was exempt from service, but he volunteered anyway, completing his service far from the front, in California and Oklahoma. By the time he finished his training, the Armistice was signed, so a year after volunteering, he returned to Birmingham and private practice.[27]

Private practice was lucrative for Hugo Black after the war. He quickly attracted a large clientele among blue-collar workers who had been injured in the mines, textile factories, and other industries in and around Birmingham. By 1925, he was earning more than $40,000 a year, largely by working on a contingency-fee basis, taking a percentage of the jury award if his client won and nothing if his client lost.[28] Between 1919 and 1925, his firm argued over one hundred cases in Alabama's appellate courts, more than half of them personal injury cases.[29]

Black also married during this time. At age thirty-four, he wed twenty-one-year-old Josephine Foster, the daughter of a socially prominent, if no longer wealthy, Birmingham family.[30] The couple moved into a two-story house on Birmingham's fashionable South Side and joined a country club.[31] Unfortunately, Josephine would die prematurely in 1951 at age fifty-two.[32]

Black hung a large skeleton in the closet of his new house when, in 1923, he joined the Robert E. Lee Klavern of Alabama's Ku Klux Klan.[33] That move signaled his interest in running for office in the near future, because the Klan controlled the voting machinery in practically all Alabama counties during the 1920s. In Jefferson County, where Black lived, the Klan was almost completely in control of local government by 1923.[34] Klansmen accounted for fifteen thousand of Birmingham's thirty-two thousand registered voters.[35] Statewide, no candidate could be elected without the Klan's support or, at least, its silence.[36]

Black's chance for the brass ring came two years later, when US Senator Oscar Underwood announced that he would not seek reelection the following year.[37] Ever the skittish race horse, Black was out of the gate six months early, campaigning statewide day and night while his rivals—like those who had run against him for county solicitor in 1914—were waiting for the official race to begin.[38] Keenly aware of his humble roots and underdog status, he appealed to ordinary people to support one of their own. On the policy front, he favored a crackdown on bootleggers and an end to immigration. Those appeals, coupled with his advocacy for working people, attracted the support of the Klan and its affiliated voters.[39] On the day of the Democratic Primary, he carried forty-two counties to win the Democratic nomination, which, because Alabama was solidly Democratic in the 1920s, virtually assured him of victory in the general election.[40]

In conformity with Senate norms in his day, Black maintained a low profile during his first term, learning the chamber's rules, listening to more experienced colleagues, and performing his committee work.[41] Perhaps the most noteworthy act of Black's first Senate term, though, was to quietly spurn the support of the Klan and the Prohibition forces that had supported his election. After publicly thanking the Klansmen for their votes three weeks after his primary win, Black never again courted their support.[42] By 1932, when he sought reelection, he neither pursued nor received Klan support.[43] Black's first term also saw him gradually join the tide of national opinion against Prohibition, as he publicly supported a referendum on the issue.[44] Despite these changes of tactics and position, Senator Black handily won his primary and general elections in 1932, winning fifty-two counties in the primary.[45]

His second term was quite different from his first. He supported newly elected President Roosevelt's New Deal programs designed to jumpstart the moribund economy through government stimulation and regulation, voting for almost every legislative measure the new administration sponsored.[46] Senator Black's most important contribution to FDR's administration, though, was as an investigator who exposed financial shenanigans by private shipping companies, the major commercial airlines, and utility holding companies.[47] His background as a trial lawyer equipped him well to investigate complex issues and to question often-reluctant witnesses. The investigation of the large airlines, which discovered that the airlines had used government subsidies for air mail delivery to reward their executives with princely salaries and stock options, on the taxpayers' dime, made the previously obscure Black the subject of nationwide newspaper headlines.[48] Later, in the wake of Senator Black's investigation of the public utility industry, Congress passed the Public Utilities Holding Company Act, which led to the dismantling of the holding companies within three years.[49]

After the investigations and Black's public support for FDR's Court-packing plan, including a radio address touting the need for the plan, the president was in Black's debt. In 1937, after almost five years in office without a chance to nominate anyone to the Supreme Court, FDR got that chance when Willis Van Devanter retired, and he sought to repay his debt by nominating Black to the Court.[50] Besides, Black satisfied FDR's criteria for a Supreme Court pick: he was relatively young (fifty-one), a son of the Deep South at a time when nobody from that region had served on the Court for many years, and likely to be confirmed by his Senate colleagues.[51] The latter was especially important to FDR, whose clout with senators was at a low point after the failure of his Court-packing plan.[52]

Although initially hesitant to leave the bustle of the Senate, Black accepted the Court nomination when FDR offered it. The Senate confirmed him by a vote of sixty-three to sixteen, with seventeen not voting, although several senators told Black beforehand that they would have voted for him had their votes been necessary.[53] One reason to vote no or not vote at all was the persistent, albeit unsubstantiated, rumors of Black's prior membership in the Ku Klux Klan.[54]

The rumors remained unsubstantiated temporarily because no FBI investigation of Black's past was undertaken before his Court nomination or confirmation.[55] But his luck seemed to have run out when *Pittsburgh Post-Gazette* reporter Ray Sprigle traveled to Alabama and located James Esdale, the former Grand Dragon of Black's klavern.[56] Esdale opened a safe that housed Black's application for Klan membership, his service card, a record of his initiation, a list of offices he had held, and his letter of resignation.[57] The reporter's visit gave Esdale an opportunity to exact revenge against Black for not awarding patronage jobs to Klan members during his Senate years.[58]

If the print media had unearthed an unsavory part of Black's past, an electronic medium—radio—would ensure he had a bright future. Black—always the capable advocate—made his case in just eleven minutes, neither denouncing the Klan nor stating his motives for having joined.[59] Instead, he said:

> I did join the Klan. I later resigned. I have never rejoined. I have never considered and I do not now consider the unsolicited card . . . as a membership of any kind in the Ku Klux Klan, I never used it. I did not even keep it. Before becoming a Senator I dropped the Klan. I have had nothing to do with it since that time.[60]

The radio address, which occurred six weeks after Black's nomination to the Court and less than two weeks after the revelation of his one-time Klan membership, was a rousing success. Before the address, 59 percent of those questioned had said that Black should resign from the Court if he had been a Klan member, but after he spoke, 56 percent said he should remain a justice.[61] Senator Black would become Justice Black after all.

C. On the Court

Free to concentrate on his judicial work after the success of his radio address, Black gradually found his place on the Court. He would serve there from October 1937 until September 1971, a month shy of thirty-four years.[62] Time and voracious reading led him to embrace the constitutional position known as "full incorporation," the view that the Fourteenth Amendment guarantees against the state governments all the constitutional protections that the Bill of Rights guarantees against the federal government.[63] Justice Black's support for full incorporation of the Bill of Rights derived from his underlying constitutional philosophy—"originalism"—which maintained that judges should interpret the Constitution according to the way in which it was understood when written.[64] Black was the first justice to articulate originalism as a constitutional theory and to explain why and how he was using it.[65] His earliest articulation of his view of the Fourteenth Amendment came in a dissent in *Adamson v. California*.[66] At issue in *Adamson* was whether the protection against compelled self-incrimination, which applied in federal court, should apply in state courts too.[67]

A five-member Court majority decided in California's favor. Justice Stanley Reed observed that despite the Fourteenth Amendment's protection against the denial by states of "liberty" without due process, a prosecutor was permitted to tell a jury in state court that it could infer guilt from a defendant's refusal to testify.[68] Black dissented in an opinion that would become famous to generations of constitutional law students for showing later courts the path toward his full-incorporation goal.[69] He argued that the Fifth Amendment—including its protection against compelled self-incrimination—should apply in both state and federal courts because the Fourteenth Amendment demanded that all the protections in the Bill of Rights extend to the states.[70]

In Black's view, the Court, beginning in 1872, had deprived the Fourteenth Amendment of its original meaning by denying that the terms "privileges and immunities" and "due process of law" within it apply the Bill of Rights to the states. Instead, the Court had held in cases such as *Lochner* (see chapter 3) that "due process" only protected property rights through "liberty of contract," which, Black stressed, had no constitutional basis.[71] To Black, *Adamson*, like *Lochner*, reflected the flawed "natural law" approach to due process championed by Justice Frankfurter; it left too much discretion to judges to decide whether a particular right was "fundamental," hence should apply to the states.[72] The only way to protect individual rights while limiting judicial discretion, Black argued, was to tie due process to specific guarantees in the Bill of Rights, such as the one against compelled self-incrimination.[73]

That philosophy ensured Black's place as a champion of individual rights during his Supreme Court tenure. His name is closely associated with the right to counsel for indigent criminal defendants, the freedom from compelled self-incrimination, and the freedom of speech.[74] Neither his "absolutist" view of the First Amendment protections nor his position that the Fourteenth Amendment made the first eight amendments applicable to the states ever became the full Court's position, but the power of his ideas and the force of his persistence moved the Court to "incorporate" (apply to the states) most of the Bill of Rights protections one at a time.[75] Indeed, by the end of Chief Justice Earl Warren's tenure in 1969, the Court had applied all of the most significant guarantees in the Bill of Rights to the states through "selective incorporation" of those guarantees into the Fourteenth Amendment's Due Process Clause. Thus, Hugo Black lived to see the Court adopt his view of due process, albeit more gradually than he would have preferred.[76]

Black's concerns about judicial discretion would cause him to break with his longtime allies on the Court—Warren and Justices Douglas and Brennan—in cases about privacy and about speech combined with conduct, which became prominent constitutional controversies in the 1960s. Black's discomfort with the idea of a constitutional right of privacy was evident in *Griswold v. Connecticut*, which concerned the constitutionality of a state law that prohibited the dissemination of contraceptive devices and information about how to use them, even to married couples. The Court struck this law down as a violation of the newly recognized right.[77] Black dissented, but struggled to write his dissent because he found the Connecticut law "abhorrent, just viciously evil, but not unconstitutional."[78] It violated no express constitutional language that protected personal privacy.

In Black's view, speech intertwined with conduct was just like the right to privacy because it invited the exercise of judicial discretion that he abhorred. Black read the First Amendment literally, that is, to protect oral and written communication, but not conduct. As a result, he believed that neither "speech plus" (e.g., speech connected to a sit-in demonstration) nor "symbolic speech" (e.g., the wearing of a black armband to protest the Vietnam War) enjoyed First Amendment protection. The government could regulate the time, place, and manner in which they occurred or could ban them completely.[79]

Black the old First Amendment warrior's last constitutional battle occurred during the Court's 1970 Term, in what came to be known as the

"Pentagon Papers Case." The Nixon administration sought to enjoin the *New York Times* and the *Washington Post* from publishing a trove of documents that chronicled the troubled history of America's military involvement in Vietnam.[80] As a First Amendment absolutist, Black naturally supported the newspapers' right to publish and joined the six-member majority that held the government had not justified the imposition of a prior restraint on publication. The group agreed to issue a one-paragraph per curiam opinion that William Brennan prepared, with each justice then writing his own opinion.[81] Black's separate opinion was a passionate defense of freedom of the press against a presidential attempt to prevent the publication of documents unflattering to the government on "national security" grounds. He wrote:

> To find that the President has "inherent power" to halt the publication of news by resort to the courts would wipe out the First Amendment and destroy the fundamental liberty and security of the very people the Government hopes to make "secure."[82]

The 1970 Term ended in late June, 1971 with the Court's decision in the Pentagon Papers Case. Twice during the summer, Black, by then eighty-five years old, was admitted to Bethesda Naval Hospital, weak, listless, and suffering from temporal arteritis, an inflammation of the blood vessels.[83] Recognizing his infirmity, he retired from the Court on September 17, 1971.[84] He died eight days later, prompting his former colleague Earl Warren to state simply but eloquently: "A great man has passed away."[85]

D. Black the Writer

Hugo Black wanted ordinary Americans to be able to read and understand his opinions, and he honed his writing toward that end. His efforts paid off because midway through his first Court term, journalist Heywood Broun wrote, "Black is certainly popular with newspaper men because he recently wrote a dissent in English as plain and simple and clear as a good running story on the first page."[86] That popularity may have resulted from Black's habit of asking nonlawyers to read his draft opinions; among his preferred readers were his second wife, Elizabeth, whom he married in 1957, and his longtime messenger, Spencer Campbell.[87]

The succeeding paragraphs will display Black's clarity of expression and legal storytelling ability in two areas of his greatest influence: criminal procedure and free speech. The featured criminal procedure cases include *Chambers v. Florida*,[88] *Adamson v. California*,[89] and *Gideon v. Wainwright*.[90] The featured free speech cases are *Beauharnais v. Illinois*,[91] *Smith v. California*,[92] and *New York Times Co. v. United States*.[93]

1. Chambers v. Florida

Hugo Black's opinion for a unanimous eight-member Court in *Chambers* (Justice Frank Murphy did not participate) illustrates his facility for arrangement, as the opinion proceeds smoothly from an introduction to a recounting of the facts to Black's reasoning to his conclusion. The opening sentence of the opinion identifies the origins of the case and the legal issue to be decided.

> The grave question presented by the petition for certiorari, granted in forma pauperis, is whether proceedings in which confessions were utilized, and which culminated in sentences of death upon four young negro men in the State of Florida, failed to afford the safeguard of that due process of law guaranteed by the Fourteenth Amendment.[94]

In one sentence the reader learns that the petitioners were four young, indigent African American men in pre–World War II Florida who were sentenced to death based on confessions of questionable validity. The imbalance of power between the defendants and the State was great, the procedures used may have been coercive, and the consequences of conviction were severe. The reader readily grasps the gravity of the case, and the potential injustice involved, from one well-crafted sentence.

Even today, eight decades later, Black's words convey in clear and compelling fashion the importance of the case and the severity of the abuses of power by law enforcement personnel. Those words resonate in the minds of modern readers in part because of contemporary interactions between the police and African American suspects, and the resulting Black Lives Matter Movement, but also because the words themselves paint a vivid and timeless picture of poor, unrepresented defendants outmatched by the resources of the State. Thus, Black's passage meets Judge Posner's definition of "legal literature," because it "can be detached from the setting in which [it was] created."[95]

Drawn into the story, the reader proceeds to the factual discussion and finds that Black is an able storyteller who can incline the reader to his position by presenting facts persuasively. He writes:

> About nine o'clock on the night of Saturday, May 13, 1933, Robert Darcy, an elderly white man, was robbed and murdered in Pompano, Florida, a small town in Broward County about twelve miles from Fort Lauderdale, the County seat. The opinion of the Supreme Court of Florida affirming petitioners' conviction for this crime stated that "It was one of those crimes that induced an enraged community. . . ."[96]

The community rage, Black continues, resulted in a sweep in which the police arrested a large number of African American males. "Between 9:30 and 10 o'clock after the murder," he wrote, "petitioner Charlie Davis was arrested, and within the next twenty-four hours from twenty-five to forty negroes living in the community, including petitioners Williamson, Chambers, and Woodward, were arrested without warrants and confined in the Broward County Jail, at Fort Lauderdale."[97]

After the arrests, round-the-clock interrogation ensued, as Black explains in stark terms.

> During the week following their arrests and until their confessions were finally acceptable to the State's attorney in the early dawn of Sunday, May 21st, petitioners and their fellow prisoners were led one at a time from their cells to the questioning room, quizzed, and returned to their cells to await another turn. So far as appears, the prisoners at no time during the week were permitted to see or confer with counsel or a single friend or relative. When carried singly from his cell and subjected to questioning, each found himself, a single prisoner, surrounded in a fourth-floor jail room by four to ten men, the county sheriff, his deputies, a convict guard, and other white officers and citizens of the community.[98]

Understandably, the defendants eventually confessed to the murder of Mr. Darcy. "After one week's constant denial of all guilt," Black writes, "petitioners 'broke.'"[99] Two days later they were indicted and arraigned.[100] "And from arrest until sentenced to death," he adds, "petitioners were never—either in jail or in court—wholly removed from the constant observation, influence, custody and control of those whose persistent pressure brought about the sunrise confessions."[101]

Black lets the facts speak for themselves by avoiding adjectives that might have injected hyperbole into the discussion. Instead, he notes the mass arrests, lack of warrants, round-the-clock interrogations, and absence of counsel, allowing the reader to infer that, based on those facts, the confessions were tainted and unreliable. This facility for "showing rather than telling," in the parlance of legal writing professors, reflects the lessons Black absorbed by studying rhetoric during and after law school. His *Chambers* opinion reflects the major lesson he learned from those studies: that "the best way to tell any story is to tell it as simply as possible, in the simplest words possible, and in the shortest way possible."[102]

Proceeding to his reasoning in *Chambers*, Black emphasizes that the drafters of the Fourteenth Amendment intended for the Due Process Clause to protect state defendants. His analysis derives from the topic of relationship and the subtopic of contraries. The behavior of the police here, in Black's view, was fundamentally incompatible with the Fourteenth Amendment's aim that the Due Process Clause should protect criminal defendants against abuse by state and local police. Appealing to pathos, he alerts the reader to the colossal mismatch in the interrogation room between the unprotected defendant untrained in the law and the considerable resources of the State.

He observes that by the time of the Fourteenth Amendment's adoption, centuries of abuse had shown that defendants could not "be safely entrusted to secret inquisitorial processes."[103] The use of the word "inquisitorial" marks the transition from facts to reasoning; in the latter, Black is unsparing in analogizing the police procedures used in *Chambers* to the atrocities imposed on powerless individuals by tyrannical governments throughout history.

> The rack, the thumbscrew, the wheel, solitary confinement, protracted questioning and cross-questioning, and other ingenious forms of entrapment of the helpless or unpopular had left their wake of mutilated bodies and shattered minds along the way to the cross, the guillotine, the stake and the hangman's noose.[104]

Note the vivid references to ancient means of torture, presented in a parallel structure ("the rack, the thumbscrew, the wheel, solitary confinement" and later "the cross, the guillotine, the stake and the hangman's noose") that injects a memorable rhythm into the sentence. Besides parallelism, Black uses isocolon to refer to the "mutilated bodies and shattered minds" that wash up in the metaphorical "wake" of torture like the abandoned cargo of a sunken ship. He uses isocolon again to emphasize that the interrogation methods in this case were "calculated to break the strongest nerves and the stoutest resistance."[105]

Finally, Black relies on metaphors at the end of his opinion to emphasize that coercive interrogation techniques are the tools of tyranny and that courts exist to counter such coercion.

> Today, as in ages past, we are not without tragic proof that the exalted power of some governments to punish manufactured crime dictatorially is the handmaid of tyranny. Under our constitutional system, courts stand against any winds that blow as havens of refuge for those who might otherwise suffer because they are helpless, weak, outnumbered, or because they are non-conforming victims of prejudice and public excitement.[106]

The metaphorical references to phony criminal charges as "the handmaid of tyranny" and to courts as "havens of refuge" show that Black's rhetorical skills went beyond arrangement. He could also employ figures of speech to highlight key facts and core values. The core value expressed here is that courts should defeat "manufactured crime," which preserves tyranny by silencing unpopular political and racial minorities. In *Chambers*, Black's opinion for a unanimous Court reversed the defendants' convictions.

2. *Adamson v. California*

Adamson produced a dramatically different outcome than *Chambers*. Instead of unanimity, *Adamson* resulted in a 5–4 decision in which Black dissented along with Justices Murphy, Rutledge, and Douglas, although only Douglas joined Black's opinion.[107] As noted earlier, California's constitution and penal code permitted the court and the prosecutor in a criminal case to comment on the defendant's failure to testify and to explain or deny damaging evidence. Both the state constitution and the penal code also permitted the trier of fact—either judge or jury—to consider the defendant's failure to testify when reaching its verdict.[108] A jury convicted Adamson of first degree murder and sentenced him to death, which sentence the California Supreme Court affirmed.[109] He did not testify.[110]

Stanley Reed's majority opinion rejected Adamson's contention that the Due Process Clause of the Fourteenth Amendment applied the Fifth Amendment's protection against compelled self-incrimination to the states.[111] To Reed, the Bill of Rights was adopted to protect individuals against the federal government, not state governments; hence, its provisions were inapplicable to the actions of the states.[112] Accordingly, the Fourteenth Amendment forbids a state from abridging the privileges and immunities of citizens of the United States, leaving a state free to abridge, within the limits of the Due Process Clause (e.g., the freedom of speech and press already applied to the states), the privileges and immunities of state citizenship.[113]

Furthermore, Reed explained, the freedom from compelled self-incrimination was not essential to a fair trial. For example, Adamson's failure to testify was not an admission of the truth of the evidence against him. Indeed, the judge had instructed the jury that despite Adamson's refusal to testify, the burden of proof remained with the state, and Adamson was presumed innocent.[114] The Court majority thus affirmed Adamson's conviction.

Hugo Black's dissent tells the story of the *Adamson* case, and highlights its significance, in the opening paragraph. Black writes:

> The appellant was tried for murder in a California state court. He did not take the stand as a witness in his own behalf. The prosecuting attorney, under purported authority of a California statute, Cal. Penal Code, § 1323 (Hilyer-Lake 1945), argued to the jury that an inference of guilt could be drawn because of appellant's failure to deny evidence offered against him. The appellant's contention in the state court and here has been that the statute denies him a right guaranteed by the Federal Constitution. The argument is that (1) permitting comment upon his failure to testify has the effect of compelling him to testify so as to violate that provision of the Bill of Rights contained in the Fifth Amendment that "No person . . . shall be compelled in any criminal case to be a witness against himself"; and (2) although this provision of the Fifth Amendment originally applied only as a restraint upon federal courts, [citation omitted] the Fourteenth Amendment was intended to, and did make the prohibition against compelled testimony applicable to trials in state courts.[115]

This paragraph is so informative that the reader could forego reading the majority opinion, yet still understand precisely what is at stake in the case.

Turning to his reasoning, Black takes aim at the natural law theory of due process, first used in *Twining v. New Jersey* and now embraced by the *Adamson* majority.[116] His argument reflects the topic of comparison and the subtopic of difference, specifically, the difference between the natural law theory and Black's "full incorporation" theory of due process. Under the former, the Court determines whether certain Bill of Rights protections apply to the states based on how "fundamental" the current Court membership thinks those protections are to due process of law. Black finds the natural law theory unacceptable because it gives the justices too much discretion to decide which provisions of the Bill of Rights are fundamental and which are not, according to their policy preferences. Employing antithesis and analogy to advance this critique, Black writes:

> Invoking this *Twining* rule, the Court concludes that although comment upon testimony in a federal court would violate the Fifth Amendment, identical comment in a state court does not violate today's fashion in civilized decency and fundamentals and is therefore not prohibited by the Federal Constitution as amended.[117]

The antithesis underscores the inexplicable incongruity, in Black's view, between enforcing the protection against compelled self-incrimination in federal court but not in state court. The analogy to "fashion" conveys Black's distaste for a standard that, in his estimation, treats constitutional protections like clothes or automobiles, to be celebrated or discarded based on shifting tastes within the Court.

Rejecting such discretion in constitutional matters, Black explains in conversational language why not only the protection against compelled self-incrimination, but all of the protections included in the first eight amendments of the Bill of Rights, apply to the states.

> My study of the historical events that culminated in the Fourteenth Amendment, and the expressions of those who sponsored and favored, as well as those who opposed its submission and passage, persuades me that one of the chief objects that the provisions of the Amendment's first section, separately, and as a whole were intended to accomplish was to make the Bill of Rights, applicable to the states.[118]

"I would therefore hold in this case," he observes, "that the full protection of the Fifth Amendment's proscription against compelled testimony must be afforded by California."[119]

Before concluding, though, Black cautions that the natural law theory is a double-edged sword; it can limit judicial power, as in *Adamson*, by preventing the Supreme Court from curbing state violations of individual constitutional rights. But, as used in *Lochner*, it can empower the Court to "roam at large in the broad expanses of policy and morals to trespass, all too freely, on the legislative domain of the States as well as the Federal Government."[120] Note the metaphorical reference to the Court "roaming at large" against legislation it dislikes, substituting personal policy preferences for constitutional jurisprudence. In Black's view, the righteous roaming and attendant trespassing would continue until the Court rejected natural law and put its faith in the constitutional text instead.

3. *Gideon v. Wainwright*

In *Gideon*, a landmark case about an indigent defendant's right to court-appointed counsel in a state felony prosecution, the majority opinion (for a unanimous Court) shows Black at his storytelling best in the opening paragraph.[121]

> Petitioner was charged in a Florida state court with having broken and entered a poolroom with intent to commit a misdemeanor. This offense is a felony under Florida law. Appearing in court without funds and without a lawyer, petitioner asked the court to appoint counsel for him, whereupon the following colloquy took place:
>
> The Court: Mr. Gideon, I am sorry, but I cannot appoint Counsel to represent you in this case. Under the laws of the State of Florida, the only time the Court can appoint Counsel to represent a Defendant is when that person is charged with a capital offense. I am sorry, but I will have to deny your request to appoint Counsel to defend you in this case.
>
> The Defendant: The United States Supreme Court says I am entitled to be represented by Counsel.[122]

The colloquy highlights Gideon's predicament. The Supreme Court's refusal to extend to the states the right to counsel for indigent defendants, except for young, uneducated persons charged with capital crimes, left Gideon unrepresented. The Court had indeed held that defendants in federal court were entitled to be represented by counsel, but only some states appointed counsel for indigent defendants in state court. Gideon knew enough about the law to attempt to represent himself, but he was no match for the county prosecutor.

Black then tells the following story of Gideon's trial: Put to trial before a jury, Gideon conducted his defense about as well as could be expected from a layman. He made an opening statement to the jury, cross-examined the State's witnesses, presented witnesses in his own defense, declined to testify himself, and made a short argument "emphasizing his innocence to the charge contained in the Information filed in this case." The jury returned a verdict of guilty, and petitioner was sentenced to serve five years in the state prison. Later, petitioner filed in the Florida Supreme Court this habeas corpus petition attacking his conviction and sentence on the ground that the trial court's refusal to appoint counsel for him denied him rights "guaranteed by the Constitution and the Bill of Rights by the United States Government." Treating the petition for habeas corpus as properly before it, the State Supreme Court, "'upon consideration thereof' but without an opinion, denied all relief."[123]

A legal writing professor could fault the alternation between "Gideon" and "petitioner" to identify the same person; using either one exclusively would have been clearer. Still, the passage describes vividly the difficulties inherent in self-representation by a nonlawyer. Indeed, those difficulties are evident in Black's clear, direct statement that "Gideon conducted his defense about as well as could be expected from a layman." Without a lawyer, Gideon was disadvantaged from the beginning of his trial to its conclusion, as any defendant untrained in the law would be, and his unfamiliarity with preparing and presenting a case made the outcome virtually inevitable.

The remainder of the paragraph reveals the roots of the issue to be decided, then identifies that issue by posing a rhetorical question, which is a trope that seeks not to elicit an answer, but rather, to assert or deny something indirectly. It induces the audience (or reader) to make the appropriate response, which can be more persuasive than a direct assertion.[124] Black writes:

> Since 1942, when *Betts v. Brady*, 316 U.S. 455, was decided by a divided Court, the problem of a defendant's federal constitutional right to counsel in a state court has been a continuing source of controversy and litigation in both state and federal courts. To give this problem another review here, we granted certiorari.[125]

After noting that the Court had appointed counsel to represent Mr. Gideon, Black identifies the question presented as: "Should this Court's holding in *Betts v. Brady*, 316 U.S. 455, be reconsidered?[126]

Proceeding to his reasoning, Black begins by recalling the natural law theory of due process, the underpinning of *Betts* on which Florida's argument in *Gideon* also relied. Here, as in *Adamson*, his analysis flows from the topic of comparison and the subtopic of difference, in particular the difference between the natural law and full incorporation theories of due process. Regarding *Betts*, he writes:

> [T]he Court held that refusal to appoint counsel under the particular facts and circumstances in the *Betts* case was not so "offensive to the common and fundamental ideas of fairness" as to amount to a denial of due process. Since the facts and circumstances of the two cases are so nearly indistinguishable,

> we think the *Betts v. Brady* holding if left standing would require us to reject Gideon's claim that the Constitution guarantees him the assistance of counsel. Upon full reconsideration we conclude that *Betts v. Brady* should be overruled.[127]

Black's rejection of the natural law theory in *Gideon* also occasioned a memorable passage about the unfairness inherent in denying counsel to indigent defendants. It is effective because of its clear language, compelling logic, and deep humanity. Black employs pathos to spur empathy in the reader for the ordinary person who is "haled into court" to defend himself in the face of fear and confusion. After noting several Court precedents that conflicted with *Betts*, Black the veteran trial lawyer writes:

> Not only these precedents but also reason and reflection require us to recognize that in our adversary system of criminal justice, any person haled into court, who is too poor to hire a lawyer, cannot be assured a fair trial unless counsel is provided for him. This seems to us to be an obvious truth. Governments, both state and federal, quite properly spend vast sums of money to establish machinery to try defendants accused of crime. Lawyers to prosecute are everywhere deemed essential to protect the public's interest in an orderly society. Similarly, there are few defendants charged with crime, few indeed, who fail to hire the best lawyers they can get to prepare and present their defenses. That government hires lawyers to prosecute and defendants who have the money hire lawyers to defend are the strongest indications of the widespread belief that lawyers in criminal courts are necessities, not luxuries. The right of one charged with crime to counsel may not be deemed fundamental and essential to fair trials in some countries, but it is in ours.[128]

This passage uses only two rhetorical techniques—polyptoton and antithesis—but both are important to its effectiveness. Polyptoton—"few defendants . . . few indeed"—emphasizes the regularity with which criminal defendants hire lawyers if they can. As for antithesis, it is the gist of the observations that: "lawyers in criminal courts are necessities, not luxuries" and "[t]he right of one charged with crime to counsel may not be . . . essential to fair trials in some countries, but it is in ours." Both figures highlight a fundamental truth about American criminal justice in 1963 and today: a fair trial requires that competent counsel represent the defendant. Thus, *Gideon* shows that figures of speech need not proliferate to persuade; indeed, one or two, if well-placed, work best.

4. *Beauharnais v. Illinois*

Mr. Beauharnais was convicted in a Chicago municipal court and fined two hundred dollars for violating a state law against the manufacture, sale, or display of, among other things, a lithograph that "portray[ed] depravity, criminality, unchastity, or lack of virtue of a class of citizens, of any race, color, creed or religion" whom the lithograph exposed to "contempt, derision, or obloquy or which is productive of breach of the peace or riots. . . ."[129] He challenged the statute on free speech and free press grounds, but the Illinois courts sustained his conviction. In a 5–4 decision, the Supreme Court affirmed. His lithograph was a leaflet that called on the mayor and city council of Chicago "to halt further encroachment, harassment and invasion of white people, their property, neighborhoods and persons, by the Negro. . . ."[130]

Writing for the majority, Justice Frankfurter recounted the ugly history of racial violence and riots in Illinois, which, in his view, made the challenged statute a reasonable legislative response designed "to curb false or malicious defamation of racial and religious groups. . . ."[131] Because the speech at issue could be punished if directed at a particular individual, it could also be outlawed when directed at a group with whom that individual "may be inextricably involved."[132] Thus, the legislature was authorized to punish such "group libel," and the Court affirmed the petitioner's conviction.

Justice Black wrote a dissent that Justice Douglas joined. Once again, Black's opening paragraph tells everything the reader needs to know about the case.

> This case is here because Illinois inflicted criminal punishment on Beauharnais for causing the distribution of leaflets in the city of Chicago. The conviction rests on the leaflet's contents, not on the time, manner or place of distribution. Beauharnais is head of an organization that opposes amalgamation and favors segregation of white and colored people. After discussion, an assembly of his group decided to petition the mayor and council of Chicago to pass laws for segregation. Volunteer members of the group agreed to stand on street corners, solicit signers to petitions addressed to the city authorities, and distribute leaflets giving information about the group, its beliefs and its plans. In carrying out this program a solicitor handed out a leaflet which was the basis of this prosecution.[133]

Proceeding to his reasoning, Black criticizes the majority for treating the Illinois statute as a traditional punishment for criminal libel because historically, criminal libel applied to expression directed at individuals, not groups. Once again, his rationale derives from "comparison" and "difference," this time the difference between traditional criminal libel and "group libel," which the case features and Black opposes. He writes:

> However tagged, the Illinois law is not that criminal libel which has been defined, limited, and constitutionally recognized time out of mind. For as constitutionally recognized that crime has provided for punishment of false, malicious, scurrilous charges against individuals, not against huge groups. This limited scope of the law of criminal libel is of no small importance. It has confined state punishment of speech and expression to the narrowest of areas

> involving nothing more than purely private feuds. Every expansion of the law of criminal libel so as to punish discussions of matters of public concern means a corresponding invasion of the area dedicated to free expression by the First Amendment. [Internal citation omitted].[134]

This passage reflects the clash between Frankfurter's dedication to legislative resolutions for societal problems and Black's commitment to the Bill of Rights. Just as the former spurred Frankfurter to support an expansion of the scope of criminal libel, the latter prompted Black to regard that expansion as a dangerous restriction on free speech.

Using metaphor and analogy to enliven his prose, Black continues:

> This Act sets up a system of state censorship which is at war with the kind of free government envisioned by those who forced adoption of our Bill of Rights. The motives behind the state law may have been to do good. But the same can be said about most laws making opinions punishable as crimes. History indicates that urges to do good have led to the burning of books and even to the burning of "witches."[135]

The reference to "state censorship" is vivid, but not excessive because it conveys the danger Black perceives in any limits to free expression about public issues. The war metaphor conveys his view that such limits violate the core values of the Constitution, as does the analogy between the Illinois law at issue and historical episodes of burning books and even women for their unorthodox ideas or behavior. The book-burning analogy in this paragraph also sets up another analogy in the next paragraph, which notes that "the same kind of state law that makes Beauharnais a criminal for advocating segregation in Illinois can be utilized to send people to jail in other states for advocating equality and nonsegregation."[136] "Nonsegregation" is an awkward word choice; still, the sentence is noteworthy in warning that speech restrictions motivated by egalitarianism in one place and time can breed speech restrictions motivated by hatred in another place and time.

Thus, Black concludes by paraphrasing Pyrrhus, the ancient Greek king whose wars against the Romans succeeded militarily, but were disastrous financially. "If there be minority groups who hail this holding as their victory," Black writes, "they might consider the possible relevancy of this ancient remark: 'Another such victory and I am undone.'"[137] For Black, the import of the analogy in the literary allusion is clear: in a democratic society, nobody wins when speech is censored, even if an errant "squeaky wheel" is temporarily silenced. Victory—the long-term vitality of democracy—lies in fostering speech on matters of public concern, not in quashing it.

5. *Smith v. California*

Smith offered Hugo Black another opportunity to articulate his absolutist view of First Amendment guarantees, this time in the context of obscenity.[138] Black joined the eight-member majority, but wrote a separate concurrence in the case, which featured a Los Angeles bookstore owner who had been convicted in a municipal court on "obscenity" charges. The city ordinance he violated prohibited the possession of "any obscene or indecent writing, [or] book ... in any place of business where . . . books . . . are sold or kept for sale."[139] A state appellate court affirmed the conviction, holding that Smith had committed a strict liability offense that consisted solely of his possession in his bookstore of a particular book that a court concluded was obscene.[140]

Writing for the majority, Justice William Brennan noted that the ordinance at issue lacked any element of *scienter*—knowledge by the petitioner of the book's content—which was why the appellate court had construed it as imposing strict liability.[141] For Brennan, the lack of a scienter requirement was fatal to the ordinance, tending to "work a substantial restriction on the freedom of speech and of the press."[142] Absent a scienter requirement, booksellers could be subject to penalties for selling books whose character they were unaware of, causing them to sell only books they had inspected and found unobjectionable. Such restraint by booksellers would, in Brennan's view, limit the distribution of constitutionally protected literature, hence the public's access to the printed word.[143] Accordingly, the Los Angeles ordinance was unconstitutional.

Black agreed that the ordinance must fall, but not because it lacked scienter. His reasoning derives from the topic of relationship and the subtopic of contraries, namely, the incompatibility between the challenged ordinance and the First Amendment's guarantee of free speech. In characteristically plain and clear language, he writes, "The grounds on which the Court draws a constitutional distinction between a law that punishes possession of a book with knowledge of its 'obscenity' and a law that punishes without such knowledge are not persuasive to me."[144] The majority's reasoning is unpersuasive because, as Black would observe later in the same paragraph, "[t]he fact is, of course, that prison sentences for possession of 'obscene' books will seriously burden freedom of the press whether punishment is imposed with or without knowledge of the obscenity."[145]

To Black, the majority had left open the possibility that government could sometimes limit the freedom of expression in favor of what Justice Brennan had termed "more important interests."[146] But in Black's view, no more important interest exists under our Constitution than freedom of expression, and the document's protection for it is absolute.

> Certainly the First Amendment's language leaves no room for inference that abridgements of speech and press can be made just because they are slight. That Amendment provides, in simple words, that "Congress shall make no law . . . abridging the freedom of speech, or of the press." I read "no law . . . abridging" to mean *no law abridging.*[147]

Thus, he continues, using polyptoton and antithesis ("court-made, not Constitution-made") to good effect,

> I do not believe that any federal agencies, including Congress and this Court, have power or authority to subordinate speech and press to what they think are "more important interests." The contrary notion is, in my judgment, court-made, not Constitution-made.[148]

Concluding his concurrence, Black again uses the word "censorship," this time along with metaphor and the first person, to underline his unwavering opposition to any limits on freedom of speech and press.

> Censorship is the deadly enemy of freedom and progress. The plain language of the Constitution forbids it. I protest against the Judiciary giving it a foothold here.[149]

"Censorship" fits Black's steadfast opposition to limits on freedom of expression. His metaphors fit it too; they depict such limits as the "deadly enemy" of freedom and progress, an enemy to which courts should deny a "foothold." The two war metaphors reflect Black's determination to prevent prosecutors from prosecuting bookstore owners on obscenity charges because the owners were familiar with the contents of the books involved and sold them anyway. If censorship is the "deadly enemy" of freedom, to Black, the scienter requirement allows the enemy's troops to land on our shores and threaten our freedom.

6. New York Times Company v. United States

In this 6–3 decision, Justice Brennan's short per curiam opinion explained that the federal government had sought to enjoin the *New York Times* and the *Washington Post* from publishing a classified study titled "History of U.S. Decision-Making Process on Viet Nam Policy," better known as the "Pentagon Papers."[150] The opinion noted that "[a]ny system of prior restraints of expression," such as the government argued for here, faced a "heavy presumption against its constitutional validity."[151] It then observed that the US District Court for the Southern District of New York in the *New York Times* case and the US District Court for the District of Columbia and the US Court of Appeals for the District of Columbia Circuit in the *Washington Post* case held that the government had not overcome that presumption. Adding "[w]e agree," the per curiam opinion reversed a decision for the government by the US Court of Appeals for the Second Circuit in the *Times* case, affirmed the D.C. Circuit's decision, and vacated the stays the Supreme Court itself had issued when the cases reached it.[152] Individual members of the Court then attached their own separate opinions.

Eighty-five years old and in frail health, Black knew that this case would likely be his swan song on the Court and he took full advantage of the opportunity it presented. His opening sentence reflects his uncompromising stance on free expression.

> [T]he government's case against the *Washington Post* should have been dismissed and the injunction against the *New York Times* should have been vacated without oral argument when the cases were first presented to this Court. I believe that every moment's continuance of the injunctions against these newspapers amounts to a flagrant, indefensible, and continuing violation of the First Amendment.[153]

The passage is powerful because of its directness; it rejects the government's arguments as without merit. Black sweeps them away as one would sweep debris from a table into a wastebasket with one hand. But the vivid reference to "every moment's continuance" of the injunctions and the parallelism in the last clause ("flagrant, indefensible, and continuing") add power to the passage too. The reader quickly senses Black's outrage at the government's efforts to prevent publication and his impatience for publication to resume.

Turning to the basis for his position, Black's analysis again reflects the topic of relationship and the subtopic of contraries, particularly the unbridgeable gap between the Nixon administration's petition to stop publication of the Pentagon Papers and the First Amendment's guarantee of a free press. Black writes that "[b]oth the history and language of the First Amendment support the view that the press must be left free to publish news, whatever the source, without censorship, injunctions, or prior restraints."[154] Note how the parallel structure at the end of the sentence proceeds from the single words "censorship" and "injunctions" to the multiword "prior restraints." As chapter 1 notes, the same rhythm (tricolon) makes so memorable the references in the Declaration of Independence to "life, liberty, and the pursuit of happiness" and to "our lives, our fortunes, and our sacred honor."

Parallelism yields to alliteration in the passage below, illuminating the watchdog function of a free press and forming the most iconic portion of Black's concurrence.

> Only a free and unrestrained press can effectively expose deception in government. And paramount among the responsibilities of a free press is the duty to prevent any part of the government from deceiving the people and sending them off to distant lands to die of foreign fevers and foreign shot and shell. In

> my view, far from deserving condemnation for their courageous reporting, the *New York Times*, the *Washington Post*, and other newspapers should be commended for serving the purpose that the Founding Fathers saw so clearly. In revealing the workings of government that led to the Vietnam War, the newspapers nobly did precisely that which the Founders hoped and trusted they would do.[155]

To Black, the press could play no more important role in a free society than to protect the citizenry against misgovernment, especially decisions that subjected it to "foreign fevers and foreign shot and shell." The alliteration adds to the gravity of the opinion, all the more important for Black in this case because of its importance and because he knew it could be his last. The vivid battlefield imagery in the alliteration clarifies for the reader the reasons why governments should not be able to censor their justifications for going to war.

E. Conclusion

Hugo Black's writing, in contrast to that of Oliver Wendell Holmes, Jr. and Robert Jackson, stands out for its arrangement rather than its style. Although he was familiar with rhetorical devices and could turn an evocative phrase on occasion, Black was best at telling a clear, simple story that led the reader seamlessly to his reasoning. He aimed to and usually succeeded in producing opinions that, despite their serious subjects and thorough analyses, ordinary people could understand. His writing therefore offers every legal writer an accessible and admirable model to study and emulate. New legal writers and experienced legal writers who favor a plain style that uses figures of speech sparingly will find Justice Black's writing an especially good model to follow.

NOTES

1. Gerald T. Dunne, *Hugo Black and the Judicial Revolution* (New York: Simon & Schuster, 1977), 43.
2. Ibid., 85–86.
3. James F. Simon, *The Antagonists: Hugo Black, Felix Frankfurter and Civil Liberties in Modern America* (New York: Touchstone/Simon & Schuster, 1989), 68.
4. Roger K. Newman, *Hugo Black: A Biography* (New York: Fordham University Press, 1997), 10–12.
5. Ibid., 11.
6. Ibid., 16.
7. Dunne, *Hugo Black and the Judicial Revolution*, 90.
8. Newman, *Hugo Black: A Biography*, 17–18.
9. Ibid.
10. Ibid. See also Noah Feldman, *Scorpions*: *The Battles and Triumphs of FDR's Great Supreme Court Justices* (New York: Twelve, 2010), 54.
11. Newman, *Hugo Black: A Biography*, 20.
12. Dunne, *Hugo Black and the Judicial Revolution*, 92.

13. Newman, *Hugo Black: A Biography*, 21.
14. Ibid.
15. Ibid.
16. Ibid., 22.
17. Ibid., 24.
18. Ibid.; Simon, *The Antagonists*, 71.
19. Newman, *Hugo Black: A Biography*, 27.
20. Ibid., 28.
21. Ibid.
22. Simon, *The Antagonists*, 73.
23. Ibid.; Newman, *Hugo Black: A Biography*, 73.
24. Simon, *The Antagonists*, 73.
25. Ibid., 74.
26. Ibid., 77.
27. Ibid.
28. Ibid., 78.
29. John P. Frank, "Hugo Black: He Has Joined the Giants," in Jesse H. Choper, ed., *The Supreme Court and Its Justices*, 2nd ed. (Chicago: ABA Publishing, 2000), 169.
30. Simon, *The Antagonists*, 81.
31. Ibid.
32. Newman, *Hugo Black: A Biography*, 406.
33. Simon, *The Antagonists*., 83.
34. Newman, *Hugo Black: A Biography*, 100.
35. Ibid., 99–100.
36. Ibid., 100.
37. Simon, *The Antagonists*, 83.
38. Ibid., 84.
39. Ibid., 86.
40. Ibid.
41. Ibid., 87.
42. Ibid., 89.
43. Ibid.
44. Ibid.
45. Ibid.; Dunne, *Hugo Black and the Judicial Revolution*, 141.
46. Simon, *The Antagonists*, 90.
47. Ibid., 90–94.
48. Ibid., 91–92.
49. Ibid., 95.
50. Ibid., 97.
51. Dunne, *Hugo Black and the Judicial Revolution*, 45.
52. Feldman, *Scorpions*, 134.
53. Newman, *Hugo Black: A Biography*, 242.
54. Dunne, *Hugo Black and the Judicial Revolution*, 45; Newman, *Hugo Black: A Biography*, 239.
55. Dunne, *Hugo Black and the Judicial Revolution*, 52.
56. Newman, *Hugo Black: A Biography*, 247–48.
57. Ibid., 248.
58. Ibid., 249.
59. Ibid., 258.
60. Dunne, *Hugo Black and the Judicial Revolution*, 73.
61. Newman, *Hugo Black: A Biography*, 259.
62. Howard Ball, *Hugo Black: Cold Steel Warrior* (New York: Oxford University Press, 1996), 5.
63. Ibid., 211.
64. Feldman, *Scorpions*, 145.
65. Ibid.

66. 332 U.S. 46 (1947).
67. Feldman, *Scorpions*, 308.
68. Ibid., 308–09.
69. Simon, *The Antagonists*, 176.
70. Feldman, *Scorpions*, 311.
71. Ibid.
72. Ball, *Hugo Black: Cold Steel Warrior*, 117.
73. Feldman, *Scorpions*, 313.
74. Frank, "Hugo Black: He Has Joined the Giants," in Choper, ed., *The Supreme Court and its Justices*, 2nd ed., 163.
75. Simon, *The Antagonists*, 179.
76. Newman, *Hugo Black: A Biography*, 530.
77. 381 U.S. 479 (1965).
78. Newman, *Hugo Black: A Biography*, 557.
79. Tinsley E. Yarbrough, "Justice Black and His Critics on Speech-Plus and Symbolic Speech," *Texas Law Review* 52 (1974): 258–59.
80. *New York Times Co. v. United States*, 403 U.S. 713 (1971).
81. Newman, *Hugo Black: A Biography*, 617.
82. 403 U.S. at 719.
83. Newman, *Hugo Black: A Biography*, 620–21.
84. Ibid., 623.
85. Ibid.
86. Ibid., 276.
87. Ball, *Hugo Black: Cold Steel Warrior*, 247.
88. 309 U.S. 227 (1940).
89. 332 U.S. 46 (1947).
90. 372 U.S. 335 (1963).
91. 343 U.S. 250 (1952).
92. 361 U.S. 147 (1959).
93. 403 U.S. 713 (1971).
94. 309 U.S. 227 (1940).
95. Richard A. Posner, *Law and Literature*, 3rd ed. (Cambridge, MA: Harvard University Press, 2009), 333.
96. *Chambers*, 309 U.S. at 229, quoting 136 Fla. at 572, 187 So. 2d. at 157.
97. *Chambers*, 309 U.S. at 229.
98. Ibid., 231.
99. Ibid., 235.
100. Ibid.
101. Ibid.
102. Newman, *Hugo Black: A Biography*, 19.
103. 309 U.S. at 237.
104. Ibid., 237–38.
105. Ibid., 238–39.
106. Ibid., 241.
107. 332 U.S. 46 (1947).
108. Ibid., 48.
109. Ibid., 47–48.
110. Ibid., 48.
111. Ibid., 50–51.
112. Ibid., 51.
113. Ibid., 52.
114. Ibid., 58.
115. Ibid., 68.
116. Ibid., 69, citing *Twining*, 211 U.S. 78 (1908).
117. 332 U.S. at 69.
118. Ibid., 71–72.

119. Ibid., 90.
120. Ibid.
121. 372 U.S. 335 (1963).
122. Ibid., 337.
123. Ibid.
124. Edward P. J. Corbett and Robert J. Connors, *Classical Rhetoric for the Modern Student* 4th ed. (New York: Oxford University Press, 1999), 404.
125. *Gideon*, 372 U.S. at 337–38.
126. Ibid., 338.
127. Ibid., 339.
128. Ibid., 344.
129. 343 U.S. 250 (1952).
130. Ibid., 252.
131. Ibid., 261.
132. Ibid., 263.
133. Ibid., 267.
134. Ibid., 271–72.
135. Ibid., 274.
136. Ibid.
137. Ibid., 275.
138. 361 U.S. 147 (1959).
139. Ibid., 148.
140. Ibid., 148–49.
141. Ibid., 149.
142. Ibid., 150.
143. Ibid., 153–54.
144. Ibid., 156.
145. Ibid.
146. Ibid., 155.
147. Ibid., 157.
148. Ibid., 159.
149. Ibid., 160.
150. 403 U.S. 713 (1971).
151. Ibid., 714.
152. Ibid.
153. Ibid., 715.
154. Ibid., 717.
155. Ibid.

Chapter Six

William Brennan

Bridge-Builder

A. Beginnings

Like Robert Jackson and Hugo Black, William Brennan lived a deluxe version of the American Dream, rising from hardscrabble blue-collar roots to claim a seat on the highest court in the land. Brennan's story, though, has the distinctly ethnic twist that flavored the stories of so many American families in the late nineteenth and early twentieth centuries. William Brennan, Sr. left County Roscommon in Ireland in 1892, at the age of twenty, seeking to escape the rural poverty of his childhood and find a more prosperous life in America.[1] He settled in New Jersey and started small, lifting a coal shovel all day to stoke the boiler in a licorice factory in Trenton.[2]

Brennan Sr. had ambition that was as strong as his back, though, and the vehicle for his ambition was Local 55 of the International Brotherhood of Stationary Engineers and Oilers. After he had stopped shoveling coal and had moved north to Newark, he became a stationary fireman, whose job was to watch boiler pressure gauges at the brewery where he worked and repair them when they malfunctioned.[3] Because the union leadership was corrupt, dissident members rallied around Brennan for leadership, and in time he became the business manager of Local 55 and a delegate to the Essex County Trades and Labor Council.[4] After spending several years involved in union politics, he ran for a seat on Newark's City Commission in 1917 and succeeded in his first try.[5] The voters returned him to office every four years until 1929, and he won more votes than any other candidate in his last two elections.[6]

The father's life would shape the son's life. William Jr. developed a social conscience rooted in his father's immigrant story. Years later, he would reflect:

> What got me interested in people's rights and liberties was the kind of family and the kind of neighborhood I was brought up in. I saw all kinds of suffering—people had to struggle. I saw the suffering of my mother, even though we were never without. We always had something to eat, we always had something to wear. But others in the neighborhood had a harder time.[7]

And when he encountered expressions of racial or ethnic prejudice, he sided with the victims because he remembered that the bigots had said the same things about Irish Americans during his boyhood.[8]

William Jr. bore a heavy burden of family expectations comfortably, earning admission to the University of Pennsylvania in 1924.[9] In one generation, a Brennan had gone from stoking a coal furnace in a licorice factory to building a stellar résumé in the Ivy League. The younger Brennan graduated with honors from Penn's prestigious Wharton School of Commerce and Finance in 1928.[10] A week before commencement, he married his high school sweetheart, Marjorie Leonard, who would stay home in New Jersey and work as a newspaper proofreader while Bill enrolled for first-year law classes at Harvard.[11] Fearing that William Sr. would disapprove of his son marrying before having earned his law degree, the couple eloped and kept the marriage a secret until Bill graduated from law school in June 1931.[12]

B. Professional Life

Bill Brennan earned good, but not superb, grades at Harvard; he was not the "star" student who seemed to be on the fast track to a federal judgeship, certainly not a seat on the Supreme Court. Indeed, one biography states that "[n]o one could have predicted that Brennan would become the most forceful and effective liberal ever to serve on the Court."[13] But he took full advantage of every opportunity he received. Before William Sr. died in 1930, he had used political connections to get his son a prestigious summer associate position with Pitney, Hardin & Skinner, a prominent Newark law firm founded in 1902, whose partners were all Protestants who had been undergraduates at Princeton. William Jr. so impressed the partners during the summer of 1930 that when he graduated from law school the following year, they offered him a full-time associate position, making him the first Irish Catholic to join the firm.[14]

Later, Brennan developed expertise in labor law, which served him well, especially after Congress enacted the National Labor Relations Act in 1935. The NLRA, which guaranteed workers' rights to organize and bargain collectively, helped to create labor law as a distinct field of law practice.[15]

Brennan's firm represented management, but his familiarity with the concerns of labor made him uniquely qualified to resolve industrial disputes. As 1938 dawned, the law firm offered him a partnership, accompanied by a significant salary increase.[16] The salary boost enabled Brennan and his family, which now included two children, to buy a house and allowed Bill to join a lawn tennis club and to play golf at another club.[17]

World War II interrupted these comfortable arrangements, but also allowed Brennan to spread his wings beyond New Jersey and to use his labor expertise to benefit his country. The Army needed skilled labor negotiators who could prevent work stoppages at munitions plants or end them quickly once they began. Assigned the rank of major, Brennan was responsible for ensuring labor peace at dozens of ammunitions plants the federal government had built, but private companies managed.[18] A "natural" for this work, Brennan received the Legion of Merit at the end of his service and a letter of commendation from Undersecretary of War Robert P. Patterson, who called him "a tower of strength in working for the Army on manpower problems."[19]

Returning to New Jersey in the fall of 1945, Brennan became a named partner of his law firm—Pitney, Hardin, Ward & Brennan.[20] He also participated in a court reform movement in New Jersey championed by Arthur Vanderbilt, the highly respected chief justice of the state supreme court.[21] In November 1947, New Jersey voters approved by referendum a restructured judiciary.[22] The new system needed new judges, and Brennan's support for it prompted the governor to appoint him to the Superior Court in January 1949.[23]

As a Superior Court judge, Brennan quickly became a favorite of Chief Justice Vanderbilt, for whom Brennan was a loyal lieutenant, leading statewide efforts to eliminate congestion and delay in the state courts.[24] As a result, he remained a trial judge for just eighteen months; in August 1950, he was promoted to become one of just six judges who served in the Superior Court's Appellate Division, which was (and still is) New Jersey's intermediate appellate court.[25] In February 1952, another promotion followed, this time to the New Jersey Supreme Court.[26]

On that Court, Brennan wrote several opinions that revealed his concern for the protection of individual rights.[27] But factors other than his concern for protecting individual rights account for Brennan's nomination to the US Supreme Court by President Eisenhower in 1956. Anyone accustomed to today's ideologically driven Supreme Court nominations will be surprised to learn that a speech about how to make courts more efficient brought Brennan to the attention of Attorney General Herbert Brownell, but that is what the historical record shows.[28] At the Department of Justice's two-day Conference on Court Congestion and Delay in May 1956, Brennan delivered a major address about New Jersey's experience with court reform and moderated a panel discussion about the court-reform experiences of his state and others.[29]

More important than ideology to President Eisenhower was Brennan's experience as a state court judge at a time of great conflict between state and federal courts about habeas corpus and federalism issues.[30] Political demographics were also important: besides being a state-court judge and a court-reform advocate, Brennan was a Catholic, a Democrat, and, at age fifty, comparatively young. Seeking to capture the Catholic vote in the heavily Democratic Northeast in the upcoming presidential election, Eisenhower, a Republican, found a middle-aged Catholic Democrat with appellate court experience to be just who he was looking for.[31] No matter that neither Felix Frankfurter, Brennan's soon-to-be colleague, nor Frankfurter's star students from Brennan's Harvard years, remembered him.[32]

A recess appointee, Brennan had been serving on the Supreme Court for four months when his Senate confirmation hearing occurred. In another striking contrast with current practices, Brennan's hearing lasted less than three hours, and the full Senate confirmed him three weeks later, with only the by-then-discredited Communist hunter Joseph McCarthy voting no.[33] Still, acknowledging his relative obscurity before being nominated to the Court, Brennan remarked that he felt like the mule at the Kentucky Derby; "I don't expect to distinguish myself but I do expect to benefit by the associations," he said.[34] On the contrary, as the following section shows, he distinguished himself beyond anyone's expectations.

C. On the Court

William Brennan would serve thirty-four years on the Supreme Court and write 1,573 opinions that fill 146 volumes of the *United States Reports*.[35] But longevity is hardly Brennan's greatest claim to fame; indeed, Supreme Court scholar Bernard Schwartz called him "the most influential associate justice in Supreme Court history."[36] A comment by Antonin Scalia, who served on the Court with Brennan from 1986 until 1990, holds at least one clue to Brennan's influence on the Court's decisions during his tenure. "Even those who were most in disagreement with him loved him," Scalia recalled.[37] Judge Patricia Wald of the D.C. Circuit wrote that "Brennan built consensus by persuasively communicating to his colleagues his sense of what was important to them and by crafting those often inconsistent viewpoints into a harmonious whole."[38] She added that "he patiently revisited and revised to absorb the varied comments of his colleagues as they flooded in."[39]

Early on in his Court tenure, Brennan was Chief Justice Earl Warren's loyal lieutenant, helping the Chief to build majorities in the many cases about which they agreed. Each week, Warren arrived in Brennan's chambers unannounced on Thursday afternoon or Friday morning, and for an hour or two they discussed the cases to be considered at the Court's next conference.[40] In the second half of the Warren Court, between 1962, when the liberal Arthur Goldberg replaced the conservative Felix Frankfurter and 1969, when Warren retired and another liberal justice, Abe Fortas, resigned, Brennan was the dominant intellectual figure in the new liberal majority that included Warren, Black, Douglas, Brennan, and Goldberg, whom Fortas replaced in 1965.[41] Brennan himself acknowledged the importance of that temporary liberal majority in stating that "[i]t was in the years from 1962 to 1969 that the face of the law changed."[42]

Brennan was a consensus-builder, but not a chameleon; he had a clear idea of his destination in constitutional cases, but he was willing to reach it incrementally, if necessary, which enhanced his long-term influence on American jurisprudence. Judge Wald observed, "This ability to plot the path he felt the law must take and to follow through with a series of opinions that served as stepping stones toward his ultimate destination gave his judicial handiwork an enduring force that made it less vulnerable to later ideological shifts on the Court."[43] Brennan always rejected "originalism"—the view that judges should interpret the Constitution according to the meaning its words had when they were written—because to him, the meaning of the Constitution lay in current needs, not in a search for the intent of its eighteenth-century drafters.[44]

Instead, Brennan based his jurisprudence on what he called "the constitutional ideal of human dignity."[45] To Brennan, that ideal was rooted in Americans' rejection of "a natural hierarchy in society," such as is embodied in a monarch or other supreme sovereign, such as the British Parliament.[46] Instead, our Constitution places sovereignty in the American people, based on an assumption of their individual equality, and makes government officials agents of the people.[47] Thus, as law professor Peter Irons has written, "Justice Brennan's judicial philosophy begins with his deep religious faith in the 'dignity' of every person, moves to the principle that government exists to serve the needs of individuals and to protect their dignity, and ends with the notion that the meaning of the Constitution must change as society changes."[48]

William Brennan's constitutional philosophy and his consensus-building skills were evident in many Supreme Court decisions, of which two are highlighted here. In *Baker v. Carr*, the Court considered whether courts could resolve challenges to legislative apportionment schemes that treated some parts of a state (and some voters) less favorably than others in awarding legislative representation.[49] Brennan's willingness to interpret the Constitution to meet changing needs was clear in *Baker*. Sixteen years earlier, in *Colegrove v. Green*,[50] Justice Frankfurter had written a majority opinion stating that voters who object to the ways in which electoral districts have been drawn should seek a remedy by lobbying or voting out of office their legislators, not by filing lawsuits.[51] In *Baker*, Brennan wrote a majority opinion holding that legislative malapportionment—which resulted in rural areas being overrepresented and urban areas being underrepresented in state legislatures—was indeed an issue that courts could decide. He opened the courtroom doors to underrepresented urban voters who had long been unable to obtain relief electorally or legislatively because the rural interests that controlled the political process had no incentive to reapportion the legislature.[52] That choice reflected Brennan's passion for democracy, which he viewed as valuing every person and fostering the capacity of every person to have a political opinion worthy of respect, in short, as honoring and promoting human dignity.[53]

Brennan's consensus-building skills were also evident in *Baker*. To retain Potter Stewart's vote, Brennan omitted from the opinion any hint of a remedy or of specific standards courts should employ to determine whether a particular legislative apportionment scheme provided equal representation. The opinion stated only that judges could apply "well developed and familiar" equal protection criteria, which, of course, did not exist for legislative districting cases because until *Baker*, courts had avoided deciding them.[54] As a result, the decision received heavy criticism for using the Equal Protection Clause as a way to avoid the appearance of departing from precedents like *Colegrove*, which said this issue was not appropriate for courts to decide.[55] But Brennan valued Stewart's vote more than doctrinal consistency. Recalling *Baker*, he said, "That's the way Potter and I very often got together. . . . He didn't want to go as far as I wanted to go and I was content just to keep his vote to get a larger majority."[56]

Brennan also gained Tom Clark's vote in *Baker*, chiefly by discussing the case with him and by circulating a chart compiled by one of Brennan's clerks that showed huge disparities between the populations of legislative districts in Tennessee, from whence the case arose. As a result, even though Brennan's position, which called for overturning *Colegrove*, originally commanded just four votes, his ability to bring Stewart and Clark into the fold produced a six-member majority for that position.[57]

Baker ushered in a bloodless revolution in American politics by establishing a foundation for the principle, which future cases would articulate, that the Constitution requires equal population as the basis for legislative districting, both state and federal.[58] As state legislatures were forced to redraw district lines in the wake of judicial mandates, power shifted from rural areas to the cities and suburbs where most people lived.[59] In Vermont, for example, no longer would the City of Burlington, with more than thirty-five thousand residents in 1962, and the tiny ski-resort town of Stratton, with just twenty-four residents, each elect one representative to the Vermont House of Representatives.[60]

The Supreme Court does not only prompt change, though; it experiences change, too. By 1972, the liberal majority of which William Brennan had been part no longer existed, as Justices Fortas, Warren, and Black were gone, replaced by the more conservative Harry Blackmun, Warren Burger, and Lewis Powell, respectively.[61] But Brennan famously continued to build majorities regularly for outcomes he favored, although after 1976, he increasingly found himself in dissent.[62] The difference between victory and defeat for Brennan often depended on Lewis Powell, who was conservative on issues of criminal procedure and federalism, but moderate-to-liberal on many others.[63]

A noteworthy example of cooperation between Brennan and Powell was affirmative action in university admissions, whose constitutionality the Court considered in *Regents of University of California v. Bakke* in 1978.[64] The Petitioner, Alan Bakke, was an aerospace engineer in his thirties who wished to attend medical school. Most schools denied him admission because they thought he was "too old" to begin medical studies. He sued one of the schools that had rejected him—the University of California at Davis—because it had reserved sixteen places in its one-hundred-member first-year medical class for "disadvantaged" minority students, which arrangement Bakke challenged on equal protection grounds.[65]

Brennan feared that his conservative colleagues would scuttle both the Davis program, which they saw as a "quota" program, and the larger concept of "affirmative action," which took race into account in admissions to improve opportunities for minorities in higher education. Recalling that during the justices' conference discussions Powell had supported some consideration of race in admissions, Brennan asked Powell if he would be amenable to affirming in part and reversing in part, which Powell agreed to do.[66] Powell's decision resulted in striking down the Davis program as an impermissible quota, while holding that universities could consider race as a factor in determining which students to admit. That conclusion enabled almost all affirmative action programs in place at that time to continue, which was Brennan's primary goal.[67]

During the 1980s Brennan owed the reduced but still evident influence that he enjoyed on the Court to Republican appointees Harry Blackmun and Lewis Powell (Nixon), and John Paul Stevens (Ford).[68] In the 1981–1982 term, Brennan and Blackmun voted together more than 70 percent of the time for the first time; they would continue to do so until Brennan's retirement in 1990.[69] The 1980s also saw Brennan and Stevens vote together between two-thirds and three-fourths of the time each term.[70]

As a result of Brennan's facility for consensus-building, his legacy has remained surprisingly intact since 1990. "The ultimate Brennan legacy," according to Bernard Schwartz, is that "no important decision of the Warren Court was overruled while the Justice sat on the Burger and Rehnquist

Courts."[71] But perhaps the legacy that Brennan would most appreciate came from Tiffany Graham, a Department of Justice paralegal and soon-to-be law student, who waited in the crowd on July 28, 1997, when pallbearers carried Brennan's casket up the steps of the Supreme Court, past an honor guard comprised of twenty-seven of his former law clerks. Asked why she was present, Graham answered, "I am a woman. I am black. What more can I say? I wouldn't have the advantages I have now. He was truly an American hero."[72]

D. Brennan the Writer

Earl Warren often tapped William Brennan to write the majority opinion in cases "that required a comprehensive and profound treatment. . . ."[73] Warren chose wisely because Brennan's opinions, despite lacking the originality and verve of Holmes and Jackson opinions, are nonetheless models of clarity and organization, making them instructive to all legal writers. If they do not sing or dance, they surely stride smoothly and converse easily with the modern reader, telling compelling stories as they go. In that way, Brennan's opinions mirror those of Hugo Black. Like Black's opinions, Brennan's opinions feature everyday language occasionally salted with a timely metaphor or a vivid turn of phrase.

Brennan's areas of greatest influence were criminal procedure, First Amendment law, and equal protection. Accordingly, this section will feature his majority opinion in *Malloy v. Hogan*,[74] his dissent in *McCleskey v. Kemp*,[75] and his majority opinions in *New York Times v. Sullivan*,[76] *Texas v. Johnson*,[77] and *Frontiero v. Richardson*.[78]

1. *Malloy v. Hogan*

Malloy was one of the cases, decided by the Supreme Court between 1962 and 1969 in which, as Brennan himself noted: "the face of the law changed."[79] In this instance, the law changed because the Court majority extended the Fifth Amendment's protection against compelled self-incrimination to the states, adopting the position that Hugo Black had championed in dissent in *Adamson v. California* in 1947.[80] Brennan's talent for arranging an opinion to tell a clear and compelling story is evident in the first two paragraphs of his majority opinion in *Malloy*, a 5–4 decision.[81] He identifies the issue at hand plainly, stating: "In this case we are asked to reconsider prior decisions holding that the privilege against self-incrimination is not safeguarded against state action by the Fourteenth Amendment."[82]

Brennan's use of the word "safeguarded" is a noteworthy rhetorical—specifically stylistic—choice. Recall that rhetorical style concerns word choice, and Brennan's word choice here reflects the high value he placed on the privilege against compelled self-incrimination. In his view, that privilege must be "safeguarded"—conserved, preserved, secured—against the state governments as well as the federal government.[83] One seeks to safeguard the things one holds dear. Thus, Brennan uses "safeguarded" rather than the more commonplace, less emotive word "protected," which enables him to convey the urgency of extending the guarantee against compelled self-incrimination to the states.

In the second paragraph, Brennan recounts the facts of the case, noting that William Malloy had been arrested for a gambling offense, pled guilty, and received a one-year jail sentence, which was suspended after ninety days, at which time he was placed on probation for two years. Sixteen months after his guilty plea, Malloy was ordered to appear before a court-appointed investigator who inquired about alleged gambling and other criminal activities in Hartford County, Connecticut. Brennan describes the questioning of Malloy as follows:

> [Malloy] was asked a number of questions related to events surrounding his arrest and conviction. He refused to answer any question "on the grounds that it may tend to incriminate me." The Superior Court adjudged him in contempt, and committed him to prison until he was willing to answer the questions. [Malloy's] application for a writ of habeas corpus was denied by the Superior Court, and the Connecticut Supreme Court of Errors affirmed. The latter court held that the Fifth Amendment's privilege against self-incrimination was not available to a witness in a state proceeding, that the Fourteenth Amendment extended no privilege to him, and that [Malloy] had not properly invoked the privilege available under the Connecticut Constitution.[84]

Then, just as clearly as he had described the facts of the case, Brennan concluded the second paragraph by holding that the Fourteenth Amendment applied the Fifth Amendment's privilege against self-incrimination to the states and that the Connecticut Supreme Court had erred in concluding that Malloy had invoked the privilege improperly.[85]

Brennan observes that the law is moving toward a single standard for federal and state cases regarding the voluntariness of confessions. Therefore, his reasoning arises from the topic of comparison and the subtopic of similarity: the similarity that increasingly exists between federal and state standards regarding the protection against compelled self-incrimination. The admissibility of a confession in a state criminal prosecution is now based on the same standard applied in federal prosecutions since 1897: "not whether the conduct of state officers in obtaining the confession was shocking, but whether the confession was free and voluntary," that is, not the product of improper influence, threats, violence, or implied promises. He uses a metaphor to illustrate this point.

> In other words the person must not have been compelled to incriminate himself. We have held inadmissible even a confession secured by so mild a whip as the refusal, under certain circumstances, to allow a suspect to call his wife until he confessed.[86]

Later, he uses antithesis effectively in writing that "[t]he shift [to the federal standard in state cases] reflects recognition that the American system of criminal prosecution is accusatorial, not inquisitorial, and that the Fifth Amendment privilege is its essential mainstay."[87]

The antithesis, which combines with parallelism here to produce "accusatorial, not inquisitorial," is effective because it shines a spotlight on a legal principle Americans hold dear: the prosecution must establish guilt by satisfying its burden of proof, thereby relieving the defense of the burden of proving the defendant's innocence. Accordingly, the prosecution cannot compel the defendant to engage in self-incrimination, a constitutional guarantee so crucial to the American system of criminal justice that it should apply in state as well as federal courts.

Having established the appropriate standard, Brennan turns his attention to whether or not Connecticut used that standard, which he concludes it did not. He first identifies, in summary form, the questions that Malloy refused to answer, which include: "(1) for whom did he work on September 11, 1959; (2) who selected and paid his counsel in connection with his arrest on that date and his subsequent conviction; (3) who selected and paid his bondsman; (4) who paid his fine; (5) what was the name of the tenant of the apartment where he was arrested; and (6) did he know John Bergoti?"[88] The Connecticut Supreme Court had concluded that Malloy's answers to the first five questions would not tend to incriminate him because the defenses of double jeopardy and the running of a one-year statute of limitations on misdemeanors would protect him.

Brennan disagreed, explaining that "the State desired to elicit from [Malloy] the identity of the person who ran the pool-selling operation in connection with which he had been arrested in 1959."[89] Therefore, Malloy's answers to the first five questions could incriminate him if the person he identified were still engaged in crime. The "disclosure of [that person's] name," Brennan writes, using a metaphor to underscore his point, "might furnish a link in a chain of evidence sufficient to connect [Malloy] with a more recent crime for which he might still be prosecuted."[90] Neither the double jeopardy nor statute-of-limitations defense would be available in those circumstances.

Brennan also rejects the Connecticut Court's conclusion that Malloy was not entitled to protection from the sixth question because he had not explained how disclosing his relationship with Bergoti would incriminate him. In Brennan's view, the State plainly thought that Bergoti was involved in the subject matter of its investigation, so an affirmative answer to the sixth question "might well have either connected [Malloy] with a more recent crime, or at least have operated as a waiver of his privilege with reference to his relationship with a possible criminal."[91] Thus, the majority reversed the Connecticut Court, concluding that it had failed to protect Malloy against compelled self-incrimination.

William Brennan's *Malloy* opinion is a model of how to arrange a judicial opinion; it proceeds smoothly and logically from introduction to facts to argument to conclusion, telling an easily understood story in the facts section and displaying the progress of its reasoning transparently throughout the argument. Brennan's argument reflects his view of the Constitution as a blueprint for the future and a means of safeguarding human freedom, as he uses the Due Process Clause to extend protection against compelled self-incrimination to defendants in state court. Several figures of speech add a splash of color, but the rhetorical beauty of the opinion lies chiefly in its arrangement, not its style. It is immensely valuable for novice legal writers, and even novice judicial-opinion writers, because it shows that one can address important constitutional doctrines and make major jurisprudential policy in clear, simple, direct language.

2. McCleskey v. Kemp

Brennan's *McCleskey* dissent displays passion and eloquence. The subject was one on which he was unwilling to compromise and unable to build a Court consensus—capital punishment. Brennan viewed the death penalty as the ultimate assault on human dignity.

Warren McCleskey, a black man, was convicted of armed robbery and murder in connection with the robbery of a furniture store and the killing of a white police officer during the robbery.[92] Unable to offer any mitigating factors to counteract those two aggravating factors, he received the death penalty. After numerous other, unsuccessful procedural moves, he filed a habeas corpus petition, which alleged that Georgia's capital sentencing was racially discriminatory in violation of the Eighth and Fourteenth Amendments. He based that claim on the so-called Baldus study, named for its lead author, Professor David C. Baldus, which, according to Justice Powell's majority opinion, "purports to show a disparity in the imposition of the death sentence in Georgia based on the race of the murder victim and, to a lesser extent, the race of the defendant."[93] Powell added that "the Baldus study indicates that black defendants, such as McCleskey, who kill white victims, have the greatest likelihood of receiving the death penalty."[94]

The Supreme Court majority declined to extrapolate from the Baldus study's data that just because, in Georgia, persons who murdered whites were more likely to receive the death penalty than persons who murdered blacks and black murderers were more likely than white murderers to receive the death penalty, Warren McCleskey was necessarily sentenced to death because of his race and that of his victim. In Powell's view, McCleskey could not make that showing because "a legitimate and unchallenged explanation for the decision [to impose a death sentence] is apparent from the record: McCleskey committed an act for which the United States Constitution and Georgia laws permit imposition of the death penalty."[95] The Court thus rejected McCleskey's equal protection claim, reasoning that the Baldus study could not show the decision makers in McCleskey's case acted with a discriminatory purpose.[96]

The majority also rejected McCleskey's claim that the Georgia capital sentencing system violated the Eighth Amendment's ban on cruel and unusual punishment. "In light of the safeguards designed to minimize racial bias in the process, the fundamental value of jury trial in our criminal justice system, and the benefits that discretion provides to criminal defendants," Justice Powell wrote, "we hold that the Baldus study does not demonstrate a constitutionally significant risk of racial bias affecting the Georgia capital sentencing process."[97]

Justice Brennan filed a dissent that Justice Marshall joined in full and Justices Blackmun and Stevens joined in part. Brennan's reasoning draws on the topic of relationship and the subtopic of contraries, here the fundamental incompatibility between Georgia's racially tainted death penalty procedures and the Eighth Amendment ban on cruel and unusual punishment. Early on, Brennan assumes the role of an observer listening to an imagined conversation between McCleskey and his counsel about the influence of racial animus on Georgia's capital sentencing system. He writes:

> At some point in this case, Warren McCleskey doubtless asked his lawyer whether a jury was likely to sentence him to die. A candid reply to this question would have been disturbing. First, counsel would have to tell McCleskey that few of the details of the crime or of McCleskey's past criminal conduct were more important than the fact that his victim was white. Furthermore, counsel would feel bound to tell McCleskey that defendants charged with killing white victims in Georgia are 4.3 times as likely to be sentenced to death as defendants charged with killing blacks. In addition, frankness would compel the disclosure that it was more likely than not that the race of McCleskey's victim would determine whether he received a death sentence: 6 of every 11 defendants convicted of killing a white person would not have received the death penalty if their victims had been black, while among defendants with aggravating and mitigating factors comparable to McCleskey's, 20 of every 34 would not have been sentenced to die if their victims had been black.[98] [Citations omitted.]

Reflecting on the significance of these numbers,

> Brennan adds: Finally, the assessment would not be complete without the information that cases involving black defendants and white victims are more likely to result in a death sentence than cases featuring any other racial combination of defendant and victim. The story could be told in a variety of ways, but McCleskey could not fail to grasp its essential narrative line: there was a significant chance that race would play a prominent role in determining if he lived or died.[99] [Citations omitted.]

Note that in the last line of the paragraph, instead of writing that race would likely affect whether [McCleskey] received "the death penalty" or "a death sentence," Brennan writes that race would likely affect whether [McCleskey] "lived or died." The words "lived or died," which plainly appeal to emotion, present the implications of Georgia's sentencing system in the starkest possible terms for the reader.

After discussing the results of the Baldus study—including that blacks who killed whites were nearly twenty-two times more likely to be sentenced to death than blacks who killed blacks and more than seven times more likely to be sentenced to death than whites who killed blacks,[100] and that prosecutors sought the death penalty for 70 percent of blacks who killed whites but just 19 percent of whites who killed blacks—Brennan concludes that its evidence makes McCleskey's risk of receiving a death sentence unacceptably high.[101] He contrasts that unacceptable risk to the acceptable risk inherent in the standard for determining guilt in a criminal case. Using antithesis, parallelism, and alliteration, he writes:

> In determining the guilt of a defendant, a State must prove its case beyond a reasonable doubt. That is, we refuse to convict if the chance of error is simply less likely than not. Surely, we should not be willing to take a person's life if the chance that his death sentence was irrationally imposed is *more* likely than not. In light of the gravity of the interest at stake, petitioner's statistics on their face are a powerful demonstration of the type of risk that our Eighth Amendment jurisprudence has consistently condemned.[102] [Emphasis in original.]

The antithesis emphasizes the contrast between a refusal to convict and a willingness to execute, the parallelism highlights the juxtaposition between "less likely than not" and "more likely than not," and the alliteration ends the sentence with the memorable "consistently condemned." Taken together, they analogize McCleskey's circumstances to those of the ordinary criminal defendant, to whom guilt will not attach when "reasonable doubt" exists. If, Brennan posits, our criminal justice system refuses to convict when reasonable doubt exists about the defendant's guilt, it should refuse to execute when a death sentence more likely results from the defendant's race and the victim's race than from the nature of the crime committed. In Brennan's view, the Eighth Amendment has long prohibited such rash and irrational punishment.

In the final paragraph of his dissent, Brennan returns to the role of observer of presumed conversations between defendants and their attorneys. He states:

> The Court's decision today will not change what attorneys in Georgia tell other Warren McCleskeys about their chances of execution. Nothing will soften the harsh message they must convey, nor alter the prospect that race undoubtedly will continue to be a topic of discussion. McCleskey's evidence will not have obtained judicial acceptance, but that will not affect what is said on death row. However many criticisms of today's decision may be rendered, these painful conversations will serve as the most eloquent dissents of all.[103]

Still, Brennan's appeals to pathos at the start and the finish of his *McCleskey* opinion, such as the metaphorical reference to "the most eloquent dissents of all" in the final sentence, should not mask the opinion's clarity and flow. The opinion identifies the illegitimate role of race in Georgia's capital sentencing early on, amasses powerful evidence to document the disparities for black and white defendants, and condemns that disparity as anathema to the Eighth Amendment's protection against cruel and unusual punishment. The *McCleskey* dissent employs more vivid words and figures of speech than Brennan's *Malloy* opinion—as *McCleskey's* facts and the opinion's status as a dissent warrant—but it shares the *Malloy* opinion's clarity, cohesiveness, forcefulness, and instructional value.

3. *New York Times Company v. Sullivan*

In March 1960, shortly after black students launched a "sit-in" movement against segregated public facilities in the South, a group of prominent black entertainers and white liberals placed a full-page ad in the *New York Times* that aimed to raise funds to support the students. One paragraph focused on Montgomery, Alabama, alleging that "truckloads of police armed with shotguns and tear-gas ringed the Alabama State College Campus."[104] Although the ad included several minor factual errors, it did not name any Montgomery city official or allege any unlawful conduct. Still, the city's police commissioner, L. B. Sullivan, sued the *New York Times* for libel and won a $500,000 judgment from an all-white jury.[105]

Libel cases like Sullivan's sought to scare the national press away from the civil rights story.[106] But in the wake of the Supreme Court's ultimate vindication of the newspaper, the national media were able to inform the American public about Dr. Martin Luther King, Jr., the struggle for civil rights, and the dogged resistance from white Southerners. Publication of this information spurred support outside the South for civil rights, ensuring the Civil Rights Movement's success in dismantling segregation. Within four months of the Court's decision in *Sullivan*, President Lyndon Johnson signed the Civil Rights Act of 1964; the Voting Rights Act followed the next year.[107]

William Brennan produced his majority opinion in *Sullivan* quickly; only two months and three days separated the argument of the case from the announcement of the decision.[108] He managed to hold the Court together without a dissent, although Justices Black, Douglas, and Goldberg wrote concurrences advocating that public officials be barred from bringing libel actions, even when they were subjected to damaging falsehoods.[109] The opinion begins in vintage Brennan fashion, with an opening sentence that states plainly the important issue before the Court. "We are required in this case," Brennan writes, "to determine for the first time the extent to which the constitutional protections for speech and press limit a State's power to award damages in a libel action brought by a public official against critics of his official conduct."[110]

Having identified Sullivan and his libel claim, Brennan points to the two paragraphs in the ten-paragraph ad that had prompted Sullivan's lawsuit.

Paragraph three stated:

> In Montgomery, Alabama, after students sang "My Country 'Tis of Thee" on the State Capitol steps, their leaders were expelled from school, and truckloads of police armed with shotguns and tear-gas ringed the Alabama State College Campus. When the entire student body protested to state authorities by refusing to re-register, their dining hall was padlocked in an attempt to starve them into submission.[111]

Paragraph six stated:

> Again and again the Southern violators have answered Dr. King's peaceful protests with intimidation and violence. They have bombed his home almost killing his wife and child. They have assaulted his person. They have arrested him seven times—for "speeding," "loitering," and similar "offenses." And now they have charged him with "perjury"—a felony under which they could imprison him for ten years.[112]

Brennan then notes that although neither statement mentioned Sullivan by name, Sullivan took offense because he thought the words "police" and "arrest" in the ad referred to him as the Police Commissioner, thereby holding him responsible for the behavior that the ad condemned."[113] Brennan acknowledges that some of the statements in the two paragraphs are inaccurate, but adds that Sullivan could show no financial loss from the alleged libel and that none of the witnesses he called at trial thought the allegations applied to him.

Turning to the law, Brennan quickly and emphatically rejects the Alabama Supreme Court's decision upholding the verdict, which decision turned on conclusions that (1) "[t]he Fourteenth Amendment is directed against state action and not private action"; and (2) the First Amendment does not apply to the challenged statements because they "were published as part of a paid 'commercial' advertisement."[114] Instead, in the most memorable language of his opinion, Brennan explains that the First Amendment is the proper measuring stick for judging speech on public issues. His reasoning derives from the topic of relationship and the subtopic of contraries: the fundamental conflict between the Alabama Supreme Court's holding and the protections for speech in the First and Fourteenth Amendments. He writes:

> Thus we consider this case against the background of a profound national commitment to the principle that debate on public issues should be uninhibited, robust, and wide-open, and that it may well include vehement, caustic, and sometimes unpleasantly sharp attacks on government and public officials. [Citations omitted.] The present advertisement, as an expression of grievance and protest on one of the major public issues of our time, would seem clearly to qualify for the constitutional protection. The question is whether it forfeits that protection by the falsity of some of its factual statements and by its alleged defamation of [Sullivan].[115]

This language is compelling, in part because of its vividness, conveyed through parallelism and tricolon ("uninhibited, robust, and wide-open" and "vehement, caustic, and sometimes unpleasantly sharp"). The latter triumvirate even reflects the gradual increase in syllables that makes the reference to "life, liberty, and the pursuit of happiness" in the Declaration of Independence so easy to recall. Here, as in earlier examples in previous chapters, tricolon produces stirring language of enduring power in a Supreme Court opinion.

But the quoted words command attention for their substance too. They instruct public officials that under our constitutional system, the First Amendment encourages and protects aggressive debate of public issues that will likely make such officials periodic targets of public vitriol. In Justice Brennan's view, the resulting anger and embarrassment experienced by the local officeholders are the price to be paid for a democracy based on Justice Holmes's marketplace of ideas. The marketplace is neither quiet nor genteel, but—because of its contentiousness—it is essential to the preservation of a free society.

In light of the American commitment to vigorous public debate, Brennan continues, the questions posed above—whether the ad is unprotected speech because it is false and defamatory—must be answered in the negative. He thus stated the rule that has come to define defamation law ever since *Sullivan*:

> The constitutional guarantees require, we think, a federal rule that prohibits a public official from recovering damages for a defamatory falsehood relating to his official conduct unless he proves that the statement was made with "actual malice"—that is, with knowledge that it was false or with reckless disregard of whether it was false or not.[116]

Applying this rule to the *New York Times*, Brennan concludes that the evidence failed to show either the recklessness necessary for actual malice or that the statements made in the ad were "of and concerning" Mr. Sullivan.[117] The Court thus reversed the Alabama Supreme Court's decision. The majority opinion is a trademark Brennan opinion: instructive, easy to follow, and inspiring too, as it creates a vast space for debate about important public issues.

4. *Texas v. Johnson*

Justice Brennan also wrote for the majority in *Texas v. Johnson*, another First Amendment case spawned by political protest, this time opposition to the policies of President Ronald Reagan and the Republican Party.[118] The case arose from the prosecution of Gregory Johnson by authorities in Dallas for burning the American flag during a protest rally held outside the 1984 Republican National Convention. The opinion reflects what former Brennan clerk Frank Michelman called Brennan's "tolerance for rumpus and hurly-burly, for disquiet and discomfiture" and his "corresponding coolness toward the bureaucratic yearning for order and control. . . ."[119]

The case produced the proverbial strange bedfellows, as Justices Kennedy and Scalia joined Brennan, Thurgood Marshall, and the increasingly liberal Harry Blackmun, in striking down the Texas law under which Johnson was prosecuted. The majority opinion begins with Brennan's characteristically clear and concise opening.

> After publicly burning an American flag as a means of political protest, Gregory Lee Johnson was convicted of desecrating a flag in violation of Texas law. This case presents the question whether his conviction is consistent with the First Amendment. We hold that it is not.[120]

Turning to the facts, Brennan recounts that toward the end of a political demonstration, Johnson unfurled an American flag in front of the Dallas City Hall, doused it with kerosene, and set it on fire. Charged with the desecration of a venerated object under a Texas statute, Johnson was tried, convicted, sentenced to a year in prison, and fined $2,000. An intermediate appellate court affirmed, but the Texas Court of Criminal Appeals reversed on First Amendment grounds.[121]

Brennan begins his analysis by noting that, as Texas had conceded for purposes of its oral argument, "Johnson's conduct was expressive conduct. . . ."[122] Because the flag-burning occurred as part of a political protest against the renomination of President Reagan, Brennan observes that it is conduct "sufficiently imbued with elements of communication . . . to implicate the First Amendment." [Citation omitted.][123] Accordingly, his reasoning again turns on the topic of relationship and the subtopic of contraries, here the contrast between the Texas law at issue and the Free Speech Clause of the First Amendment.

Brennan then examines the government's right to restrict expressive conduct. He notes that "[t]he government generally has a freer hand in restricting expressive conduct than it has in restricting the written or spoken word," but that "[i]t may not, however, proscribe particular conduct *because* [that conduct] has expressive elements." [Emphasis in original.][124] Therefore, to determine whether or not particular expressive conduct is subject to regulation, one must consider not "the verbal or nonverbal nature of the expression, but the governmental interest at stake," which "helps to determine whether a restriction on that expression is valid."[125]

Texas, Brennan observes, offers two interests to justify its conviction of Johnson: preventing breaches of the peace and preserving the flag as a symbol of nationhood and national unity. The first interest is not implicated here because, as Texas admitted in its brief, no actual breach of the peace occurred during or after the flag-burning. The second interest, which punishes Johnson's political expression because of its content (mistreatment of a venerated object designed to seriously offend other individuals), warrants, in Brennan's words, "the most exacting scrutiny."[126] That scrutiny produces perhaps the best-known words in Brennan's opinion, which are noteworthy for their metaphorical reference to a "bedrock principle" of the First Amendment.

> If there is a bedrock principle underlying the First Amendment, it is that the government may not prohibit the expression of an idea simply because society finds the idea itself offensive or disagreeable.[127]

The principle, Brennan observes, extends to expression of hostility to the flag and the ideas it represents. "In short," he writes, "nothing in our precedents suggests that a State may foster its own view of the flag by prohibiting expressive conduct relating to it."[128]

In powerful language reflective of his tolerance for "rumpus and hurly-burly," in Professor Michelman's words, Brennan explains that to permit flag-burning is to celebrate American democracy rather than to endanger it.[129] He writes:

> We are fortified in today's conclusion by our conviction that forbidding criminal punishment for conduct such as Johnson's will not endanger the special role played by our flag or the feelings it inspires. To paraphrase Justice

> Holmes, we submit that nobody can suppose that this one gesture of an unknown man will change our Nation's attitude toward its flag.[130]

The next paragraph continues in the same vein:

> We are tempted to say, in fact, that the flag's deservedly cherished place in our community will be strengthened, not weakened, by our holding today. Our decision is a reaffirmation of the principles of freedom and inclusiveness that the flag best reflects, and of the conviction that our toleration of criticism such as Johnson's is a sign and source of our strength. Indeed, one of the proudest images of our flag, the one immortalized in our own national anthem, is of the bombardment it survived at Fort McHenry. It is the Nation's resilience, not its rigidity, that Texas sees reflected in the flag—and it is that resilience that we reassert today.[131]

Both paragraphs emphasize that the flag's meaning lies in the values it represents, most notably, tolerance for dissent, even dissent expressed in flag-burning. Both paragraphs also display several stylistic devices to underscore that point: the vivid word "fortified" in the first paragraph to denote resolve in the decision reached, antithesis in the second paragraph ("strengthened, not weakened" and "resilience, not rigidity"), and alliteration ("sign and source" and "resilience," "rigidity," "reflected," and "reassert") in the third and the final sentences of that paragraph, respectively. The most powerful use of rhetorical style in these paragraphs, though, is the image of the flag withstanding the bombardment at Fort McHenry during the War of 1812. Presumably, that image is a metaphor for Brennan's deep belief that the United States will best withstand the "bombardment" of political protest by protecting speech, not punishing it.

Thus, neither Texas's interest in preventing breaches of the peace nor its interest in preserving the flag as a symbol of nationhood and national unity warranted punishing Gregory Johnson for engaging in political expression. The Court therefore affirmed the decision of the Texas Court of Criminal Appeals.

5. Frontiero v. Richardson

Lieutenant Sharon Frontiero, an Air Force officer, challenged a statutory scheme that assumed the wives of male service members were financially dependent on their husbands, thereby allowing the men to qualify for a larger housing allowance and additional medical and dental benefits. The same statutory scheme, though, forced married female service members to prove the financial dependency of their husbands in order to qualify for extra benefits. Justice Brennan wrote a plurality opinion for himself and Justices Douglas, White, and Marshall, in which Chief Justice Burger and Justices Powell and Blackmun concurred.[132] Its rationale flows from the topic of comparison and the subtopic of difference, more precisely, the difference between the ways in which the challenged statutes treated male and female military personnel despite the promise of the Equal Protection Clause.

The opening paragraph describes the case at hand clearly and simply.

> The question before us concerns the right of a female member of the uniformed services to claim her spouse as a "dependent" for the purposes of obtaining increased quarters allowances and medical and dental benefits under 37 U.S.C. ss. 401, 403, and 10 U.S.C. ss. 1072, 1076, on an equal footing with male members. Under these statutes, a serviceman may claim his wife as a "dependent" without regard to whether she is in fact dependent upon him for any part of her support. 37 U.S.C. s. 401(1); 10 U.S.C. s. 1072(2)(A). A servicewoman, on the other hand, may not claim her husband as a "dependent" under these programs unless he is in fact dependent upon her for over one-half of his support. 37 U.S.C. s. 401; 10 U.S.C. s. 1072(2)(C). Thus, the question for decision is whether this difference in treatment constitutes an unconstitutional discrimination against servicewomen in violation of the Due Process Clause of the Fifth Amendment.[133]

Equally clear is the plurality's preference for the application of strict scrutiny to gender-based classifications. In this regard, Brennan writes:

> At the outset, appellants contend that classifications based upon sex, like classifications based upon race, alienage, and national origin, are inherently suspect and must therefore be subjected to close judicial scrutiny. We agree and, indeed, find at least implicit support for such an approach in our unanimous decision only last Term in *Reed v. Reed*, 404 U.S. 71 (1971) [declaring unconstitutional an Idaho statute providing that, when two persons are otherwise equally entitled to appointment as the administrator of an estate, the male applicant must be preferred to the female].[134]

Reed represents a necessary change from rational-basis analysis in such circumstances, Brennan continues, because historically, courts had almost always found a "rational basis" to treat women as unequal to men. He writes:

> There can be no doubt that our Nation has had a long and unfortunate history of sex discrimination. Traditionally, such discrimination was rationalized by an attitude of "romantic paternalism" which, in practical effect, put women, not on a pedestal, but in a cage. Indeed, this paternalistic attitude became so firmly rooted in our national consciousness that, 100 years ago, a distinguished Member of this Court was able to proclaim: " . . . The paramount destiny and mission of woman are to fulfill the noble and benign offices of wife and mother. This is the law of the Creator."[135]

Note the effective use of antithesis in the second sentence ("not on a pedestal, but in a cage") to distinguish the supposedly protective intent of romantic paternalism from its discriminatory result. Note also Brennan's reference to the musty language of *Bradwell v. Illinois*—odd-sounding and antiquated even in the early 1970s—to emphasize the degree to which paternalistic practices toward women of the current day were rooted in the residual values and assumptions of a bygone era.

"As a result of notions such as these," Brennan observes, statutes came to reflect "gross, stereotyped distinctions between the sexes" and even though "the position of women in America has improved markedly in recent decades . . . women still face pervasive, although at times more subtle, discrimination in our educational institutions, in the job market and, perhaps most conspicuously, in the political arena."[136] For those reasons and because Congress had of late become increasingly critical of sex-based classifications (e.g. Title VII of the 1964 Civil Rights Act, 42 U.S.C. § 2000e-2(a), (b), and (c); the Equal Pay Act of 1963, 29 U.S.C. § 206(d); and Section 1 of the Equal Rights Amendment, H.R.J. Res. No. 208, 92nd Cong., 2d Sess. (1972)), Brennan writes that "we can only conclude that classifications based upon sex, like classifications based upon race, alienage, or national origin, are inherently suspect, and must therefore be subjected to strict judicial scrutiny."[137]

The only remaining step was to invalidate the statutory scheme of which Sharon Frontiero and her husband complained. The government conceded that the reason for the disparate treatment based on sex here might well have been "administrative convenience"; in other words, Congress could have concluded that presuming the wives of male service members were dependent, but requiring the husbands of female service members to prove that status was cheaper and easier than treating male and female service members the same.[138] But, Brennan notes, the government offered "no concrete evidence . . . tending to support its view that such differential treatment in fact saves the Government any money."[139] Besides, he adds, "the Constitution recognizes higher values than speed and efficiency."[140]

Thus, the majority, with four members (including Brennan) applying strict scrutiny and three using the rational basis test, held that the challenged statutes violated the Due Process Clause of the Fifth Amendment by requiring female service members to prove their husbands' dependency.[141] Once again Justice Brennan used his bridge-building skills and his crystalline prose to champion social progress that would have been delayed, if not denied, without him.

E. Conclusion

In criminal procedure, the First Amendment, equal protection, and numerous other areas of law, William Brennan's influence was enormous, as great as or perhaps greater than that of any other associate justice in Supreme Court history. The well-known sources of that influence were his intellect, his fundamental decency as a human being, and his willingness to work toward consensus, or at least compromise. But his prose deserves close study in its own right because it offers a primer for the beginning law student, the newly seated judge, and everyone in between on how to craft a clear, concise, and coherent legal argument that can inform, persuade, and even inspire.

NOTES

1. David Halberstam, "The Common Man as Uncommon Man," in E. Joshua Rosenkranz and Bernard Schwartz, eds., *Reason and Passion: Justice Brennan's Enduring Influence* (New York: W.W. Norton and Company, 1997), 28.
2. Peter Irons, *Brennan vs. Rehnquist: The Battle for the Constitution* (New York: Alfred A. Knopf, 1994), 25.
3. Seth Stern and Stephen Wermiel, *Justice Brennan: Liberal Champion* (Boston, MA: Houghton Mifflin Harcourt, 2010), 6.
4. Halberstam, "The Common Man as Uncommon Man," in Rosenkranz and Schwartz, eds., *Reason and Passion*, 28; Irons, *Brennan vs. Rehnquist: The Battle for the Constitution*, 25.
5. Irons, *Brennan vs. Rehnquist*, 26.
6. Ibid.
7. Nat Hentoff, "Profiles: the Constitutionalist," *New Yorker*, March 12, 1990, 45–46, cited in Hunter R. Clark, "In Memoriam: The Pulse of Life in Justice Brennan's Jurisprudence," *Drake Law Review* 46 (1997): xxii.
8. Halberstam, "The Common Man as Uncommon Man," in Rosenkranz and Schwartz, eds., *Reason and Passion*, 28.
9. Stern and Wermeil, *Justice Brennan*, 8.
10. Irons, *Brennan vs. Rehnquist*, 26.
11. Ibid.
12. Stern and Wermiel, *Justice Brennan*, 25.
13. Ibid., xiii.
14. Ibid., 23.
15. Ibid., 32.
16. Ibid., 33.
17. Ibid., 34.
18. Ibid., 37–38.
19. Ibid., 40.
20. Ibid.
21. Ibid., 45.
22. Ibid.
23. Ibid., 46.
24. Stephen J. Wermiel, "The Nomination of Justice Brennan: Eisenhower's Mistake? A Look at the Historical Record," *Constitutional Commentary* 11 (1995): 515.
25. Stern and Wermiel, *Justice Brennan*, 52.
26. Ibid., 54.
27. See, for example, *In re Pillo*, 93 A.2d 176 (1952), in which Brennan held that New Jersey's statutory privilege against self-incrimination absolved a witness in a gambling investigation from having to answer a grand jury's questions; *Adams Theatre Co. v. Keenan*, 96 A.2d 519 (1953), in which he held that because a licensing official could not show that the plaintiff, who sought a license to run a theater that offered burlesque shows, planned to present "lewd and indecent" entertainment, no basis existed to exercise prior restraint and deny the plaintiff a license; and *State v. True*, 98 A.2d 881 (1953), in which he dissented from the majority's refusal to permit an accused murderer to inspect his own confession. In *True*, he wrote that the same liberal discovery rules that by then applied in civil cases in New Jersey should apply in

criminal cases too. "It shocks my conscience," he wrote, "that in these circumstances counsel for an accused facing a possible death sentence should be denied inspection of his confession which, were this a civil case, could not be denied." 98 A.2d at 896.

28. Rosenkranz and Schwartz, eds., *Reason and Passion*, 23.

29. Wermiel, "The Nomination of Justice Brennan: Eisenhower's Mistake? A Look at the Historical Record," 522.

30. Ibid., 534.

31. E. Joshua Rosenkranz, Morton Horwitz, Daniel O'Hearn, Roy Schotland, and Patricia Wald, "Remembering a Constitutional Hero," *New York Law School Law Review* 43 (1999): 13.

32. Rosenkranz, and Schwartz, eds., *Reason and Passion*, 24.

33. Stern and Wermiel, *Justice Brennan*, 119.

34. Rosenkranz and Schwartz, eds., *Reason and Passion*, 24.

35. Rosenkranz, Horwitz, O'Hearn, Schotland, and Wald, "Remembering a Constitutional Hero," 28.

36. Bernard Schwartz, "How Justice Brennan Changed America," in Rosenkranz and Schwartz, eds., *Reason and Passion*, 31.

37. Clark, "In Memoriam: The Pulse of Life in Justice Brennan's Jurisprudence," x.

38. Rosenkranz, Horwitz, O'Hearn, Schotland, and Wald, "Remembering a Constitutional Hero," 30.

39. Ibid.

40. Stern and Wermeil, *Justice Brennan*, 183.

41. Rosenkranz, Horwitz, O'Hearn, Schotland, and Wald, "Remembering a Constitutional Hero," 15.

42. Kim Isaac Eisler, *A Justice for All: William J. Brennan, Jr. and the Decisions That Transformed America* (New York: Simon & Schuster, 1993), 179.

43. Rosenkranz, Horwitz, O'Hearn, Schotland, and Wald, "Remembering a Constitutional Hero," 30–31.

44. Rosenkranz and Schwartz, eds., *Reason and Passion*, 41.

45. Ibid.

46. William J. Brennan, Jr., "Reason, Passion, and 'The Progress of the Law,'" *Cardozo Law Review* 10 (1988): 14.

47. Ibid.

48. Irons, *Brennan vs. Rehnquist*, 38–39.

49. 369 U.S. 186 (1962).

50. 328 U.S. 459 (1946).

51. David E. Marian, *The Jurisprudence of Justice: William J. Brennan, Jr.* (Lanham, MD: Rowman & Littlefield Publishers, Inc., 1997), 27.

52. Ibid.

53. Frank I. Michelman, *Brennan and Democracy* (Princeton, NJ: Princeton University Press, 1999), 62.

54. Stern and Wermiel, *Justice Brennan*, 187.

55. Ibid.

56. Ibid., 189.

57. Rosenkranz, Horwitz, O'Hearn, Schotland, and Wald, "Remembering a Constitutional Hero," 34.

58. See, for example, *Reynolds v. Sims*, 377 U.S. 533 (1964) (holding that both houses of state legislatures had to be comprised of districts that were equal in population) and *Wesberry v. Sanders*, 376 U.S. 1 (1964) (holding that the one-person, one-vote principle applied to congressional districts, too).

59. Rosenkranz and Schwartz, ed., *Reason and Passion*, 34.

60. Michael Sherman, Gene Sessions, and P. Jeffrey Potash, *Freedom and Unity: A History of Vermont* (Barre, VT: Vermont Historical Society, 2004), 509.

61. Rosenkranz, Horwitz, O'Hearn, Schotland, and Wald, "Remembering a Constitutional Hero," 34–35.

62. Ibid., 15.

63. Stern and Wermiel, *Justice Brennan*, 496.
64. 438 U.S. 265.
65. Irons, *Brennan vs. Rehnquist*, 258.
66. Stern and Wermiel, *Justice Brennan*, 449.
67. Rosenkranz and Schwartz, eds., *Reason and Passion*, 37. See also Stern and Wermiel, *Justice Brennan*, 455.
68. Stern and Wermiel, *Justice Brennan*, 495.
69. Ibid.
70. Ibid.
71. Bernard Schwartz, "How Justice Brennan Changed America," in Rosenkranz and Schwartz, eds., *Reason and Passion*, 41.
72. Stern and Wermiel, *Justice Brennan*, 543.
73. Jonathan Turley, "The 9 Greatest Supreme Court Justices," *American History Magazine* (July 29, 2009), accessed November 24, 2018, http://www.historynet.com/the-9-greatest-supreme-court-justices.htm.
74. 378 U.S. 1 (1964).
75. 481 U.S. 279 (1987).
76. 376 U.S. 254 (1964).
77. 491 U.S. 397 (1989).
78. 411 U.S. 677 (1973). Because of the length of several of the opinions to be discussed, this section will examine five of Justice Brennan's opinions, even though previous chapters examined six opinions of the featured justice.
79. Eisler, *A Justice for All*, 179.
80. 332 U.S. 46.
81. 378 U.S. 1 (1964).
82. Ibid., 2.
83. *Pocket Oxford American Dictionary & Thesaurus*, 3rd ed. (New York: Oxford University Press, 2010), 688.
84. 378 U.S. at 3.
85. Ibid.
86. Ibid., 7.
87. Ibid.
88. Ibid., 12.
89. Ibid., 13. Pool-selling is the sale or distribution of chances in a betting pool.
90. Ibid.
91. Ibid., 14.
92. 428 U.S. 279 (1986).
93. Ibid., 286.
94. Ibid., 287.
95. Ibid., 297.
96. Ibid.
97. Ibid., 313.
98. Ibid., 321.
99. Ibid.
100. Ibid., 327.
101. Ibid.
102. Ibid., 328.
103. Ibid., 344–45.
104. The title of the ad was "Heed Their Rising Voices." The ad appeared on the editorial page of the *New York Times* on March 29, 1960 and is reprinted in the appendix to the *Sullivan* decision.
105. Irons, *Brennan vs. Rehnquist*, 156.
106. Ibid.
107. Clark, "In Memoriam: The Pulse of Life in Justice Brennan's Jurisprudence," xx–xxi.
108. 376 U.S. 254 (1964); Lewis, "The Press: Free But Not Exceptional," in Rosenkranz and Schwartz, eds., *Passion and Reason*, 56.

109. Lewis, "The Press: Free But Not Exceptional," in Rosenkranz and Schwartz, eds., *Passion and Reason*, 56.
110. 376 U.S. at 256.
111. Ibid., 257.
112. Ibid., 257–58.
113. Ibid., 258.
114. Ibid., 265.
115. Ibid., 270–71.
116. Ibid., 279–80.
117. Ibid., 287–88.
118. 491 U.S. 397 (1989).
119. Michelman, *Brennan and Democracy*, 72.
120. 491 U.S. at 399.
121. Ibid., 399–400.
122. Ibid., 405.
123. Ibid., 406.
124. Ibid.
125. Ibid., 406–7.
126. Ibid., 412.
127. Ibid., 414.
128. Ibid., 415.
129. Michelman, *Brennan and Democracy*, 72.
130. Ibid., 418–19 (citing *Abrams v. United States*, 250 U.S. 616, 628 [1919] [Holmes, J., dissenting]).
131. Ibid., 419.
132. 411 U.S. 677 (1973).
133. Ibid., 678–79.
134. Ibid., 682.
135. Ibid., 684–85 (quoting *Bradwell v. State of Illinois*, 16 Wall. 130, 141 [1873] [Bradley, J., concurring]).
136. Ibid., 685–86.
137. Ibid., 688.
138. Ibid., 688–89.
139. Ibid., 689.
140. Ibid., 690 (quoting *Stanley v. Illinois*, 405 U.S. 645, 656 (1972)).
141. Ibid., 690–91.

Chapter Seven

Antonin Scalia

Originalist in Style Too

A. Beginnings

Just as William Brennan's death in 1997 prompted many tributes, from allies as well as opponents, so did Antonin Scalia's death in February 2016. His personal friend, but ideological foe—Justice Elena Kagan—said of Scalia's influence on American law:

> The fact of the matter is, you wake up in 100 years and most people are not going to know most of our names. I think that is really not the case with Justice Scalia, who I think is going to go down as one of the most important, most historic figures on the Court.[1]

The parallels between Brennan and Scalia do not end with tributes after death, though. Like Brennan, Scalia exceeded the considerable accomplishments of an immigrant father to breathe the rarefied air atop the US government. Antonin's father, Salvatore, left Sicily at age seventeen, arriving at Ellis Island in December of 1920 with his parents and younger sister.[2]

Salvatore, or "Sam," as his friends called him, lived the American dream. He studied voice for a time and worked as a journalist temporarily before earning a bachelor's degree from Rutgers University in 1931, followed by a master's degree from Columbia University the next year.[3] In 1939, three years after Antonin's birth, the elder Scalia, who by then had married and lived with his family in Queens, began working as an instructor at Brooklyn College, teaching French, Italian, and Spanish, while pursuing a doctorate at Columbia. His completion of his doctorate in 1950 resulted in a promotion from instructor to assistant professor at Brooklyn College.[4] He taught there for thirty years, retiring in 1969.[5] Justice Scalia recalled his father as "severe" and "demanding,"[6] wondering why every "A" grade that young Antonin earned in school was not an "A+."[7]

But such disappointments were rare for Sam Scalia because Antonin was a model student. At Xavier High School, an all-boys school in lower Manhattan run by Jesuit priests, Antonin studied Latin and Greek and the great rhetoricians.[8] His flair for the dramatic served him well as an orator and actor,[9] but his star shone brightest in the classroom, as he was the class valedictorian[10] and won a Naval ROTC scholarship to college.[11] In college, at Georgetown University, also a Jesuit institution, he continued to be active in drama and debate and remained an academic star, graduating first in his class in 1957.[12]

The young Antonin Scalia exhibited many of the personal traits that would become trademarks of Justice Scalia. His "knack for levity," storytelling, and "sense of showmanship," as described by biographer Joan Biskupic, reflected the vibrancy of his mother's family, the Panaros, who also supplied a role model in Antonin's Uncle Vince, a lawyer who became a county prosecutor, mayor, and state legislator in New Jersey.[13]

Juxtaposed to Scalia's fun-loving side were his devout Catholicism and academic rigor. The latter reflected his father's similar orientation; indeed, the younger Scalia's emphasis on the close reading of texts seems traceable not only to the influence of a Catholic education, but also to the insistence of his father, who published several works of translation, on the literal reading of texts.[14] All of these traits and influences would exhibit themselves at Harvard, where Scalia enrolled in law school in 1957.

B. Professional Life

While at Harvard, Scalia became a proponent of the philosophy of Professor Herbert Wechsler, who advocated judging based on "neutral principles," because only the elected branches of government should make "value" choices based on a political ideology.[15] Wechsler taught at Columbia, but gave a famous lecture at Harvard in 1959 that shaped Scalia's thinking profoundly.[16] Wechsler insisted that despite his disapproval of racial segregation in public schools, he thought the Supreme Court had erred when it held in *Brown v. Board of Education* in 1954 that segregated schools were unconstitutional because segregation harmed black children psychologically.[17] Such value-based policy choices, Wechsler argued, were the province of the legislative and executive branches, not the judiciary. During his judicial career, Scalia would voice a similar distaste for "judicial activism" and would seek to determine the literal meaning of statutory language and the original public meaning of constitutional provisions he was called upon to interpret.

Scalia's performance at Harvard destined him for the top rungs of the legal ladder. He graduated magna cum laude in 1960, having served as Notes Editor of the *Harvard Law Review.*[18] After graduation, he married Maureen McCarthy, a Radcliffe graduate,[19] and the couple, who would eventually have nine children and more than thirty grandchildren, set off for a year of travel in Europe, thanks to Scalia's receipt of a Sheldon Fellowship from Harvard.[20]

After returning to the United States, Antonin Scalia joined a large law firm, specifically, Jones, Day, Cockley & Reavis in Cleveland.[21] Six years later, he stepped off the law-firm track about a year before he could have become a partner, opting instead to teach at the University of Virginia Law School. He would remain there for just four years, though, because he wished to be closer to the political fray in Washington, D.C. Joan Biskupic has observed:

> Scalia's political savvy, natural combativeness, and allegiance to the executive were ideally suited for the post-Watergate time. His authoritarian bent, rooted in a rule-oriented father and Catholic upbringing, fostered his concern for the erosion of the executive branch and encroachments on the presidency.[22]

First, he joined the Office of Telecommunications in President Richard Nixon's White House in 1971, where he was instrumental in negotiating a "consensus agreement" between the nascent cable television industry, broadcast networks, movie producers, and the Federal Communications Commission that allowed cable television to expand beyond small rural markets while protecting the copyrights held by the broadcast networks.[23] From 1972 until 1974, Scalia chaired the Administrative Conference of the United States, an independent research agency within the federal government that evaluated the efficiency and fairness of federal agency procedures and recommended improvements to Congress and the White House.[24] In 1974, after Gerald Ford became president, Scalia became the assistant attorney general in charge of the White House Office of Legal Counsel, a prestigious division of the Department of Justice responsible for producing legal opinions regarding the powers of the executive branch.[25]

Three years later, after Democrat Jimmy Carter won the presidency, Scalia returned to teaching, this time at the University of Chicago Law School, where he began working in the fall of 1977.[26] Hoping to return to the government after Ronald Reagan's election to the presidency in 1980, Scalia gladly accepted, in 1982, President Reagan's offer of a seat on the US Court of Appeals for the District of Columbia Circuit.[27]

Antonin Scalia enjoyed being an appellate judge. He told a television interviewer: "I like the intellectual endeavor. I like playing with ideas and words and analyzing the meaning of statutes."[28] He quickly established an assertive and consistently conservative judicial philosophy. Judge Scalia was skeptical of legislation that he thought impinged on the prerogatives of the executive branch. He construed grants of individual rights narrowly, and he opposed affirmative action laws designed to benefit individuals based on their race or gender.[29] He sought to erect higher barriers to prevent consumers and other groups from bringing class-action lawsuits. He opposed what he saw as a judicial tendency to look beyond the text of a statute to determine its reach, which coincided with his firm belief that elected officials, not courts, should address society's ills.[30] A particular bugaboo for Scalia was judges' use of "legislative history" to divine the purpose of a statute; Members of Congress voted on bills, not committee reports, he argued, so statutory interpretation should be based on the text itself, not the artifacts of its production.[31]

The conservative lawyers in the Reagan administration had been following Judge Scalia's work on the D.C. Circuit closely for almost four years when, in May of 1986, the Supreme Court's Chief Justice—Warren Burger—informed President Reagan that he intended to retire at the end of the current term in June.[32] Scalia immediately became a prime candidate to fill the seat of Associate Justice William Rehnquist, whom Reagan nominated to replace Burger.

President Reagan did not look far to find candidates for the Rehnquist seat, as Scalia's main rival for the post was his colleague on the D.C. Circuit, Robert Bork, also an assertive conservative and former law professor.

The credentials of both men qualified them for service on the Court, but Scalia enjoyed several advantages. Some members of the administration viewed Judge Bork as a longevity risk because he was fifty-nine years old, overweight, and a heavy smoker.[33] Scalia exhibited the conservative values of the Reagan administration as much as Bork did, and he was nine years younger. Beyond that, Scalia—the son of a Sicilian immigrant—offered the administration a compelling story to tell because he would be the first Italian American to serve on the Supreme Court.

Once nominated, Scalia cruised to confirmation, ultimately receiving a 98–0 endorsement by the Senate.[34] Senate Democrats had spent themselves trying to prevent Rehnquist's ascent to the center chair, based on their fears that he would steer the Court sharply to the right.[35] Rehnquist's hearings had consumed four days instead of the originally scheduled two, and the Senate Judiciary Committee's vote to send his nomination to the full Senate was a relatively tight 13–5 in favor.[36] The confirmation vote by the full Senate was also a reasonably close 65–33 in favor, as Rehnquist received more "No" votes than any confirmed justice to that point.[37] Democrats who opposed both Rehnquist and Scalia knew that if they could block Rehnquist's promotion, they could deny Scalia a seat on the Court too. They therefore questioned Rehnquist aggressively and gave Scalia a free pass so as not to appear hostile to every Reagan nominee.[38] Ironically, as Joan Biskupic has noted, Rehnquist—the Democrats' main target—moved to the center somewhat in later years, but Scalia, whom they waived through the gate, remained a committed conservative throughout his Court tenure.[39] In another irony, Scalia's candidacy for the Court benefited from his ethnic heritage, despite his long-standing opposition to affirmative action programs.[40]

C. On the Court

Antonin Scalia was as confident about and as aggressive in promoting his jurisprudential convictions on the Supreme Court as he had been on the D.C. Circuit. Never shy, he requested changes big and small in the opinion drafts of his colleagues when he was in the majority. If the author did not adopt Scalia's suggestion, Scalia would refuse to sign the full opinion and would use a concurrence to state his objection to a particular paragraph or even a particular footnote.[41]

When assigned to write the majority opinion, Scalia's rigidity sometimes cost him the majority support he originally enjoyed. Such circumstances taught Rehnquist that when a single vote appeared to have won a case, he should not assign the majority opinion to Scalia, lest the latter's intransigence turn victory into defeat.[42] Unlike Brennan, Scalia was unwilling to make the compromises that were often necessary to build and hold a majority. In Joan Biskupic's words, "[He would not] yield on things that mattered."[43]

Textualism and originalism—the twin pillars of his jurisprudential edifice—mattered most. Textualism is an approach to statutory interpretation that considers primarily the words of and the tradition associated with the document being interpreted. In the textualist's view, when construing a statute, a judge is obligated to apply the statute's words when clear and, when they are unclear, to rely instead on the legal tradition of the statute: what it meant to the society that adopted it.[44] Professor Mark Tushnet has observed:

> Before Scalia, until the late '80s, the justices would issue a ruling and say, "Here is why our opinion makes sense," and then support it with some law and history. But now everyone is much more conscious about looking at what the text says—and quite often less conscious about how that might fit into a social or practical context.[45]

As Professor Tushnet's comment suggests, Scalia's emphasis on statutory (and constitutional) texts changed the way lawyers and judges structured their analyses of statutes and of constitutional provisions. Justice Elena Kagan perhaps made this point best when she stated in a 2015 lecture at Harvard: "We are all textualists now."[46]

Scalia offered three related reasons for his primary reliance on statutory text and canons of construction instead of legislative history when reading statutes. First, legislative history may be unreliable, enabling judges to be selective in deciding which history to honor and which to ignore; second, legislative history does not represent the views of even a majority of the legislators, and may represent only the views of a select few who championed the legislation; third, reliance on legislative history causes courts to exceed their power because the only "law" they are authorized to interpret is that contained in the statutory text.[47]

Regarding constitutional interpretation, Scalia wrote: "What I look for in the Constitution is precisely what I look for in a statute: the original meaning of the text, not what the original draftsmen intended."[48] In other words, Scalia's originalism—a method of interpretation that seeks to determine the meaning of a constitutional provision at the time of its adoption—was rooted in textualism.

Scalia acknowledged originalism's imperfections, not the least of which is that it is "a task sometimes better suited to the historian than the lawyer," but embraced it nonetheless because of the lack of an acceptable alternative.[49] He analogized originalism to the reference librarian who speaks too softly, which is occasionally problematic, but not nearly so as the reference librarian who speaks too loudly.[50] In Scalia's view, judges who rejected originalism were susceptible to "judicial personalization of the law," meaning that they interpreted the Constitution according to their own policy preferences, such as by striking down death sentences as inherently unconstitutional even though the Constitution refers explicitly to the death penalty.[51] Their "judicial legislating" had three unfortunate consequences, Scalia maintained: (1) to make the Constitution mean whatever one wants it to mean results in it not meaning much at all; (2) if the Constitution means whatever one wants it to mean, no criteria exist by which to interpret its words; and (3) under these circumstances, the Supreme Court is exposed to the same political pressures and partisan critiques as Congress and the presidency.[52]

Antonin Scalia's reliance on textualism and originalism usually led him to support conservative outcomes in individual cases. His methodology found no abortion rights in the Constitution, yet located there strict prohibitions on affirmative action programs and on laws designed to regulate the financing of political campaigns.[53] At the end of the 2012–2013 Court Term, he wrote in a dissent in *United States v. Windsor*[54] that the Court possessed "no power under the Constitution to invalidate this democratically adopted legislation," referring to the federal Defense of Marriage Act, whose definition of "marriage" as open only to opposite-sex couples the majority had held unconstitutional.[55] The previous day, though, in *Shelby County v. Holder*, he had voted with the majority to strike down a key component of the Voting Rights Act, which since 1965 had required federal approval of changes in election law made by states and localities with a history of racial discrimination in voting.[56] In short, despite his frequent refrain that judges should defer to the decisions of legislative majorities, Scalia was selectively deferential; his deference extended to laws restricting abortion, preserving the death penalty and political patronage, and fostering religious observances, but not to laws promoting affirmative action, campaign finance reform, or, as *Windsor* shows, gay rights.[57]

Still, Scalia was not a knee-jerk conservative; for example, his textualism and originalism sometimes led him to support the claims of criminal defendants. Perhaps the clearest examples of Scalia's jurisprudence favoring criminal defendants were cases that featured the Confrontation Clause of the Sixth Amendment. In *Crawford v. Washington*, Scalia wrote a majority opinion holding that the defendant's Confrontation Clause rights were violated when the prosecutor played at trial a tape-recorded statement to police by the defendant's wife describing how her husband had stabbed a man who had raped her, even though the marital privilege deprived the defendant of the right to cross-examine her.[58] Five years later, in *Melendez-Diaz v. Massachusetts*, Scalia again wrote for the majority, holding that the Confrontation Clause gives defendants the right to cross-examine the preparers of forensic (e.g., blood, ballistic, etc.) reports used in prosecutions. Therefore, prosecutors could no longer automatically introduce those reports at trial in written form; instead, the preparer must affirmatively present the results in live testimony, unless the defense agrees otherwise.[59]

Such occasional departures from his usual conservative orthodoxy were not enough to silence Scalia's critics, though. Some of them charged that he was not always faithful to the "neutral principles" of statutory construction and constitutional interpretation as he claimed to be, permitting much more discretion to seep into his conclusions than he would ever admit. For example, Professor Catherine Langford, who studied Scalia's Eighth Amendment and Establishment Clause jurisprudence, concluded that he was "opportunistic" because he used his interpretative methodology "to achieve particular legal results rather than to limit judicial interpretation to the textual parameters of the Constitution."[60]

Whether Antonin Scalia was a visionary or an opportunist, his talent as a writer was a key to his influence on American law. A discussion of his writing follows.

D. Scalia the Writer

Scalia stands out as much for his writing as for his jurisprudence. More than most judges, he seems to have internalized Aristotle's admonition that how one expresses ideas is as important as the ideas expressed. Indeed, he thought about writing, as the following quote, related by his biographer, Joan Biskupic, reveals:

> Writing is a very painful process. . . . But I love having written, to have a product that I have sweated over . . . honed to . . . perfection.[61]

He even wrote about writing, with coauthor Bryan Garner, advising legal writers to make their prose interesting by using figures of speech such as simile, metaphor, analogy, and antithesis, but cautioning that such devices help "only if they cause the serious legal points you're making to be more vivid, more lively, and hence more memorable."[62] Scalia and Garner also advised legal writers to "enliven" their word choices, "mix up" their sentence structures, and "vary" their sentence lengths.[63]

Scalia's writing, like his jurisprudence, had both devoted friends and ardent foes. The former praised him for the clarity, simplicity, and directness of his prose, whereas the latter chided him for opinions—especially dissents—that were spiked with sarcasm, often aimed at his colleagues. Scalia noted in a 1994 lecture that writing dissents was "fun" because "you just write for yourself," but his fun often seemed to occur at his colleagues' expense.[64] Joan Biskupic has observed that "Scalia wrote with a recriminatory tone that often undercut his effectiveness" and that he was "hyperbolic and almost entirely dismissive of arguments from the other side."[65] For example, in several dissents, he described the majority's reasoning as "nothing short of ludicrous" and "beyond the absurd,"[66] as [not passing] "the most gullible scrutiny,"[67] and as "entirely irrational."[68] Even in a concurrence, he wrote that Justice O'Connor's reasoning "cannot be taken seriously" and "preserves a chaos that is evident to anyone who can read and count."[69]

In fairness to Justice Scalia, though, the caustic language quoted above, albeit indefensible, was largely confined to dissents, obscuring his majority opinions (and some dissents) that use the tools of classical rhetoric wisely and effectively. The remainder of this section will illustrate his effective use of rhetorical techniques in *Crawford*,[70] *Melendez-Diaz*,[71] *Vernonia School District 47J v. Acton*,[72] *National Treasury Employees Union v. Von Raab*,[73] and *Johnson v. Transportation Agency, Santa Clara County, Cal.*[74]

1. *Crawford v. Washington*

At issue in *Crawford* was whether the prosecution had violated Mr. Crawford's Confrontation Clause rights by playing at his trial for assault and attempted murder a tape-recorded statement by his wife in which she described how he had stabbed a man who had allegedly raped her. The defense claimed that admission of the recording violated the Confrontation Clause because Mr. Crawford had no opportunity to cross-examine Ms. Crawford. She had not testified in person because of the State of Washington's marital privilege, which generally barred a spouse from testifying without the other spouse's consent. But the trial court had admitted into evidence Ms. Crawford's recorded statement to the police under *Ohio v. Roberts*,[75] which held that a court may admit an unavailable witness's statement against a criminal defendant if the statement bears "adequate indicia of reliability,"[76] meaning that it fits within "a firmly rooted hearsay exception" or bears "particularized guarantees of trustworthiness."[77] A jury convicted Crawford of assault; an intermediate appellate court reversed, but the Washington Supreme Court reinstated the conviction, reasoning that Ms. Crawford's statement was reliable because it was almost identical to her husband's description of the stabbing.

Writing for a unanimous Court, Justice Scalia, true to his textualism and originalism, begins by quoting the Confrontation Clause's promise that "the accused shall enjoy the right . . . to be confronted with the witnesses against him," and by noting Mr. Crawford's claim that the "indicia of reliability" standard of *Ohio v. Roberts* "strays from the original meaning of the Confrontation Clause"; hence, the Court should reconsider *Roberts*.[78] His reasoning derives from the topic of relationship and the subtopic of contraries, notably, the irreconcilable conflict between the "indicia of reliability" standard announced in *Roberts* and the requirements of the Confrontation Clause. Scalia observes that the constitutional text does not resolve the case because "witnesses against" a defendant could mean persons who testify at trial, persons whose statements are offered at trial, or "something in between."[79] Therefore, one has to examine the historical background of the Clause to discern its meaning.

Scalia examines the pertinent history at length, especially the 1603 treason trial in England of Sir Walter Raleigh, which ended with a death sentence. The accused was prohibited from confronting his alleged accomplice, who had implicated him by letter and in an examination before the Privy Council. The historical record leads Scalia to two conclusions about the meaning of the Confrontation Clause. "First," he writes, "the principal evil at which the Confrontation Clause was directed was the civil-law mode of criminal procedure, and particularly its use of ex parte examinations as evidence against the accused."[80] Second, "the Framers would not have allowed admission of testimonial statements of a witness who did not appear at trial unless he was unavailable to testify, and the defendant had had a prior opportunity for cross-examination."[81] The *Roberts* standard, however, would condition the admission of ex parte testimony not on those criteria, but rather, in Scalia's words, "upon a mere finding of reliability."[82] In other words, the *Roberts* rule "allows a jury to hear evidence, untested by the adversary process, based on a mere judicial determination of reliability."[83]

Scalia underscores the failings of *Roberts* with an effective use of analogy and isocolon. He writes:

> Dispensing with confrontation because testimony is obviously reliable is akin to dispensing with jury trial because a defendant is obviously guilty. That is not what the Sixth Amendment prescribes.[84]

The analogy, of course, is between foregoing confrontation and foregoing a jury trial. It is effective, especially with the reader who is less familiar with the right of confrontation than with the better known right to a jury trial, because equating the two magnifies the importance of the confrontation right. Nonetheless, it may be overdrawn because "obvious guilt" is not a constitutionally permissible basis for denying a jury trial, whereas since *Roberts*, the Confrontation Clause had permitted the admission of evidence furnished by an unavailable witness if the evidence passed a test of reliability. The two circumstances are not equivalent because the first would surely deny due process, whereas the second would not. Still, Scalia saw them as equivalent, so the analogy served his jurisprudential purpose well.

The isocolon serves Scalia's purpose too. It links "dispensing with confrontation because testimony is obviously reliable" to "dispensing with jury trial because a defendant is obviously guilty," strongly suggesting equivalence between the two scenarios. Rhythm also figures prominently in the passage, in which the longer, more explanatory first sentence precedes a shorter, more direct and dramatic second sentence ("That is not what the Sixth Amendment prescribes") that underscores the incompatibility between the *Roberts* rule and the Confrontation Clause.

Scalia also notes the *Roberts* rule's unpredictability because of the "amorphous, if not entirely subjective" nature of its core concept: reliability.[85] Then, using a metaphor, antithesis, and a bit of hyperbole at the same time, Scalia writes that "[t]he unpardonable vice of the *Roberts* test, however, is not its unpredictability, but its demonstrated capacity to admit core testimonial statements that the Confrontation Clause plainly meant to exclude."[86] Therefore, reliability is immaterial absent the opportunity for cross-examination. Scalia addresses this point using metaphor and antithesis. He writes:

> That inculpating statements are given in a testimonial setting [e.g., under oath before a grand jury] is not an antidote to the confrontation problem, but rather the trigger that makes the Clause's demands most urgent. It is not enough to point out that most of the usual safeguards of the adversary process attend the statement, when the single safeguard missing is the one the Confrontation Clause demands.[87]

The "antidote" and "trigger" metaphors enliven the first sentence of the passage. The antidote metaphor instructs the reader that just because someone who is under oath provides incriminating evidence against the defendant does not mean that the "confrontation" requirement has been met. The trigger metaphor adds that far from solving the confrontation problem, such testimony highlights it. In the second sentence, antithesis emphasizes the missing confrontation safeguard under the *Roberts* rule. Thus, the indispensible protection that the Sixth Amendment provides for criminal defendants is the right of confrontation.

Turning to the *Crawford* case, Scalia charges that the missing confrontation safeguard was evident in the admission of Ms. Crawford's statement, which she had made "while in police custody, herself a potential suspect" and "[i]n response to often leading questions from police detectives. . . ."[88] Despite these red flags, "the trial court admitted her statement, listing several reasons why it was reliable" and the State Supreme Court upheld that decision because the wife's statement corroborated the husband's testimony.[89]

Based on the previous reasoning, Justice Scalia concludes that with respect to testimonial evidence, "the Sixth Amendment demands what the common law required: unavailability and a prior opportunity for cross-examination."[90] He does not attempt a "comprehensive definition of 'testimonial,' leaving that task 'for another day.'"[91] Instead, he explains:

> Whatever else the term covers, it applies at a minimum to prior testimony at a preliminary hearing, before a grand jury, or at a former trial; and to police interrogations. These are the modern practices with closest kinship to the abuses at which the Confrontation Clause was directed.[92]

The kinship metaphor nicely links those modern practices to the historic abuses, such as the Raleigh trial, that prompted adoption of the Confrontation Clause. Based on that kinship, the Court reversed the Washington Supreme Court and remanded for further proceedings.

2. *Melendez-Diaz v. Massachusetts*

Five years after *Crawford*, the Supreme Court again faced a Confrontation Clause case, and Antonin Scalia again wrote for the Court, although this time in a 5–4 decision featuring an unlikely majority: Justices Scalia, Ginsburg, Souter, Stevens, and Thomas.[93] In a clear, concise opening paragraph, Scalia noted that Massachusetts courts "had admitted into evidence affidavits reporting the results of forensic analysis which showed that material seized by the police and connected to the defendant was cocaine."[94] The resulting question for the Court was "whether those affidavits [we]re 'testimonial,' rendering the affiants 'witnesses' subject to the defendant's right of confrontation under the Sixth Amendment."[95]

The petitioner, charged with cocaine trafficking and distribution, had objected to admission of the "certificates of analysis"—showing the results of tests on seized substances—because, he claimed, under *Crawford*, the analysts must testify about the results in person. The trial court overruled the objection, after which the certificates were admitted into evidence and a jury convicted the petitioner. An intermediate appellate court affirmed, and the state's Supreme Judicial Court denied review.

Scalia begins his analysis by pointing out that the "certificates" are affidavits—written declarations of facts sworn to by the declarant, functionally identical to courtroom testimony, and made under circumstances that would lead one to conclude they would be used at a future trial.[96] Thus, under *Crawford*, unless the analysts were unavailable to testify at trial and petitioner had a prior opportunity to cross-examine them, he was entitled to confront the analysts at trial.[97] The legal analysis is based on the topic of testimony, which, unlike the other topics, derives its information from external sources, here the authority of the forensic analyst, instead of from the nature of the question a case presents."[98]

In Scalia's mind, then, *Melendez-Diaz* featured a "rather straightforward application of [the Court's] holding in *Crawford*," despite "the potpourri of analytic arguments" to the contrary by Massachusetts and the dissenters.[99] "Potpourri of analytic arguments" illustrates the use of metaphor (potpourri, usually meaning a pleasant fragrance produced by several sources) to add color to a sentence. Notwithstanding those arguments, Scalia continues:

> At least this much is entirely clear: In faithfully applying *Crawford* to the facts of this case, we are not overruling 90 years of settled jurisprudence [as the dissent charged]. It is the dissent that seeks to overturn precedent by resurrecting [*Ohio v.*] *Roberts* a mere five years after it was rejected in *Crawford*.[100]

In the second sentence, the metaphor of resurrection makes clear Scalia's point that the majority is properly—even "faithfully"—applying the controlling precedent, *Crawford*, whereas the dissenters seek to exhume a relic the Court buried five years earlier. In Scalia's view, the dissenters—not the majority—are acting irresponsibly. By making this point, he seeks to buttress the argument from testimony and authority with the now familiar argument from relationship and contraries (the *Roberts* rule's incompatibility with the Confrontation Clause) relied on in *Crawford*.

After considering several arguments offered by Massachusetts and the dissenters, Scalia concedes that they may be right that other, perhaps even better, ways to challenge forensic results are available, but "the Constitution guarantees one way: confrontation."[101] An aphorism makes his point: "We do not have license to suspend the Confrontation Clause when a preferable trial strategy is available."[102] To Massachusetts's claim that forensic results, as distinguished from testimony, are not subject to distortion and manipulation that necessitates confrontation, Scalia responds with another aphorism: "Forensic evidence is not uniquely immune from the risk of manipulation."[103] Indeed, he observes that the prospect of confrontation can ensure accuracy in forensic analysis, which may be compromised by pressure to alter evidence to favor the prosecution. Using analogy, he writes: "Like the eyewitness who has fabricated his account to the police, the analyst who provides false results may, under oath in open court, reconsider his false testimony."[104]

Neither could Massachusetts persuade Scalia that the petitioner's ability to subpoena the analysts avoided a Confrontation Clause violation in this case. Using antithesis, he writes:

> [T]he Confrontation Clause imposes a burden on the prosecution to present its witnesses, not on the defendant to bring those adverse witnesses into court. Its value to the defendant is not replaced by a system in which the prosecution presents its evidence via *ex parte* affidavits and waits for the defendant to subpoena the affiants if he chooses.[105]

The use of antithesis in the first sentence emphasizes that the right of confrontation is meant to confer a benefit on the defendant and to impose a burden on the prosecution, not the reverse. In Scalia's mind, the alternative that Massachusetts suggested—the defendant's right to subpoena the analyst's testimony—would shift the burden of presenting prosecution witnesses from prosecution to defense, contrary to the Confrontation Clause.

Finally, Scalia addresses the claim by Massachusetts that requiring forensic analysts to present their test results at trial would make the trial process more burdensome, noting that the Court could not forego the right of confrontation, just as it could not forego the right to a jury trial or the privilege against self-incrimination. Continuing the analogy and closing with a memorable aphorism, he writes, "The Confrontation Clause—like those other constitutional provisions—is binding, and we may not disregard it at our convenience."[106]

Besides, he adds, using a familiar metaphor designed to dispel predictions of gloom and doom, "[p]erhaps the best indication that the sky will not fall after today's decision is that it has not done so already."[107] The sky remains aloft because defendants in drug prosecutions rarely object to the admission of forensic certificates in lieu of live testimony. They see no benefit to be gained by doing so. Thus, Scalia concludes, "there is little reason to believe that our decision today will commence the parade of horribles [Massachusetts] and the dissent predict."[108] The sky-is-falling and parade-of-horribles metaphors are a bit worn, but still apt, because they counter the adverse consequences that Massachusetts claims will result if the Court requires forensic analysts to testify at trial. They also highlight Scalia's contention that such consequences will not flow from the Court's decision because few defendants will insist on confronting live witnesses from the State forensic lab. The Court thus reversed and remanded.

3. *Vernonia School District 47J v. Acton*

A seventh-grader who wanted to play football in the Vernonia, Oregon School District challenged the constitutionality of the District's "Student-Athlete Drug Policy," which authorized random urinalysis of students who participate in its athletic programs.[109] A federal district court upheld the policy, but the US Court of Appeals for the Ninth Circuit reversed, and the Supreme Court granted cert. Justice Scalia wrote for a six-member majority that found the drug-testing program constitutional under the Fourth and Fourteenth Amendments.

At the start of his opinion, Scalia makes a rhetorical choice to note the rural, small-town setting in which the case arises. Then, despite having lived his entire life in and around large cities and not having been a high school athlete, he shows sensitivity for places like Vernonia, writing that there, "[a]s elsewhere in small-town America, school sports play a prominent role in the town's life, and student athletes are admired in their schools and in the community."[110] In this instance, sensitivity was also strategy (*pathos*) because the athletes' visibility in town and at school would figure prominently in the school district's rationale for adopting drug testing and in the Court's rationale for upholding it.

The "expressed purpose" of the drug-testing program, Scalia notes, employing parallelism, is "to prevent student athletes from using drugs, to protect their health and safety, and to provide drug users with assistance programs."[111] His reasoning rests on the topic of comparison and the subtopic of similarity, here the similarity between the school district's drug-testing program for athletes and the requirements of the Fourth Amendment. The testing program was adopted in 1989, a result of the school administration having reached, in the District Court's words, "its wits end" after witnessing rampant, brazen drug use by students and a spike in classroom disruptions and disciplinary actions during the previous few years.[112] The program was limited to athletes because, as Justice Scalia explained, "[n]ot only were student athletes included among the drug users but, as the District Court found, athletes were the leaders of the drug culture," causing administrators to fear an increased risk of sports-related injuries.[113]

Scalia then turns to the constitutional issues the program raises. He begins by reminding the reader that drug tests without probable cause already exist in several settings outside of public schools (e.g., railroad workers after train accidents, certain Customs Service employees, suspected drunk drivers, etc.) when "special needs, beyond the normal need for law enforcement, make the warrant and probable-cause requirement impracticable."[114] And the Court has found "special needs" justifying searches without probable cause in schools.[115]

Nevertheless, Scalia continues, the Court must consider "the nature of the privacy interest upon which the search here at issue intrudes."[116] He observes that public school students "have a lesser expectation of privacy than members of the population generally," as they "are routinely required to submit to various physical examinations, and to be vaccinated against various diseases."[117] And, he stresses, privacy expectations are further reduced for athletes. Using an aphorism and irony, he writes:

> School sports are not for the bashful. They require "suiting up" before each practice or event, and showering and changing afterwards. Public school locker rooms, the usual sites for these activities, are not notable for the privacy they afford.[118]

The aphorism in the first sentence encapsulates the majority's conclusion that privacy interests are reduced for high school athletes, making drug tests for athletes less intrusive than they might be for the general student body. The irony in the last sentence reinforces this point with a dash of wry humor.

Besides surrendering a measure of privacy, high school athletes "voluntarily subject themselves to a degree of regulation even higher than that imposed on students generally."[119] Scalia uses parallelism to corral a large body of information. He writes:

> In Vernonia's public schools, [athletes] must submit to a preseason physical exam . . . , they must acquire adequate insurance coverage or sign an insurance waiver, maintain a minimum grade point average, and comply with any "rules of conduct, dress, training hours and related matters as may be established for each sport by the head coach and athletic director with the principal's approval."[120]

Then, using an analogy, Scalia equates athletes in the Vernonia School District to adults who work in a highly regulated industry, such as the public utility industry. "Somewhat like adults who choose to participate in a 'closely regulated industry,'" he writes, "Students who voluntarily participate in school athletics have reason to expect intrusions upon normal rights and privileges, including privacy."[121] At first glance, the analogy between extracurricular athletic participation and a career decision may seem strained. But recall that an analogy compares two fundamentally different things that, nevertheless, have something in common. The common thread here is a willingness to abide by certain rules in return for enjoying the psychic, social, or material benefits derived from playing a particular sport or working in a particular industry.

Furthermore, not only is the athletes' privacy interest reduced, but the intrusion caused by the drug tests is minimal. Boys produce test samples at a urinal along a wall, fully clothed and observed only from behind, if at all, and girls do so inside a closed stall, "with a female monitor standing outside listening only for sounds of tampering."[122] Therefore, the privacy interest affected by the testing program is "negligible."[123]

Finally, Scalia turns to the school district's interest in curbing drug use among athletes. To underscore that interest, he notes the District Court's findings that before drug testing, "[d]isciplinary actions had reached epidemic proportions . . . "[124] School administrators could have designed a testing program based on individual suspicion, but that alternative was unrealistic. Using a metaphor and antithesis, Scalia writes:

> It may be impracticable, for one thing, simply because the parents who are willing to accept random drug testing for athletes are not willing to accept accusatory drug testing for all students, which transforms the process into a badge of shame.[125]

The badge-of-shame metaphor illuminates a strong argument in favor of suspicionless drug testing of athletes: it makes no assumptions and casts no aspersions, but rather, shows an appropriate concern for health and safety. And one can opt out by choosing not to play a sport. In contrast, suspicion-based testing would likely make assumptions and cast aspersions. Besides, Scalia warns, it assigns to teachers "the new function of spotting and bringing to account drug abuse, a task for which they are ill prepared, and which is not readily compatible with their vocation."[126] Thus, the rhetoric of Justice Scalia's majority opinion exhibits pathos not only for the place of school sports in small towns, but also for three groups that are often on opposite sides in litigation. Those groups include public school administrators, who seek to ensure a safe, orderly learning environment; teachers, who do not wish to be assigned a law enforcement role too; and parents, who may not trust school authorities to operate fairly a suspicion-based drug-testing program. All of these considerations factored into the Court's decision to reverse the Ninth Circuit's decision and remand for further proceedings.

4. *National Treasury Employees Union v. Von Raab*

This case also features a Fourth Amendment challenge to a drug-testing program, but unlike in the previous case, the drug testing here applied to employees of the US Customs Service who sought a transfer or a promotion to certain positions.[127] And in this case, Justice Scalia dissented. Justice Kennedy wrote for a five-member majority that upheld drug testing—without probable cause—of employees who sought positions involving the interdiction of drugs or that required carrying a firearm.[128]

In 1986, the Commissioner of Customs announced a drug-testing program in which submission to testing was made a condition of placement or employment for positions that met one or more of three criteria. The criteria were: (1) direct involvement in drug interdiction or enforcement of related laws; (2) a requirement that the employee carry firearms; and (3) a requirement that the employee handle "classified" material.[129] Customs employees who tested positive for drugs and could offer no satisfactory explanation were subject to dismissal from the Customs Service, but the results could not be shared with any other agency, including prosecutors, without the employee's written consent.[130]

A union of federal employees and a union official challenged the drug-testing program as violating the Fourth Amendment, and a federal district court in Louisiana agreed, enjoining the program. But the US Court of Appeals for the Fifth Circuit reversed, and the Supreme Court granted cert. It upheld the drug tests for employees who were directly involved in drug interdiction or were required to carry firearms, but voided them for employees who handled classified material.[131]

Justice Kennedy began his analysis by stating that the government had "a compelling interest in ensuring that front-line interdiction personnel are physically fit, and have unimpeachable integrity and judgment."[132] He stated that "the public should not bear the risk that employees who may suffer from impaired perception and judgment will be promoted to positions where they may need to employ deadly force."[133] Besides, he continued, Customs employees who are directly involved in drug interdiction or who must carry firearms in the line of duty "have a diminished expectation of privacy in respect to the intrusions occasioned by a urine test."[134] "[S]uccessful performance of their duties depends uniquely on their judgment and dexterity"; therefore, these employees cannot reasonably expect to conceal from their employer information, such as evidence of drug use, that is closely related to their fitness.[135]

Justice Kennedy concluded that the government's interests outweighed personal privacy interests for Customs Service employees "who seek to be promoted to positions that directly involve the interdiction of illegal drugs or that require the incumbent to carry a firearm."[136] Thus, drug testing of those employees was compatible with the Fourth Amendment. But because the record did not define clearly the universe of Customs employees required to handle "classified material," the Court vacated that portion of the Fifth Circuit's decision and remanded for further proceedings.

Justice Scalia penned a dissent in which Justice Stevens joined. Using antithesis to identify the gist of the case, Scalia begins his dissent as follows:

> The issue in this case is not whether Customs Service employees can constitutionally be denied promotion, or even dismissed, for a single instance of unlawful drug use, at home or at work. They assuredly can. The issue here is what steps can constitutionally be taken to *detect* such drug use.[137] [Emphasis in original.]

Besides antithesis, this passage features a rhythmic cadence achieved by employing two longer sentences as bookends for a shorter, more direct sentence. The latter reminds the reader rather emphatically that the Customs Service can lawfully discipline its employees for using illegal drugs, provided that discipline flows from constitutionally permissible methods of detection.

Later, by means of a pungent metaphor, Scalia describes the drug-testing program as "a kind of immolation of privacy and human dignity in symbolic opposition to drug use."[138] The word "immolation," which means to kill or sacrifice by burning, jars the reader, as does the term "human dignity," Justice Brennan's touchstone and an unlikely one for Scalia the textualist and originalist. Both seem hyperbolic in the context of a governmental drug-testing program for a narrow class of employees seeking promotions. To Scalia, though, that program is anathema. His rationale derives from the topic of relationship and the subtopic of contraries because, in his mind, a fundamental incompatibility exists between the Customs Service's drug-testing program and the Fourth Amendment.

He dismisses the majority's reasoning that the Customs Service's compelling interest in ensuring the good judgment and physical fitness of its drug-interdicting and firearms-carrying employees warrants its drug-testing program. Combining antimetabole, antithesis, and a historical reference, he observes: "To paraphrase Churchill, all this contains much that is obviously true, and much that is relevant; unfortunately, what is obviously true is not relevant, and what is relevant is not obviously true."[139] Then, using an analogy to argue that the "compelling interest" claimed by the government is speculative, he writes:

> It is not apparent to me that a Customs Service employee who uses drugs is significantly more likely to be bribed by a drug smuggler, any more than a Customs Service employee who wears diamonds is significantly more likely to be bribed by a diamond smuggler—unless, perhaps, the addiction to drugs is so severe, and requires so much money to maintain, that it would be detectable even without benefit of a urine test.[140]

To buttress that analogy, Scalia follows it with an example of polyptoton, repeating a word to disparage what he sees as the Customs Service's flimsy justification for its drug-testing program. He writes:

> What is absent in the Government's justifications—notably absent, revealingly absent, and as far as I am concerned dispositively absent—is the recitation of *even a single instance* in which any of the speculated horribles actually occurred: an instance, that is, in which the cause of bribe-taking, or of poor aim, or of unsympathetic law enforcement, or of compromise of classified information, was drug use.[141] [Emphasis in original.]

The careful reader will note that polyptoton is not the only "poly" that Scalia uses in the above passage. He also uses polysyndeton, which features the conjunction "or" to link the various "horribles" that, in his view, drug testing will not prevent. By repeating the conjunction, he slows the cadence of the sentence, planting firmly in the reader's mind each "horrible" that the federal government has predicted will occur absent drug testing, but has not shown actually occurred.

Scalia's view did not prevail, though. The Customs Service drug-testing program survived, at least for employees who sought promotions to positions that involved carrying firearms and interdicting drugs.[142]

5. *Johnson v. Transportation Agency, Santa Clara County, Cal.*

Antonin Scalia also dissented in *Johnson*, in which Justice Brennan wrote for the majority.[143] Responding to gender imbalances in its workforce, the Agency devised an affirmative action plan in 1978 that applied to employee promotions, among other things. In choosing a new road dispatcher, the Agency passed over Paul Johnson, a male employee, in favor of Diane Joyce, a female employee. Under the Plan, when filling a vacancy in a job classification in which women were significantly underrepresented (such as road dispatcher), the Agency was authorized to consider as one factor the sex of a qualified applicant. At issue in Mr. Johnson's lawsuit was whether that consideration of gender violated Title VII of the Civil Rights Act of 1964.

Nine candidates were deemed qualified for the job, including Johnson and Joyce; of the nine, seven scored above 70 on their interviews with the hiring board, as Johnson tied for second with a score of 75 and Joyce finished third with a score of 73.[144] After a second interview, Agency supervisors recommended that Johnson be hired, but the Agency's Affirmative Action Coordinator intervened and advised the Director to hire Joyce, which he did. Johnson then filed a complaint with the Equal Employment Opportunity Commission, received a right-to-sue letter, and filed suit.

Justice Brennan first addressed whether underrepresentation of women in Skilled Crafts jobs—the category that included road dispatchers—warranted consideration of the sex of applicants. He pointed out that when the job vacancy at issue arose, none of the Agency's Skilled Craft Workers and just one of its 110 Road Maintenance Workers (Joyce) was a woman.[145] Under those circumstances, he explained, the Agency had reasonably determined that "it was appropriate to consider as one factor the sex of Ms. Joyce in making its decision."[146]

Brennan next considered "whether the Agency Plan unnecessarily trammeled the rights of male employees or created an absolute bar to their advancement."[147] He concluded that it did not, emphasizing that the Plan included numerical goals for increasing job opportunities within the Agency for minorities and women, but no quotas. Instead, it "merely authorize[d] that consideration be given to affirmative action concerns when evaluating qualified applicants."[148] Besides, Brennan added, the Plan was temporary because it was designed to achieve a more diverse work force for the Agency, but not "to maintain a permanent racial and sexual balance."[149] Thus, the majority concluded that the Agency had appropriately taken gender into account as one factor in hiring Ms. Joyce as a road dispatcher. Its Affirmative Action Plan was "fully consistent with Title VII. . . ."[150]

Justice Scalia dissented, joined by Chief Justice Rehnquist and, in part of his dissent, by Justice Byron White. True to his textualism, Scalia begins by quoting Title VII, which prohibits discrimination in compensation, terms, conditions, or privileges of employment based on an array of demographic categories, including sex.[151] He then uses antithesis to express his opposition to the majority's decision. He writes: "The Court today completes the process of converting this [meaning Title VII] from a guarantee that race or sex will *not* be the basis for employment determinations, to a guarantee that it often *will*.[152] [Emphasis in original.]

To Scalia, the Affirmative Action Plan does not exist to remedy past sex discrimination by the Agency; indeed, no such sex discrimination had existed. The latter conclusion reflects Scalia's view that because women had not historically trained for and applied for jobs such as road dispatcher, their extreme underrepresentation in those jobs is not sex discrimination. In other words, he does not regard their historic lack of access as "discrimination" within the meaning of Title VII. But using affirmative action to aid their selection for the jobs surely is.

Scalia's argument originates in the topic of testimony and the subtopic of "laws"; in this instance, the latter refers to the text of Title VII of the 1964 Civil Rights Act, which, in Scalia's view, the Court majority ignores. He sees the Agency's Plan as "imposed racial and sexual tailoring that would . . . give each protected racial and sexual group a governmentally determined 'proper' proportion of each job category."[153] He stresses that the "traditionally segregated job category" in this case is not traditionally segregated in the sense of past exclusion of minorities or women, "but in the sense that, because of longstanding social attitudes, it has not been regarded *by women themselves* as desirable work."[154] [Emphasis in original.] Using antithesis and isocolon, Scalia the textualist chides the majority for straying from the words of Title VII. He writes:

> [T]oday's decision is a demonstration not of stability and order but of the instability and unpredictable expansion which the substitution of judicial improvisation for statutory text has produced.[155]

The antithesis lies in the early reference to "a demonstration not of stability and order, but of the instability and unpredictable expansion . . ." and the isocolon is the juxtaposition of "judicial improvisation" to "statutory text" later in the sentence.[156]

The majority's claim that the Plan does not automatically exclude any qualified candidate from being considered irks Scalia, who is certain that "if there was any minimally qualified applicant from one of the favored groups, [the white male] candidate would be rejected."[157] Indeed, he draws an analogy between the majority's claim and an exchange from Shakespeare's King Henry the Fourth, Part I:

> GLENDOWER: I can call spirits from the vasty Deep.
>
> HOTSPUR: Why, so can I, or so can any man. But will they come when you call for them? Act III, Scene I, lines 53–55.[158]

This analogy may be ill-advised nowadays because the audience for Supreme Court opinions is likely to be less familiar with Shakespeare than its predecessors. Nonetheless, it illustrates Scalia's point that the presence of white males in the candidate pool belied their slim chances of being hired in the face of an affirmative action plan.

Later, using a metaphor ("engine of racism and sexism") and a dose of hyperbole ("practically compelled" race and sex discrimination), Scalia offers a lament for textualism. He writes:

> A statute designed to establish a color-blind and gender-blind workplace has thus been converted into a powerful engine of racism and sexism, not merely *permitting* intentional race- and sex-based discrimination, but often making it, through operation of the legal system, practically compelled.[159] [Emphasis in original.]

Finally, Scalia uses pathos to create sympathy and support for the white working-class men whom he views as the casualties of affirmative action programs. He writes:

> In fact, the only losers in the process are the Johnsons of the country, for whom Title VII has been not merely repealed but actually inverted. The irony is that these individuals—predominantly unknown, unaffluent, unorganized—suffer this injustice at the hands of a Court fond of thinking itself the champion of the politically impotent.[160]

Hyperbole and antithesis are featured in the statement that for men like Paul Johnson, Title VII has been "not merely repealed, but actually inverted." The hyperbole is misleading because the Court did not repeal Title VII, but rather, interpreted it to encompass affirmative action. Polyptoton and parallelism are reflected in the reference to the "unknown," "unaffluent," [and] "unorganized" persons who suffer under Affirmative Action. Irony features prominently in Scalia's charge that the Court imposes "injustice" on politically powerless white, working-class men while it perceives itself as "the champion of the politically impotent."[161] Scalia would have reversed the Ninth Circuit, invalidating the Agency's Affirmative Action Program, but his position commanded just three votes, including his own.

E. Conclusion

Only time will tell if, one-hundred years after his death, Antonin Scalia will be remembered as, in Justice Kagan's words, "one of the most important, most historic figures on the [Supreme] Court."[162] If he is so remembered, his skill as a writer, including his creative use of rhetorical techniques, will have contributed mightily to his enduring legacy. In the meantime, despite its occasional excesses, Scalia's writing bears careful study by contemporary legal writers for its vividness and its creative use of figures of speech.

NOTES

1. R. David Lat, "How Justice Scalia's Writing Style Affected American Jurisprudence," Above the Law, November 21, 2016, accessed December 22, 2016, http://abovethelaw.com/2016/11/how-justice-scalia's-writing-style-affected -american-jurisprudence/.
2. Joan Biskupic, *American Original: The Life and Constitution of Supreme Court Justice Antonin Scalia* (New York: Farrar, Strauss & Giroux, 2009), 13.
3. Ibid., 13–14.
4. Ibid., 15.
5. Bruce Allen Murphy, *Scalia: A Court of One* (New York: Simon & Schuster, 2014), 11.
6. Biskupic, *American Original*, 15.
7. Ibid., 20.
8. Ibid., 21.
9. Ibid.
10. Ibid., 6
11. Ibid., 25.
12. Ibid. See also Murphy, *Scalia: A Court of One*, 21–22.
13. Biskupic, *American Original*, 17.
14. Ibid., 191. See also George Kannar, "The Constitutional Catechism of Antonin Scalia," *Yale Law Journal* 99 (1990): 1297 and Murphy, *Scalia: A Court of One*, 8.
15. Biskupic, *American Original*, 27.
16. Murphy, *Scalia: A Court of One*, 36–37.
17. Biskupic, *American Original*, 27.
18. Ralph A. Rossum, *Antonin Scalia's Jurisprudence: Text and Tradition* (Lawrence, KS: University Press of Kansas, 2006), 3.
19. Biskupic, *American Original*, 31.
20. Rossum, *Antonin Scalia's Jurisprudence*, 3. See also Murphy, *Scalia: A Court of One*, 39.
21. Murphy, *Scalia: A Court of One*, 39.
22. Biskupic, *American Original*, 64.
23. Murphy, *Scalia: A Court of One*, 51–52.
24. Ibid., 55–57.

25. Biskupic, *American Original,* 34.
26. Ibid., 65.
27. Ibid., 80.
28. Ibid., 89.
29. Ibid., 91.
30. Ibid.
31. Ibid., 93.
32. Ibid., 104.
33. Ibid., 108.
34. Ibid., 121.
35. Murphy, *Scalia: A Court of One*, 130–31.
36. Rossum, *Antonin Scalia's Jurisprudence*, 19.
37. Ibid.
38. Ibid.
39. Biskupic, *American Original*, 121.
40. Murphy, *Scalia: A Court of One*, 124.
41. Biskupic, *American Original*, 130.
42. Ibid., 131
43. Ibid., 132.
44. Rossum, *Antonin Scalia's Jurisprudence*, 2.
45. Ibid., 2–3.
46. Richard L. Hasen, *The Justice of Contradictions: Antonin Scalia and the Politics of Disruption* (New Haven, CT: Yale University Press, 2018), 10.
47. Ibid., 20–21.
48. Antonin Scalia, *A Matter of Interpretation: Federal Courts and the Law* (Princeton, NJ: Princeton University Press, 1997), 38; see also Antonin Scalia and Bryan Garner, *Reading Law: The Interpretation of Legal Texts* (St. Paul, MN: Thomson/West, 2012), 435.
49. Antonin Scalia, "Originalism: The Lesser Evil," *University of Cincinnati Law Review* 57 (1989): 857.
50. Ibid., 863.
51. Ibid.
52. Catherine L. Langford, *Scalia v. Scalia: Opportunistic Textualism in Constitutional Interpretation* (Tuscaloosa, AL: University of Alabama Press, 2017), 32.
53. Biskupic, *American Original*, 352.
54. 133 S.Ct. 2675 (2013).
55. Ibid., 2697–98. See also Hasen, *The Justice of Contradictions*, x.
56. 133 S.Ct. 2612 (2013). See Hasen, *The Justice of Contradictions*, x.
57. David A. Schultz and Christopher E. Smith, *The Jurisprudential Vision of Justice Antonin Scalia* (Lanham, MD: Rowman & Littlefield Publishers, 1996), 56. See also Biskupic, *American Original*, 355.
58. 541 U.S. 36 (2004).
59. 557 U.S. 305 (2009).
60. Langford, *Scalia v. Scalia*, 119.
61. Biskupic, *American Original*, 133.
62. Antonin Scalia and Bryan Garner, *Making Your Case: The Art of Persuading Judges* (St. Paul, MN: Thomson/West 2008), 112.
63. Ibid.
64. Antonin Scalia, "A Look Back: 1994 William O. Douglas Lecture Series Transcript," *Gonzaga Law Review* 51 (2016): 598. See also Hasen, *The Justice of Contradictions*, 67.
65. Biskupic, *American Original*, 343.
66. *Lee v. Weisman*, 505 U.S. 577.
67. *Morgan v. Illinois*, 504 U.S. 719 (1992).
68. *Austin v. Michigan Chamber of Commerce*, 494 U.S. 652 (1990).
69. *Webster v. Reproductive Health Services*, 492 U.S. 490 (1989).
70. 541 U.S. 36 (2004).
71. 557 U.S. 305 (2009).

72. 515 U.S. 646 (1995).
73. 489 U.S. 656 (1989).
74. 480 U.S. 616 (1987).
75. 448 U.S. 56 (1980).
76. Ibid., 66.
77. Ibid.
78. 541 U.S. at 42.
79. Ibid., 42–43.
80. Ibid., 50.
81. Ibid., 53–54.
82. Ibid., 60.
83. Ibid., 62.
84. Ibid.
85. Ibid., 63.
86. Ibid., 65–66.
87. Ibid., 65.
88. Ibid.
89. Ibid.
90. Ibid., 68.
91. Ibid.
92. Ibid.
93. 557 U.S. at 306.
94. Ibid., 307.
95. Ibid.
96. Ibid., 310.
97. Ibid. 311.
98. Corbett and Connors, *Classical Rhetoric for the Modern Student*, 4th ed., 112.
99. 557 U.S. at 312.
100. Ibid., 313.
101. Ibid., 318.
102. Ibid.
103. Ibid.
104. Ibid., 319.
105. Ibid., 324–25.
106. Ibid., 325.
107. Ibid.
108. Ibid., 328.
109. 515 U.S. 646 (1995).
110. Ibid., 648.
111. Ibid., 650.
112. Ibid., 649–50.
113. Ibid., 649.
114. Ibid., 653.
115. Ibid.
116. Ibid., 654.
117. Ibid., 656–57.
118. Ibid., 657.
119. Ibid.
120. Ibid.
121. Ibid.
122. Ibid., 658.
123. Ibid.
124. Ibid., 663.
125. Ibid.
126. Ibid., 664.
127. 489 U.S. 656 (1989).

128. Ibid., 679.
129. Ibid., 660–61.
130. Ibid., 663.
131. Ibid., 664–65.
132. Ibid., 670.
133. Ibid., 671.
134. Ibid., 672.
135. Ibid.
136. Ibid., 677.
137. Ibid., 680.
138. Ibid., 681.
139. Ibid., 682.
140. Ibid.
141. Ibid., 683.
142. On the same day that the Court decided *Von Raab*, it also decided *Skinner v. Railway Labor Executives' Association*, 489 U.S. 602 (1989), in which it upheld similar testing of railroad employees involved in train accidents. Justice Scalia joined the majority opinion because of evidence showing drug and alcohol use by railroad employees and a connection between such use and accidents. Six years after *Von Raab* and *Skinner*, he would write the majority opinion that upheld such testing of high school athletes in the *Acton* case. For Scalia, *Skinner* and *Acton* presented the evidence necessary to justify drug testing without probable cause, but *Von Raab* did not.
143. 480 U.S. 616 (1987). Justices Marshall, Blackmun, Powell, and Stevens joined Justice Brennan's opinion. Justice O'Connor wrote separately, but concurred in the judgment.
144. Ibid., 623–24.
145. Ibid., 634.
146. Ibid., 637.
147. Ibid., 637–38.
148. Ibid., 638.
149. Ibid., 640.
150. Ibid., 642.
151. 42 U.S.C. § 2000e-2(a) (2012).
152. 480 U.S. at 658.
153. Ibid., 660.
154. Ibid., 668.
155. Ibid., 672.
156. Ibid., 674.
157. Ibid.
158. Ibid.
159. Ibid., 677.
160. Ibid.
161. Ibid.
162. Lat, "How Justice Scalia's Writing Style Affected American Jurisprudence," Above the Law, November 21, 2016, accessed December 22, 2016, http://abovethelaw.com/2016/11/how-justice-scvalia's-writing-style-affected-american-jurisprudence/ .

Chapter Eight

Rhetoric and the Supreme Court

Past, Present, and Future

A. Voices for the Ages

This book set out to show how classical rhetorical techniques can enhance the persuasiveness of Supreme Court opinions by making their language clear, lively, and memorable. The words of the featured justices achieve that goal, irrespective of accompanying commentary. Indeed, they underscore the Aristotelian aphorism that began the book, namely, that it is not enough to know what to say; one must know how to say it.[1] Despite differences in their writing styles, the five justices knew both what to write and how to write it. The opinions presented here have endured, at least in part, because their authors used invention (logos, pathos, and ethos), arrangement, and style to great effect.

Even today, long after Justice Holmes's Court service and death, Americans recognize and often paraphrase his famous aphorism: "The most stringent protection of free speech would not protect a man in falsely shouting fire in a theatre and causing a panic."[2] Similarly, contemporary discussions of free speech regularly prompt advocates who favor broad protection for speech to quote or paraphrase Robert Jackson's historic aphorism: "Freedom to differ is not limited to things that do not matter much."[3] In both instances, the modern speaker may not recall the author of the original statement, but that speaker understands and embraces the idea it expresses. Time will tell whether Justice Scalia's observation that "[d]ispensing with confrontation because testimony is obviously reliable is akin to dispensing with jury trial because a defendant is obviously guilty" achieves comparable resonance in the public mind.

Whether it does or not, it could still be a wonderful teaching tool. Many years ago, in an undergraduate constitutional law class I taught, a student complained that in numerous cases, the Supreme Court often sided with a "minority view" (e.g., Jehovah's Witnesses, civil rights demonstrators, flag burners, etc.) even though the will of the majority is supposed to govern in the United States. I explained that unlike legislative questions about budget or tax policy, where majority rule applies, questions of individual rights presented in a lawsuit are resolved by judicial interpretations of the pertinent law, not by the views of an electoral majority. To illustrate, I read to the class Justice Jackson's timeless reminder about our constitutional rights: "One's right to life, liberty, and property, to free speech, a free press, freedom of worship and assembly, and other fundamental rights may not be submitted to vote; they depend on the outcome of no elections."[4] Jackson's words answered the student's question beautifully.

The examples cited from Justices Holmes, Jackson, and Scalia show in microcosm what this book has sought to convey in greater detail: words still matter in our increasingly technological world. Indeed, they matter for the ages in Supreme Court opinions.

The justices featured here contributed to the Court's rhetorical legacy in different ways. In broad terms, they represent at least two different writing styles, although all five rejected the magisterial opinion style of the eighteenth and nineteenth centuries in favor of a more personal and conversational format. Justices Holmes, Jackson, and Scalia adorned their writing with aphorisms and literary allusions, along with figures of speech such as metaphors, similes, and anaphora. Their opinions thus illustrate the rhetorical concept of style, which, in the hands of a skilled writer, can turn pedestrian prose into legal literature.

Justice Holmes's opinions stand out for their brevity, directness, and freedom from legal jargon, although their best-known features are aphorisms and metaphors, such as "The Fourteenth Amendment does not enact Mr. Herbert Spencer's Social Statics,"[5] "Every idea is an incitement,"[6] and "Eloquence may set fire to reason."[7] These examples show Holmes as a master at conveying ideas concisely, vividly, and memorably. He had an uncanny ability to express profound thoughts in a few words. His eloquent brevity illustrates Professor Michael Frost's observation that "successful legal arguments depend as much on deliberate stylistic choices as they do on substantive choices."[8]

Holmes's writing also represents a transition from an older, more magisterial style of judicial writing, in which the author issued pronouncements from "on high," to the modern style, in which the author engages the reader in a conversation about a case, thereby revealing the process of resolution. Holmes's opinions exhibited the relative lack of case law and detailed explanation common in the older style, which often made his reasoning opaque.[9]

But they were stylish and flowed in a conversational way, which lent them a distinctly modern flavor too.[10]

A prime example of the conversational style in Holmes's opinions is his dissent in *Lochner v. New York*.[11] In the first sentence, he asserts that the majority has erred by deciding the case according to its fondness for laissez faire economics. Then he confides in the reader:

> If it were a question whether I agreed with that theory, I should desire to study it further and long before making up my mind. But I do not conceive that to be my duty, because I strongly believe that my agreement or disagreement has nothing to do with the right of a majority to embody their opinions in law.[12]

Among Holmes's many contributions to American jurisprudence, then, was a modern writing style that substituted conversation for pronouncement, making the reader of the opinion somewhat more equal in stature to the author in the twentieth century than previously. The Holmesian literary influence is evident in the writings of his successors on the Court.

Robert Jackson shared Holmes's talent for vivid, evocative prose expressed concisely. Holmes relied primarily on aphorisms and metaphors, though, whereas Jackson employed a wide variety of rhetorical techniques. For example, Jackson used parallelism and isocolon to great effect in writing, "A person gets from a symbol the meaning he puts into it, and what is one man's comfort and inspiration is another's jest and scorn."[13] He used polyptoton in warning, "Compulsory unification of opinion achieves only the unanimity of the graveyard."[14] And he dazzled with antimetabole in reminding Americans, "It is not the function of our Government to keep the citizen from falling into error; it is the function of the citizen to keep the Government from falling into error."[15]

Antonin Scalia exhibited both Holmes's academic bent and Jackson's ear for language. Like his two predecessors, he is known as much for his writing as for his jurisprudence. Scalia's opinions feature similes, metaphors, and aphorisms. Perhaps his most memorable, and surely his most humorous, figure of speech is the simile he displayed in a concurring opinion[16] that criticized the much-maligned *Lemon* test, a means for determining whether a particular government program or rule violates the Establishment Clause of the First Amendment.[17] Specifically, Scalia charged that the Court used this test when convenient to do so, but otherwise ignored it, thereby muddying the waters of church-state jurisprudence. According to Scalia,

> Like some ghoul in a late-night horror movie that repeatedly sits up in its grave and shuffles abroad, after being repeatedly killed and buried, *Lemon* stalks our Establishment Clause jurisprudence once again, frightening the little children and school attorneys of Center Moriches Union Free School District.[18]

But style, for all its vividness and imagination, is no substitute for clarity, as the opinions of Justices Black and Brennan show. Beginning in law school, and continuing through his early years on the Court, Hugo Black worked hard to improve his skills as a writer. He never became a great stylist in the mold of Holmes, Jackson, or Scalia, but he did become a first-rate storyteller, as his opinions discussed in chapter 5 demonstrate. His description of the interrogations of the arrestees in *Chambers v. Florida* highlights those storytelling skills, as does his recounting of the colloquy between the accused and the trial judge in *Gideon v. Wainwright* concerning the availability of counsel for an indigent defendant in a felony prosecution. The new legal writer in particular should study Black's *Chambers* and *Gideon* opinions, focusing on the simplicity of their language and the clarity of their arrangement. Those opinions qualify as legal literature not only for their substantive conclusions, but for the elegant storytelling they represent.

William Brennan's writing style, like Hugo Black's, was more functional than flashy, but its clarity and comprehensiveness led to Brennan's authorship of the majority opinions in many landmark cases. Also like Black, Brennan was a master of arrangement, which is especially evident in his majority opinions in *New York Times Company v. Sullivan* and *Frontiero v. Richardson.* The new legal writer should study those opinions as models of storytelling through careful arrangement.

Each of the five featured justices, then, has used classical rhetorical techniques to burnish the literary tradition at the Supreme Court. To be sure, they have done so in different ways. Holmes, Jackson, and Scalia wrote for the legal literati, or at least appeared to, employing figures of speech and literary allusions to add spice and verve to their prose. Black and Brennan, on the other hand, wrote as much for the layperson as for the lawyer, presenting compelling stories and proceeding transparently from introduction to facts to reasoning to conclusion. Taken together, the five featured justices have left professional and amateur students of the Court alike a rich trove of legal literature.

As a result, although this book is not intended as a "how to" manual for legal writing, law students and new lawyers can use the opinions presented here as guides when devising arguments and arranging them for maximum clarity. Experienced lawyers can use these opinions to enhance the power of their writing with timely and evocative figures of speech. Both law students and experienced lawyers can benefit from creating a list or a chart of the various topics and subtopics subsumed under the canon of invention, to remind them of the origins of legal arguments and perhaps help them to generate arguments from time to time. They can also benefit from preparing a list of figures of speech, divided into schemes and tropes, and consulting it when editing a judicial opinion, pleading, law review article, or law school paper.

The opinions presented here can also benefit legal writing teachers by providing models of rhetorical skill to recommend to students, assign as required reading, or discuss in class to illustrate invention, arrangement, and style. Such material fits well in a course segment about the nature and sources of legal arguments or about how legal writing need not be dull. And legal writing teachers can use the opinions to show students how judicial opinion writing has changed over time by comparing them to the work of earlier justices, such as John Marshall or Joseph Story. Teachers of certain history, political science, and communications courses, respectively, can use them for similar ends.

Thus, the literary legacy left by the five featured justices has many beneficiaries. Both novice and veteran legal writers can use the work of these justices as a template for improving their own legal writing. Teachers can use the featured work to emphasize the continuing importance of classical rhetoric to persuasive legal communication. Happily, as the next section will show, the influence of classical rhetoric on Supreme Court opinions did not end with Justice Scalia's death.

B. Passing the Baton

Justices Holmes, Jackson, Black, Brennan, and Scalia no longer walk the halls of the Supreme Court's marble temple. Still, classical rhetoric is alive and well in those halls, thanks to the writing talents of two current members of the Court, Chief Justice John Roberts and Associate Justice Elena Kagan. Although this book focuses primarily on the writings of former justices, Roberts and Kagan deserve honorable, if brief, mention here because, like well-trained sprinters in a 4 × 100-meter relay race, they have accepted the rhetorical baton from their predecessors in a seamless transfer. Since their respective arrivals at the Court (2005 for Roberts and 2011 for Kagan), they have demonstrated mastery of the canons of classical rhetoric, suggesting that for perhaps the next twenty years, the Supreme Court's rhetorical legacy is in capable hands.

One majority opinion written by each justice will illustrate this point and perhaps whet the reader's appetite to read more. The two opinions follow, first one written by Chief Justice Roberts and then one by Justice Kagan. Both cases originated in Florida, but that is all they have in common; the Roberts opinion concerns the limits of free speech for judicial candidates, and the Kagan opinion pertains to the constitutionality of a drug search under the Fourth Amendment.

1. *Williams-Yulee v. Florida Bar*

Chief Justice Roberts's opinion, for a bare majority of five justices, is plainly an appeal to ethos because the case arose from an effort by the Florida Bar to, in his words, "preserve public confidence in the integrity of [its judiciary]. . . ."[19] Toward that end, Florida, along with other states, "prohibit[s] judges and judicial candidates from personally soliciting funds for their [election] campaigns."[20] The question for the Court to answer was "whether the First Amendment permits such restrictions on speech."[21]

Concluding that it does, the Chief Justice draws his reasoning from the topic of comparison and the subtopic of difference, specifically the difference between judges and "politicians." He writes:

> Judges are not politicians, even when they come to the bench by way of the ballot. And a State's decision to elect its judiciary does not compel it to treat judicial candidates like campaigners for political office. A State may assure its people that judges will apply the law without fear or favor—and without having personally asked anyone for money.[22]

Roberts enhances his appeal to ethos with an aphorism ("Judges are not politicians. . . ." and alliteration ("the bench by way of the ballot" and "without fear or favor"), grabbing the reader's attention and holding it.

Having introduced his subject and his thesis, Roberts proceeds, in classical rhetorical fashion, to a discussion of the facts, noting that Canon 7C(1) of Florida's Code of Judicial Conduct prohibits judges and candidates for elected judgeships from "personally solicit[ing] campaign funds"[23] and from "solicit[ing] attorneys for publicly stated support," although they may establish campaign committees to do so.[24] Judicial candidates may also learn the identities of donors to their campaigns and send thank you notes to them.[25]

The Petitioner, Lanell Williams-Yulee, who calls herself "Yulee," ran for a judgeship in Hillsborough County, Florida, in 2009. The letter announcing her campaign stated, "An early contribution of $25, $50, $100, $250, or $500, made payable to 'Lanell Williams-Yulee Campaign for County Judge,' will help raise the initial funds needed to launch the campaign and get our message out to the public."[26] The following sentence directly requested the recipients' financial support in the forthcoming primary election. Yulee signed the letter, mailed it to local voters, and posted it on her campaign's website.

The foray into politics did not end well for Yulee. She lost the primary election to the incumbent, and the Florida Bar Association charged her with violating its Code of Judicial Conduct.[27] She contested the charge on First Amendment grounds, saying she had a right to solicit funds in an election campaign, and the Florida Supreme Court appointed a referee to hold a hearing and recommend a finding. The referee recommended that Williams-Yulee be sanctioned, and the Florida Supreme Court adopted that recommendation.[28] It reasoned that Canon 7C(1) was narrowly tailored to serve the compelling interest of preserving the public's perception of judicial impartiality by insulating judicial candidates from solicitation while allowing alternative means of raising campaign funds.[29]

Moving to his reasoning, Roberts notes that the parties agree Canon 7C(1) restricts speech based on its content, but disagree about the appropriate level of scrutiny to be applied. Emphasizing that "speech about public issues and the qualifications of candidates for elected office commands the highest level of First Amendment protection," he concludes that "a State may restrict the speech of a judicial candidate only if the restriction is narrowly tailored to serve a compelling interest."[30] Then, despite acknowledging that "[t]he Florida Bar faces a demanding task in defending Canon 7C(1) against Yulee's First Amendment challenge," the Chief Justice determines that the Canon advances Florida's "compelling interest in preserving public confidence in the integrity of the judiciary" by "means narrowly tailored to avoid unnecessarily abridging speech."[31] "This is therefore one of the rare cases," he writes, "in which a speech restriction withstands strict scrutiny."[32]

Returning to his ethical theme, Roberts uses polyptoton and alliteration to highlight the justification for that unusual conclusion. "Simply put," he observes, "Florida and most other States have concluded that the public may lack confidence in a judge's ability to administer justice without fear or favor if he comes to office by asking for favors."[33] "Fear or favor," as seen earlier, illustrates alliteration, and the use of "favor" and "favors" in the same sentence shows polyptoton at work. These devices also serve Roberts's goal of preventing elected judges from being beholden to their campaign donors. The reason to apply strict scrutiny here, Roberts continues, is that "the role of judges differs from the role of politicians"; that is, judges are not supposed to be responsive to their supporters in deciding cases, so campaign finance decisions applicable to political officeholders do not apply in judicial elections.[34] Besides, Roberts adds, the risk of undue influence or the appearance thereof is great in judicial elections because the donors are likely to be lawyers or litigants who may appear before the judge to whom they have donated. For the same reason, potential donors whom judicial candidates solicit may fear retaliation if they do not donate.[35]

Defending the Florida Bar's decision to limit the speech of judicial candidates but not their campaign committees, Chief Justice Roberts notes that solicitation by the candidate is different from solicitation by the candidate's committee. Using aphorism and analogy, he writes, "The identity of the solicitor matters, as anyone who has encountered a Girl Scout selling cookies outside a grocery store can attest."[36] The aphorism in the first independent clause ("The identity of the solicitor matters") gets the reader's attention, and the analogy that follows makes Roberts's point plainly. Judicial candidates seeking support for their campaigns may be as difficult for lawyers to resist as Girl Scouts selling cookies are for shoppers outside a supermarket. And the consequences of the former, unlike those of the latter, can be dangerous for justice and democracy. "The same person who signed the fundraising letter might one day sign the judgment," Roberts observes.[37] Once again the Chief Justice uses polyptoton to underscore his point: a judge should never feel beholden to a litigant who donated to the judge's election campaign.

Toward the end of the opinion, Roberts switches from an argument based on the topic of comparison and the subtopic of difference to an argument based on the topic of relationship and the subtopic of antecedent/consequence, here the adverse consequences of an unwise proposal. He rejects Yulee's suggestion that the best means of ensuring the public's confidence in judicial integrity is not to prohibit solicitation by judicial candidates, but instead, to require judges to recuse themselves from cases involving their donors and supporters. Using metaphor, Roberts writes that such an arrangement "could create a perverse incentive for litigants to make campaign contributions to judges solely as a means to trigger their later recusal—a form of peremptory strike against a judge that would enable transparent forum shopping."[38] The "peremptory strike" metaphor (like the forum shopping metaphor) is instantly recognizable to the legal community. Peremptory strikes are permissible when used to remove from the pool prospective jurors suspected of bias. Forum shopping—searching for a congenial court in which to bring one's case—is generally frowned upon and surely would be if it took the form of orchestrated efforts to spur recusals. In other words, Yulee's suggested solution would create an ethical problem instead of solving one.

Thus, in *Williams-Yulee*, the US Supreme Court affirmed the Florida Supreme Court's decision, which sanctioned Yulee for her violation of the personal solicitation ban. Chief Justice Roberts's majority opinion is rich in the influences of classical rhetoric. It appeals to ethos, and it features arguments that derive from "Comparison" ("difference") and "Relationship" (antecedent/consequence"), respectively. Its arrangement proceeds easily from the ethical theme at hand to the facts to the Chief Justice's reasoning and rebuttal of Yulee's arguments to the judgment affirming the Florida Supreme Court. It also employs alliteration, analogy, aphorism, metaphor, and polyptoton to enhance those arguments. Rhetoric lives on in the Chief Justice's chambers.

2. *Florida v. Harris*

Like Chief Justice Roberts, Justice Elena Kagan is no stranger to the techniques of classical rhetoric, as her majority opinion in *Florida v. Harris* shows.[39] Her reasoning, for a unanimous Court, derives from the topic of comparison, like the Roberts opinion in *Williams-Yulee*, but unlike that opinion, draws on the subtopic of similarity instead of difference. In this case, the similarity is between the standard for achieving probable cause from informant-provided information and the standard for doing so from information obtained by a dog sniff. At issue in *Harris* was how to determine if the "alert" of a drug-detection dog, during a traffic stop, furnished probable cause to search a vehicle. The Florida Supreme Court had held that in every case, the State must present, in Justice Kagan's words, "an exhaustive set of records, including a log of the dog's performance in the field, to establish the dog's reliability."[40] Justice Kagan rejects that view, finding it "inconsistent with the 'flexible, common-sense standard' of probable cause" that applies to information obtained from informants.[41]

The underlying facts were unremarkable. A Florida K-9 officer stopped a truck bearing an expired license plate. On approaching the driver's side door, he noticed that the driver was "unable to sit still, shaking, and breathing rapidly"; an open can of beer sat in the cup holder.[42] The officer requested permission to search the truck, but the driver refused, so the officer retrieved his canine partner from the patrol car and walked the dog around the truck. The dog, which was trained to detect several drugs, alerted at the driver's side door.[43] A subsequent search did not reveal any drugs the dog was trained to detect, but instead revealed numerous ingredients for making methamphetamine, which resulted in Harris's arrest.

Harris moved to suppress the evidence found in his truck, arguing that the dog's alert had not given the officer probable cause to search. At a hearing on the motion, the officer testified about his—and "Aldo" the dog's—training in drug detection; Monthly Canine Detection Training Logs showed that Aldo had performed "satisfactorily" (the higher of two possible assessment standards) in each training session.[44] On cross-examination, the officer conceded that Aldo's one-year certification from "Drug Beat," a private company that trains and certifies K-9 dogs, had expired, but he noted that Florida did not require such certification. The officer also conceded that he did not maintain complete records of Aldo's performance in the field, just records of alerts that resulted in arrests. The trial court concluded that probable cause for the search existed, and an intermediate appellate court affirmed, but the Florida Supreme Court reversed, holding that the State must present evidence of the dog's performance history, including records that showed how often the dog had alerted in the field without drugs having been found.[45]

Beginning her analysis, Justice Kagan shows her familiarity with classical rhetoric. Arrangement is reflected in a smooth progression from presenting the facts to discussing the current standard for establishing probable cause regarding informant-supplied evidence to analyzing why the same standard should govern dog-sniff evidence too. The logos element of invention is reflected in her effort to devise one test for achieving probable cause from information provided by both sources. She describes the test for probable cause to conduct a search as a "practical and common-sensical standard" based on "the totality of the circumstances."[46] She writes:

> We have rejected rigid rules, bright-line tests, and mechanistic inquiries in favor of a more flexible, all-things-considered approach. In [*Illinois v.*] *Gates*, for example, we abandoned our old test for assessing the reliability of informants' tips because it had devolved into a "complex superstructure of evidentiary and analytical rules," any one of which, if not complied with, would derail a finding of probable cause. We lamented the development of a list of "inflexible, independent requirements applicable in every case." Probable cause, we emphasized, is a fluid concept—turning on the assessment of possibilities, in particular factual contexts—not readily, or even usefully, reduced to a neat set of legal rules.[47]

Besides the logos evident in Justice Kagan's reasoning for applying the same probable-cause standard to both informant-provided evidence and dog sniffs is an appeal to ethos. The latter establishes her credibility by showing the practicality of the test she favors, which already applies to informant-supplied information. Several figures of speech are present too, including parallelism and tricolon ("rigid rules, bright-line tests, and mechanistic inquiries"), along with the analogy of dog sniffs to informants' tips. She also uses hyperbole—in the form of slightly exaggerated verbs such as "abandoned," "derail," and "lamented"—to emphasize that the Court has replaced its old, rigid standard with a new, flexible one for evaluating whether informants' tips produce probable cause. Later, instead of writing that the Florida Supreme Court departed from or failed to apply the newer standard in this case, she writes that the Florida Court "flouted" it, indicating open disregard, not inadvertence or excusable error.

Noting that under the Florida Court's rule, "[n]o matter how much other proof the State offers of the dog's reliability, the absent field performance records will preclude a finding of probable cause," Justice Kagan characterizes that rule as "the antithesis of a totality-of-the-circumstances analysis."[48] She adds,

> It is, indeed, the very thing we criticized in *Gates* when we overhauled our method for assessing the trust-worthiness of an informant's tip. A gap as to any one matter, we explained, should not sink the State's case; rather, that "deficiency . . . may be compensated for, in determining the overall reliability of a tip, by a strong showing as to . . . other indicia of reliability."[49]

Justice Kagan chooses her words carefully to magnify the Florida Supreme Court's deviation from the probable-cause standard announced in *Gates*. Besides referring to the Florida Court's reasoning as the "antithesis" of the proper standard, she again uses hyperbole—in the form of a slightly overheated verb—to remind the Florida Court that *Gates* had "overhauled" the standard for establishing probable cause based on informants' tips. Then she stresses that because the Florida Court had "flouted" the overhaul, it had allowed "a gap as to any one matter" concerning a K-9 dog's reliability to "sink" (another vivid verb) the State's case despite a strong showing of reliability based on other indicators. In short, the State's case could fail, despite the dog's reliability, because the Florida Court plainly disregarded the governing standard.

In the future, Justice Kagan continues, the State can establish the dog's reliability by showing that an appropriate organization certified the dog after suitable testing or, absent certification, that "the dog has recently and successfully completed a training program that evaluated his proficiency in locating drugs."[50] If the State makes such a showing and the defense fails to challenge it, the trial court should find probable cause; otherwise, the court should weigh the competing evidence. Summing up, Justice Kagan writes:

> The question—similar to every inquiry into probable cause—is whether all the facts surrounding a dog's alert, viewed through the lens of common sense, would make a reasonably prudent person think that a search would reveal contraband or evidence of a crime. A sniff is up to snuff when it meets that test.[51]

A metaphorical "lens of commonsense" in the first sentence and a playful bit of alliteration in the final sentence ("a sniff is up to snuff") enliven an otherwise mundane discussion of probable cause.

Under the Supreme Court's new standard, as evidenced by the monthly training logs, Aldo was a reliable detector of drugs when Mr. Harris's case arrived in the trial court. Accordingly, the Court concludes that the officer had probable cause to search the truck, thereby reversing the decision below.

Like Chief Justice Roberts's opinion in *Williams-Yulee*, Justice Kagan's opinion in *Harris* makes ample use of classical rhetoric. It relies on logos, emphasizing adherence to a common-sense standard for determining probable cause to search in dog-sniff cases. Ethos is also at work, though, because the practicality of the standard the opinion announces likely enhances its credibility with readers. Finally, style is evident in the forms of parallelism, tricolon, hyperbole, metaphor, and alliteration, which add flavor to Justice Kagan's reasoning.

Perhaps the most important similarity between the Roberts and Kagan opinions, however, is that they exhibit a measure of rhetorical verve and panache despite being majority opinions, which invariably subordinate self-expression to the building of consensus or, failing that, a majority. Both opinions are highly professional, yet include vibrant and occasionally playful language. The reader can anticipate even more vibrancy and playfulness in dissents by these two justices. Thus, as long as Chief Justice Roberts and Justice Kagan are on the bench, the Supreme Court's rhetorical legacy will be in good hands.

C. Conclusion

Lawyers, law professors, and the subset of social scientists and historians who study the Supreme Court all have occasion to ponder why certain opinions (and opinion writers) have attained iconic status. But practicing lawyers are too preoccupied with clients and cases to consider this question as carefully as they might like. Even lawyers who developed an interest in rhetoric while in school are likely to find that the daily demands of drafting bills, prosecuting criminal defendants, or representing an environmental organization or utility companies leave little time for pursuing that interest. An occasional continuing legal education seminar may touch on rhetoric, but lawyers often feel pressured to attend only those seminars most relevant to their areas of practice.

Most law professors sidestep rhetoric too because their teaching and scholarship usually focus on decisions reached, doctrines followed, modified, or rejected, and policies reflected in the Court's decisions rather than the precise words used. For these professors, the "wall" of separation between church and state or the "fruit-of-the-poisonous-tree" doctrine is more important for how it affects Establishment Clause or Fourth Amendment jurisprudence than for how it affects persuasion.

Social scientists who study the Court are even farther removed from the words than law professors are. For example, much contemporary political science scholarship about the Court collects large numbers of the justices' votes in various case categories over time and measures, via statistical techniques, the effects of certain "independent variables" (e.g., personal policy preferences, a desire to preserve the Court's institutional integrity, attachment to precedent, etc.) on those votes.[52] One need not focus on the words in Supreme Court opinions to investigate these types of questions. The words are only relevant to the extent that they reveal a justice's vote for or against affirmative action, same-sex marriage, or restrictions on gun ownership, for example. Put another way, the "data" on which political scientists rely as the raw materials for their scholarly work are the justices' votes, not their words.

Therefore, this book has sought to fill a void in literature about the Court. It begins from the premise that—notwithstanding the prominence of doctrine, ideology, and social science methodology—the words still matter in Supreme Court opinions. Indeed, they are the coin of the realm for the justices, whose business is persuasion. Because the words are so important, the rhetorical techniques that can enhance them, enliven them, and make them persuasive are worthy of greater attention by anyone who studies the Supreme Court or whose work the Court affects. Doctrines and policies surely contribute to the lasting power of Supreme Court opinions, but so does the author's rhetorical fluency. This book shows that many of the most memorable opinions are the work of authors who were talented rhetoricians.

Indeed, those opinions are memorable—at least in part—*because* the justices who wrote them were talented rhetoricians. Their rhetorical skill has crafted solutions to momentous disputes, whose resolution, in turn, has shaped the contours of the American political community for generations.

Accordingly, law professors, as well as social scientists and historians who study the Supreme Court, can use the opinions presented here to better appreciate how classical rhetoric can enhance the persuasive power of Court opinions. Law students and practicing lawyers can use them to learn rhetorical techniques that will enhance the persuasiveness of their own writing. The justices who wrote those opinions have much to teach both novice and veteran legal writers.

NOTES

1. Aristotle, *On Rhetoric*, Trans. W. Rhys Roberts (New York: Barnes & Noble Classics, 2005), Bk. 3, Ch. 1, p. 397.
2. *Schenck v. United States,* 249 U.S. at 52.
3. *West Virginia State Board of Education v. Barnette,* 319 U.S. at 642.
4. Ibid., 638.
5. *Lochner v. New York*, 198 U.S. at 75.
6. *Gitlow v. New York*, 268 U.S. at 673.
7. Ibid.
8. Michael Frost, "Greco-Roman Analysis of Metaphoric Reasoning," *Legal Writing: Journal of the Legal Writing Institute* 2 (1996): 128.
9. William D. Popkin, *Evolution of the Judicial Opinion: Institutional and Individual Styles* (New York: NYU Press, 2007), 152. According to Professor Popkin, Holmes's style "was ideally suited to a transitional period of declining faith in judicial ability to access first principles (associated with the growing influence of Legal Realism) while the judge still remained anchored in the older formalist vision of the law, in which courts declared the law."
10. Sheldon M. Novick, *Honorable Justice: The Life of Oliver Wendell Holmes* (Boston, MA: Little, Brown, and Co., 1989), 256–57.
11. 198 U.S. 45 (1905).
12. Ibid., 75.
13. *West Virginia State Board of Education v. Barnette*, 319 U.S. at 632–33.
14. Ibid., 641.
15. *American Communications Association v. Douds*, 339 U.S. at 442–43.
16. *Lamb's Chapel v. Center Moriches Union Free School District*, 508 U.S. 384 (1993).
17. The *Lemon* test derives from the Supreme Court's decision in *Lemon v. Kurtzman*, 403 U.S. 602 (1971). A challenged statute satisfies the test if (1) it has a secular purpose; (2) its principal or primary effect neither advances nor inhibits religion; and (3) it does not foster an excessive entanglement between church and state. Ibid., 612–13.
18. *Lamb's Chapel*, 508 U.S. at 398.
19. 135 S. Ct. at 1662.
20. Ibid.
21. Ibid.
22. Ibid.
23. Ibid., 1663.
24. Ibid.
25. Ibid., 1663.
26. Ibid., 1663–64.
27. Ibid., 1664.

28. Ibid., 1665.
29. Ibid.
30. Ibid., 1666.
31. Ibid.,
32. Ibid.
33. Ibid.
34. Ibid., 1667.
35. Ibid., 1667–68.
36. Ibid., 1669.
37. Ibid.
38. Ibid., 1672.
39. 568 U.S. 237 (2013).
40. Ibid., 240.
41. Ibid. (quoting *Illinois v. Gates*, 462 U.S. 213 [1983]).
42. Ibid.
43. Ibid.
44. Ibid., 2441–42.
45. Ibid., 242–43.
46. Ibid., 244.
47. Ibid., citing *Gates*, 462 U.S. at 232, 235.
48. Ibid., 245.
49. Ibid.
50. Ibid., 247.
51. Ibid., 248.
52. Some examples of contemporary political science scholarship about the Supreme Court include Matthew E. K. Hall, *What Justices Want: Goals and Personality on the U.S. Supreme Court* (New York: Cambridge University Press, 2018); Richard L. Pacelle, Jr., Brett W. Curry, and Bryan W. Marshall, *Decision Making by the Modern Supreme Court* (New York: Cambridge University Press, 2011); and Thomas G. Hansford and James G. Spriggs, II, *The Politics of Precedent on the Supreme Court* (Princeton, NJ: Princeton University Press, 2006).

Bibliography

Abrams v. United States, 250 U.S. 616 (1919).
Adams Theatre Co. v. Keenan, 96 A.2d 519 (1953).
Adamson v. California, 332 U.S. 46 (1947).
Aldisert, Ruggero. *Opinion Writing*, 3rd ed. (Durham, NC: Carolina Academic Press, 2012).
Alschuler, Albert W. *Law Without Values: The Life, Work, and Legacy of Justice Holmes* (Chicago: University of Chicago Press, 2000).
Alton, Stephen R. "Loyal Lieutenant, Able Advocate: The Role of Robert H. Jackson in Franklin Roosevelt's Battle with the Supreme Court," *William & Mary Bill of Rights Journal* 5 (1997): 527–618.
American Communications Association v. Douds, 339 U.S. 382 (1950).
Aristotle. *On Rhetoric*, Trans. H. Rhys Roberts (New York: Barnes & Noble Classics, 2005).
Austin v. Michigan Chamber of Commerce, 494 U.S. 652 (1990).
Baker, Liva. *The Justice from Beacon Hill: The Life and Times of Oliver Wendell Holmes* (New York: HarperCollins, 1991).
Baker v. Carr, 369 U.S. 186 (1962).
Ball, Howard. *Hugo Black: Cold Steel Warrior* (New York: Oxford University Press, 1996).
Barrett, John Q. "Albany in the Life Trajectory of Robert H. Jackson," *Albany Law Review* 68 (2005): 513–537.
Beauharnais v. Illinois, 343 U.S. 250 (1952).
Berger, Linda. "What Is the Sound of a Corporation Speaking? How the Cognitive Theory of Metaphor Can Help Lawyers Shape the Law," *Journal of the Association of Legal Writing Directors* 2 (2004): 169–208.
Berkey v. Third Avenue Railway Company, 155 N.E. 58 (1926).
Betts v. Brady, 316 U.S. 455 (1942).
Biskupic, Joan. *American Original: The Life and Constitution of Supreme Court Justice Antonin Scalia* (New York: Farrar, Strauss & Giroux, 2009).
Bosmajian, Haig. *Metaphor and Reason in Judicial Opinions* (Carbondale, IL: Southern Illinois University Press, 1992).
Bradwell v. State of Illinois, 16 Wall. 130 (1873).
Brennan, William J., Jr. "Reason, Passion, and 'The Progress of the Law,'" *Cardozo Law Review* 10 (1988): 3–23.
Brown v. Allen, 344 U.S. 443 (1953).
Buck v. Bell, 274 U.S. 200 (1927).
Cather, Willa. *My Antonia* (New York: Penguin Classics, 2014).
Chafee, Zechariah. "Freedom of Speech in Wartime," *Harvard Law Review* 32 (1919): 932–973.

Chambers v. Florida, 309 U.S. 227 (1940).

Clark, Hunter R. "In Memoriam: The Pulse of Life in Justice Brennan's Jurisprudence," *Drake Law Review* 46 (1997): i–xxiv.

Choper, Jesse H., ed. *The Supreme Court and Its Justices* (Chicago: American Bar Association Publishing, 2000).

Cicero, Marcus Tullius. *De Oratore*, Trans. H. Rackham (Cambridge, MA: Harvard University Press, 1942).

Colegrove v. Green, 328 U.S. 459 (1946).

Connors, Robert J., Ede, Lisa S., and Lunsford, Andrea A. *Essays on Classical Rhetoric and Modern Discourse* (Carbondale, IL: Southern Illinois University Press, 1984).

Corbett, Edward P. J., and Connors, Robert J. *Classical Rhetoric for the Modern Student*, 4th ed. (New York: Oxford University Press, 1999).

———. *Classical Rhetoric for the Modern Student*, 2nd ed. (New York: Oxford University Press, 1971).

Crawford v. Washington, 541 U.S. 36 (2004).

Currie, David P., "The Constitution in the Supreme Court: 1910–1921," *Duke Law Journal* 34 (1985): 1111–1162.

Debs v. United States, 249 U.S. 211 (1919).

Desmond, Charles S., Freund, Paul A., Stewart, Potter, and Shawcross, Lord. *Mr. Justice Jackson: Four Lectures in His Honor* (New York: Columbia University Press, 1969).

Domnarski, William. *The Great Justices 1941–1954: Black, Douglas, Frankfurter and Jackson in Chambers* (Ann Arbor, MI: University of Michigan Press, 1996).

Dozier, Curtis, and Honeycutt, Lee H., eds. Quintilian. *Institutes of Oratory*, Trans. John Selby Watson (Published by the Editors, 2015).

Dunne, Gerald T. *Hugo Black and the Judicial Revolution* (New York: Simon & Schuster, 1977).

Edwards, Linda H. *Readings in Persuasion: Briefs That Changed the World* (New York: Wolters Kluwer 2012).

Eisler, Kim Isaac. *A Justice for All: William J. Brennan, Jr. and the Decisions That Transformed America* (New York: Simon & Schuster, 1993).

Feldman, Noah. *Scorpions: The Battles and Triumphs of FDR's Great Supreme Court Justices* (New York: Twelve, Hatchett Book Group, Inc. 2010).

Ferguson, Robert A. "Holmes and the Judicial Figure," *University of Chicago Law Review* 55 (1988): 506–547.

Florida v. Harris, 133 S. Ct. 1050 (2013).

Frank, John P. "Hugo Black: He Has Joined the Giants," in Jesse H. Choper, ed., *The Supreme Court and Its Justices*, 2nd ed. (Chicago: American Bar Association Publishing, 2000), 162–174.

Frank v. Mangum, 237 U.S. 309 (1915).

Freund, Paul A. *On Law and Justice* (Cambridge, MA: Harvard University Press, 1968).

Frontiero v. Richardson, 411 U.S. 677 (1973).

Frost, Michael H. *Introduction to Classical Legal Rhetoric: A Lost Heritage* (Burlington, VT: Ashgate Publishing Company, 2005).

———. "Greco-Roman Analysis of Metaphoric Reasoning," *Legal Writing: Journal of the Legal Writing Institute* 2 (1996): 113–141.

Garner, Bryan A. *Garner on Language and Writing* (Chicago: American Bar Association, 2009).

Gerhart, Eugene C. *Robert H. Jackson: Country Lawyer, Supreme Court Justice, America's Advocate* (Buffalo, NY: William S. Hein & Co., 2003).

Gitlow v. New York, 268 U.S. 652 (1925).

Grey, Thomas C. "Holmes and Legal Pragmatism," *Stanford Law Review* 41 (1989): 787–870.

Griswold v. Connecticut, 381 U.S. 479 (1965).

Halberstam, David, "The Common Man as Uncommon Man," in Joshua E. Rosenkranz and Bernard Schwartz, eds. *Reason and Passion: Justice Brennan's Enduring Influence* (New York: W.W. Norton and Company, 1997), 22–30.

Hall, Matthew E. K. *What Justices Want: Goals and Personality on the U.S. Supreme Court* (New York: Cambridge University Press, 2018).
Hammer v. Dagenhart, 247 U.S. 251 (1918).
Hansford, Thomas G., and Spriggs, James G., II. *The Politics of Precedent on the Supreme Court* (Princeton, NJ: Princeton University Press, 2006).
Hasen, Richard L. *The Justice of Contradictions: Antonin Scalia and the Politics of Disruption* (New Haven, CT: Yale University Press, 2018).
Hemingway, Ernest. *For Whom the Bell Tolls* (New York: Charles Scribner's Sons, 1968).
Hentoff, Nat. "Profiles: The Constitutionalist," *New Yorker*, March 12, 1990, 45–46.
Hockett, Jeffrey D. *New Deal Justice: The Constitutional Jurisprudence of Hugo L. Black, Felix Frankfurter and Robert H. Jackson* (Lanham, MD: Rowman & Littlefield, 1996).
Holmes, Oliver Wendell, Jr. *The Common Law* (Boston: Little, Brown, and Co., 1881, 1923).
Howe, Mark DeWolfe, ed. *The Occasional Speeches of Justice Oliver Wendell Holmes* (Cambridge, MA: Harvard University Press, 1962).
Illinois v. Gates, 462 U.S. 213 (1983).
In re Pillo, 93 A.2d 176 (1952).
Irons, Peter. *Brennan vs. Rehnquist: The Battle for the Constitution* (New York: Alfred A. Knopf, 1994).
Jackson, Robert H. "Final Report to the President Concerning the Nurnberg War Crimes Trial," *Temple Law Quarterly* 20 (1946): 338–344.
Jaffe, Louis L. "Mr. Justice Jackson," *Harvard Law Review* 68 (1955): 940–996.
Jewell, Lucille A. "Old School Rhetoric and New School Cognitive Science: The Enduring Power of Logocentric Categories," *Legal Communication & Rhetoric: Journal of the Association of Legal Writing Directors* 13 (Fall 2016): 39–77.
Johnson v. Transportation Agency, Santa Clara County, Cal., 480 U.S. 616 (1987).
Johnson v. United States, 333 U.S. 10 (1948).
Kannar, George. "The Constitutional Catechism of Antonin Scalia," *Yale Law Journal* 99 (1990): 1297–1357.
Kapgan, Yury. "Of Golf and Ghouls: The Prose Style of Antonin Scalia," *Legal Writing: The Journal of the Legal Writing Institute* 9 (2003): 71–107.
Keith, William M., and Lundberg, Christian O. *The Essential Guide to Rhetoric* (Boston: Bedford/St. Martin's, 2008).
Kelley, Patrick J. "The Life of Oliver Wendell Holmes, Jr.," *Washington University Law Quarterly* 68 (1990): 429–483.
Kennedy, George A. *Classical Rhetoric and Its Christian and Secular Tradition from Ancient to Modern Times*, 2nd ed. (Chapel Hill, NC: University of North Carolina Press, 1999).
Kennedy, John F. *Inaugural Address*, January 20, 1961.
Korematsu v. United States, 323 U.S. 214 (1944).
Lamb's Chapel v. Center Moriches Union Free School District, 508 U.S. 384 (1993).
Langford, Catherine L. *Scalia v. Scalia: Opportunistic Textualism in Constitutional Interpretation* (Tuscaloosa, AL: University of Alabama Press, 2017).
Lat, R. David. "How Justice Scalia's Writing Style Affected American Jurisprudence," Above the Law, November 21, 2016, http://abovethelaw.com/2016/11/how-justice-scalias-writing-style-affected-american-jurisprudence.
Lavine, Linda, and Saunders, Kurt M. "Thinking Like a Rhetor," *Journal of Legal Education* 43 (1993): 108–122.
Lee v. Weisman, 505 U.S. 577 (1992).
Lewis, Anthony. "The Press: Free but Not Exceptional," in Joshua E. Rosenkranz and Bernard Schwartz, eds. *Reason and Passion: Justice Brennan's Enduring Influence* (New York: W.W. Norton and Company, 1997), 53–63.
Lief, Alfred. *Representative Opinions of Mr. Justice Holmes* (New York: Vanguard Press, 1931).
———. *The Dissenting Opinions of Mr. Justice Holmes* (New York: Vanguard Press, 1929).
Lincoln, Abraham. *Second Inaugural Address*, March 4, 1865.
Lochner v. New York, 198 U.S. 45 (1905).
Malloy v. Hogan, 378 U.S. 1 (1964).

Marian, David E. *The Jurisprudence of Justice: William J. Brennan, Jr.* (Lanham, MD: Rowman & Littlefield Publishers, Inc., 1997).
McCollum v. Board of Education, 333 U.S. 203 (1948).
Michelman, Frank I. *Brennan and Democracy* (Princeton, NJ: Princeton University Press, 1999).
Minersville School District v. Gobitis, 310 U.S. 586 (1940).
Moore v. Dempsey, 261 U.S. 86 (1923).
Morgan v. Illinois, 504 U.S. 719 (1992).
Murphy, Bruce Allen. *Scalia: A Court of One* (New York: Simon & Schuster, 2014).
Murphy, James J., Katula, Richard A., Hill, Forbes I., and Ochs, Donovan J. *A Synoptic History of Classical Rhetoric*, 3rd ed. (Mahwah, NJ: Lawrence Erlbaum Associates, 2003).
Murphy, James J., ed. *The Rhetorical Tradition and Modern Writing* (New York: Modern Language Association of America, 1982).
Nater, Swen, and Gallimore, Ronald. *You Haven't Taught Until They Have Learned: John Wooden's Teaching Principles and Practices* (Morgantown, WV: Fitness Information Technology, 2010).
Newman, Roger K. *Hugo Black: A Biography* New York: Fordham University Press, 1997).
New York Times Co. v. Sullivan, 376 U.S. 254 (1964).
New York Times Co. v. United States, 403 U.S. 713 (1971).
Novick, Sheldon M. *Honorable Justice: The Life of Oliver Wendell Holmes* (Boston: Little, Brown, and Co., 1989).
Obama, Barack, *Remarks at the 50th Anniversary of the Selma Marches*, Selma, AL, March 7, 2015.
O'Brien, David M. *Justice Robert Jackson's Unpublished Opinion in Brown v. Board* (Lawrence, KS: The University Press of Kansas, 2017).
Ohio v. Roberts, 448 U.S. 56 (1980).
Oseid, Julie. *Communicators in Chief: Lessons in Persuasion from Five Eloquent American Presidents* (Durham, NC: Carolina Academic Press, 2017).
Pacelle, Richard L., Jr., Curry, Brett W., and Marshall, Bryan W. *Decision Making by the Modern Supreme Court* (New York: Cambridge University Press, 2011).
Phelps, Theresa Godwin. "The New Legal Rhetoric," *Southwestern Law Journal* 40 (1986): 1089–1102.
Philips, Harlan, ed. *The Reminiscences of Robert H. Jackson* (New York: Columbia University Oral History Research Office, 1955).
Popkin, William D. *Evolution of the Judicial Opinion: Institutional and Individual Styles* (New York: NYU Press, 2007).
Posner, Richard A. *Law and Literature*, 3rd ed. (Cambridge, MA: Harvard University Press, 2009).
———. *Law and Literature: A Misunderstood Relation* (Cambridge, MA: Harvard University Press, 1988).
Rappaport, Bret. "Using the Elements of Rhythm, Flow, and Tone to Create a More Effective and Persuasive Acoustic Experience in Legal Writing," *Legal Writing: The Journal of the Legal Writing Institute* 16 (2010): 65–115.
Ray, Laura Krugman. "Judicial Personality: Rhetoric and Emotion in Supreme Court Opinions," *Washington & Lee Law Review* 59 (2002): 193–234.
———. "A Law Clerk and His Justice: What William Rehnquist Did Not Learn from Robert Jackson," *Indiana Law Review* 29 (1996): 535–592.
Reed v. Reed, 404 U.S. 71 (1971).
Regents of the University of California v. Bakke, 438 U.S. 265 (1978).
Reimann, Matthias. "Why Holmes?" *Michigan Law Review* 88 (1990): 1908–1924.
Robbins, Kristen K. "Philosophy vs. Rhetoric in Legal Education: Understanding the Schism Between Doctrinal and Legal Writing Faculty," *Journal of the Association of Legal Writing Directors* 3 (2006): 108–128.
———. "Paradigm Lost: Recapturing Classical Rhetoric to Validate Legal Reasoning," *Vermont Law Review* 27 (2003): 483–563.

Robbins-Tiscione, Kristen K. *Rhetoric for Legal Writers* (St. Paul, MN: West Publishing Company, 2009).
Rosenkranz, E. Joshua, Horowitz, Morton, O'Hearn, Daniel, Schotland, Roy, and Wald, Patricia. "Remembering a Constitutional Hero," *New York Law School Law Review* 43 (1999): 13–39.
Rosenkranz, E. Joshua, and Schwartz, Bernard, eds. *Reason and Passion: Justice Brennan's Enduring Influence* (New York: W.W. Norton and Company, 1997).
Rossum, Ralph A. *Antonin Scalia's Jurisprudence: Text and Tradition* (Lawrence, KS: University Press of Kansas, 2006).
Scalia, Antonin. "A Look Back": William O. Douglas Lecture Series Transcript, *Gonzaga Law Review* 51 (2016): 583–599.
———. *A Matter of Interpretation: Federal Courts and the Law* (Princeton, NJ.: Princeton University Press, 1997).
———. "Originalism: The Lesser Evil," *University of Cincinnati Law Review* 57 (1983): 849–865.
———. and Garner, Bryan A. *Reading Law: The Interpretation of Legal Texts* (St. Paul, MN: Thomson/West, 2012).
———. *Making Your Case: the Art of Persuading Judges* (St. Paul, MN: Thomson/West, 2008).
Schenck v. United States, 249 U.S. 47 (1919).
Schultz, David A. and Smith, Christopher E. *The Jurisprudential Vision of Justice Antonin Scalia* (Lanham, MD: Rowman & Littlefield Publishers, 1996).
Schwartz, Bernard, "How Justice Brennan Changed America," in Joshua E. Rosenkranz and Bernard Schwartz, eds, *Reason and Passion: Justice Brennan's Enduring Influence* (New York: W.W. Norton and Company), 31–44.
Shelby County v. Holder, 133 S. Ct. 2612 (2013).
Sherman, Michael, Sessions, Gene, and Potash, P. Jeffrey. *Freedom and Unity: A History of Vermont* (Barre, VT: Vermont Historical Society, 2004).
Simon, James F. *The Antagonists: Hugo Black, Felix Frankfurter and Civil Liberties in Modern America* (New York: Touchstone/Simon & Schuster, 1989).
Smith, Michael R. *Advanced Legal Writing: Theories and Strategies in Persuasive Writing*, 3rd ed. (New York: Wolters Kluwer, 2013).
———. "Levels of Metaphor in Persuasive Legal Writing," *Mercer Law Review* 58 (2007): 919–947.
———. "Rhetoric Theory and Legal Writing: An Annotated Bibliography," *Journal of the Association of Legal Writing Directors* 3 (2006): 129–144.
Smith v. California, 361 U.S. 147 (1959).
Stanley v. Illinois, 405 U.S. 645 (1972).
State v. True, 98 A.2d 881 (1953).
Stern, Seth, and Wermiel, Stephen. *Justice Brennan: Liberal Champion* (Boston, MA: Houghton Mifflin Harcourt, 2010).
Streifford, Howard. *An Axiological Analysis of the Rhetorical Implications in Selected Supreme Court Decisions* (Unpublished Doctoral Dissertation, Southern Illinois University-Carbondale, 1967).
Terminiello v. Chicago, 337 U.S. 1 (1949).
Texas v. Johnson, 491 U.S. 397 (1989).
Tiscione, Kristen Konrad. *Rhetoric for Legal Writers*, 2nd ed. (St. Paul, MN: West Academic Publishing, 2016).
Turley, Jonathan. "The 9 Greatest Supreme Court Justices," *American History Magazine* (July 29, 2009), http://www.historynet.com/the-9-greatest-supreme-court-justices.htm.
Tushnet, Mark, "The Logic of Experience: Oliver Wendell Holmes on the Supreme Judicial Court," *Virginia Law Review* 63 (1977): 975–1052.
Twining v. New Jersey, 211 U.S. 78 (1908).
United States v. Windsor, 133 S. Ct. 2675 (2013).
Vernonia School District 47J v. Acton, 515 U.S. 646 (1995).

Wald, Patricia M. "The Rhetoric of Results and the Results of Rhetoric: Judicial Writings," *University of Chicago Law Review* 62 (1995): 1371–1419.
Webster v. Reproductive Health Services, 492 U.S. 490 (1989).
Wermiel, Stephen. "The Nomination of Justice Brennan: Eisenhower's Mistake? A Look at the Historical Record," *Constitutional Commentary* 11 (1995): 515–537.
West Virginia State Board of Education v. Barnette, 319 U.S. 624 (1943).
White, G. Edward. *Oliver Wendell Holmes, Jr.* (New York: Oxford University Press, 2006).
White, James Boyd. "Law as Rhetoric, Rhetoric as Law: The Arts of Cultural and Communal Life," *University of Chicago Law Review* 52 (1985): 684–702.
Williams-Yulee v. Florida Bar, 135 S. Ct. 1656 (2015).
Youngstown Sheet and Tube Company v. Sawyer, 343 U.S. 579 (1952).
Yarbrough, Tinsley E. "Justice Black and His Critics on Speech-Plus and Symbolic Speech," *Texas Law Review* 52 (1974): 257–284.
Zinsser, William. *On Writing Well: The Classic Guide to Writing Nonfiction* (New York: HarperCollins, 2006).

Index

About the Author

Brian L. Porto is professor of law at Vermont Law School, where he has taught courses in legal writing since 2006. He holds a JD from Indiana University-Bloomington and a PhD in political science from Miami University (Ohio). He has worked as an attorney in both state government and private practice, and continues to practice law by writing appellate briefs for Vermont attorneys. With those attorneys in mind, he has published several articles about brief-writing and about the use of rhetorical techniques in Supreme Court opinions in the *Vermont Bar Journal*. A veteran sports-law scholar, he has published two books and numerous law review articles on legal issues in college sports. *Rhetoric, Persuasion, and Modern Legal Writing: The Pen Is Mightier* is his fifth book.

Ingram Content Group UK Ltd.
Milton Keynes UK
UKHW041811210323
418919UK00004B/127

9 781498 568913